# IMPROVISING OTHERWISE

# Improvising Otherwise

## A Decolonial Feminist Approach to Improvisation in Early Modern English Culture

*Fatima Lahham*

https:openbookpublishers.com
©2025 Fatima Lahham

This work is licensed under a Creative Commons Attribution 4.0 International (CC BY 4.0). This license enables users to distribute, remix, adapt, and build upon the material in any medium or format, so long as attribution is given to the creator. The license allows for commercial use providing attribution is made to the author (but not in any way that suggests that they endorse you or your use of the work). Attribution should include the following information:

Fatima Lahham, *Improvising Otherwise: A Decolonial Feminist Approach to Improvisation in Early Modern English Culture*. Cambridge, UK: Open Book Publishers, 2025, https://doi.org/10.11647/obp.0451

Further details about CC BY licenses are available at https://creativecommons.org/licenses/by/4.0/

Copyright and permissions for the reuse of many of the images included in this publication differ from the above. This information is provided in the captions and in the list of illustrations. Every effort has been made to identify and contact copyright holders and any omission or error will be corrected if notification is made to the publisher.

All external links were active at the time of publication unless otherwise stated and have been archived via the Internet Archive Wayback Machine at https://archive.org/web

Updated digital material and resources associated with this volume are available at https://doi.org/10.11647/obp.0451#resources

ISBN Paperback: 978-1-80511-520-5
ISBN Hardback: 978-1-80511-521-2
ISBN PDF: 978-1-80511-522-9
ISBN HTML: 978-1-80511-524-3
ISBN EPUB: 978-1-80511-523-6

DOI: 10.11647/obp.0451

Cover image: 'Abdullah Bukhari, 'Two Nightingales in a Rose Bush', Double-Sided Illustrated Leaf from an Ottoman Album, ca. 1725–45. Purchase, Ravi and Seran Trehan Gift, in celebration of Turkey's Centennial, 2023, The Met, public domain
Cover design: Jeevanjot Kaur Nagpal

To Mama Dula

# Contents

| | |
|---|---|
| Acknowledgements | ix |
| List of Figures | xi |
| List of Audio Recordings | xiii |
| Introduction | 1 |
| 1. Improvising the Human: Extemporary Practice and the Body in Early Modern England | 17 |
| 2. Improvising Encounter: Travelogue Reading as World-Making | 53 |
| Interlude: Bees on the Moon | 87 |
| 3. Improvising Nature: Transposable Tongues of the Nightingale | 97 |
| 4. Improvising Text: Historical Performance and a Decolonial Imaginary | 123 |
| Epilogue | 151 |
| Bibliography | 157 |
| Index | 173 |

# Acknowledgements

I am here writing this only through Allah's mercy and permission, and the huge generosity shown to me. I have (to varying degrees) been thinking about improvisation, decolonial feminism and early modern histories since the end of 2018, and I wish that I could list every single person who has shared ideas and ears with me over the last seven years. Any shortcomings and errors remain my own, and I pray that despite them, this book will still be useful in some small way.

To my PhD supervisor Dr. Bettina Varwig, thank you for your constant support and guidance while I worked on my PhD project from 2018–22.

To Alessandra, Adèle, Laura, Jeevan and Raegan at Open Book Publishers, thank you for all your invaluable support in the process of writing this book.

To the Cambridge AHRC DTP, thank you for the full scholarship that allowed me the time and freedom to read and learn during my PhD studies, as well as for funding the album that accompanies this book.

To the wonderful librarians and archivists at Christ's College Library Cambridge, the Cambridge Music Faculty Library, the National Archives at Kew, and the British Library in London, thank you for all your help finding and reading the sources in this book.

To Myles Eastwood, thank you for your expertise in recording my improvisatory ideas.

To Julieta Chaparro Buitrago and to all the members of our feminist writing group, thank you for creating a space where many of the ideas and creativities in this book took shape.

To Mustafa Beg, thank you for giving me the computer on which I wrote and edited huge sections of this manuscript when mine stopped working days before a big deadline.

To Elaine Brown, thank you for all your constant support during the past years.

To Jess, thank you for reading this before it got released into the world, I am really grateful for all your wisdom.

To all my friends and family members who I have not mentioned, but who I hold in my heart with so much gratitude: thank you for your love and generosity and support.

I am writing this in April 2025, in the middle of several genocides. This book is about some of the historical processes that have enabled some of the violent atrocities we are currently witnessing to take place. Mahmoud Darwish writes: Gaza does not propel people to cool contemplation; rather she propels them to erupt and collide with the truth.

May we be propelled to collide with the truth. May we be propelled to name the truth. May we be propelled to hold the people of Gaza and all oppressed people with love in our hearts and with truth in our actions.

# List of Figures

Fig. 1    Christopher Simpson, *The Division Viol* (London: Printed by    p. 22
          Mr Godbid, and sold by John Playford, 1659), p. 22, public
          domain.

Fig. 2    John Walsh, *The Division Flute* (London: Playford, 1706),    p. 23
          Part 2, p. 11, public domain.

Fig. 3    Christopher Simpson, *The Division Viol* (London: Printed by    p. 25
          Mr Godbid, and sold by John Playford, 1659), p. 32, public
          domain.

Fig. 4    Nicola Matteis, *Ayrs*, Book 2 (n.d.: n.p.), p. 24, public    p. 31
          domain.

Fig. 5    Nicola Matteis, *Ayrs*, Book 3 (n.d.: n.p.), p. 2, public domain.    p. 32

Fig. 6    Henry Maundrell, *A Journey from Aleppo to Jerusalem at Easter,*    p. 76
          *A.D. 1697* (Oxford: Printed at the Theatre, 1703), https://
          archive.org/details/gri_journeyfroma00maun, p. 23, public
          domain.

Fig. 7    Henry Maundrell, *A Journey from Aleppo to Jerusalem at Easter,*    p. 79
          *A.D. 1697* (Oxford: Printed at the Theatre, 1703), https://
          archive.org/details/gri_journeyfroma00maun, p. 108, public
          domain.

Fig. 8    SP 10/73, part 2, folio 73v, National Archives, Kew    p. 85
          (reproduced with permission, all rights reserved).

Fig. 9    Charles Butler, *The Feminine Monarchie* (Oxford: Printed    p. 88
          by Ioseph Barnes, 1609), p. 104, https://archive.org/
          details/bim_early-english-books-1475-1640_the-feminine-
          monarchie-_butler-charles_1609, public domain.

Fig. 10   Charles Butler, *The Feminine Monarchie* (London: Printed by    p. 91
          John Haviland, 1623), p. 96, https://archive.org/details/
          RAM2023-1081/page/n3/mode/2up, public domain.

| | | |
|---|---|---|
| Fig. 11 | Francis Godwin, *The Man in the Moone* (London: Printed by John Norton, to be sold by Ioshua Kurton and Thomas Warren, 1657), pp. 94–5, https://archive.org/details/bim_early-english-books-1641-1700_the-man-in-the-moone_godwin-francis_1657/page/n1/mode/2up, public domain. | p. 95 |
| Fig. 12a | Jacob van Eyck, 'Engels Nachtegael', in *Der Fluyten Lusthof*, 2nd edn (Amsterdam: Paulus Matthysz, 1644), p. 31, https://s9.imslp.org/files/imglnks/usimg/d/d3/IMSLP354037-PMLP201599-van_eyck_1_edicao_tif.pdf, public domain. | p. 116 |
| Fig. 12b | Jacob van Eyck, 'Engels Nachtegael' (cont.), *Der Fluyten Lusthof*, 2nd edn (Amsterdam: Paulus Matthysz, 1644), p. 32, https://s9.imslp.org/files/imglnks/usimg/d/d3/IMSLP354037-PMLP201599-van_eyck_1_edicao_tif.pdf, public domain. | p. 116 |
| Fig. 13 | Fragment from John Covel's collected papers. British Library, London, MS Add MS 22911 (reproduced with permission, all rights reserved). | p. 119 |
| Fig. 14 | Thomas Mace, 'A Fancy-Prelude', *Musick's Monument* (London: T. Ratcliffe and N. Thompson, 1676), p. 210, https://archive.org/details/bim_early-english-books-1641-1700_musicks-monument-_mace-thomas_1676/page/n231/mode/2up, public domain. | p. 131 |
| Fig. 15 | Thomas Mace, *Musick's Monument* (London: T. Ratcliffe and N. Thompson, 1676), p. 121, https://archive.org/details/bim_early-english-books-1641-1700_musicks-monument-_mace-thomas_1676/page/n231/mode/2up, public domain. | p. 135 |
| Fig. 16 | Thomas Mace, *Musick's Monument* (London: T. Ratcliffe and N. Thompson, 1676), p. 150, https://archive.org/details/bim_early-english-books-1641-1700_musicks-monument-_mace-thomas_1676/page/n231/mode/2up, public domain. | p. 141 |
| Fig. 17 | 'Readings Ground', in John Walsh, *The Division Flute* (London: Walsh, 1706), p. 1, public domain. | p. 143 |

# List of Audio Recordings

| | | |
|---|---|---|
| Audio Recording 1 | 'Division for Flute'. Track 2 from Fatima Lahham, *bulbul*, FS Records (2022). | p. 22 |
| Audio Recording 2 | 'Huseyni Semaii'. Track 3 from Fatima Lahham, *bulbul*, FS Records (2022). | p. 66 |
| Audio Recording 3 | 'The Bee'. Track 6 from Fatima Lahham, *bulbul*, FS Records (2022). | p. 89 |
| Audio Recording 4 | 'Engels Nachtegaeltje'. Track 4 from Fatima Lahham, *bulbul*, FS Records (2022). | p. 115 |
| Audio Recording 5 | 'Asfour tal men el shebbak'. Track 1 from Fatima Lahham, *bulbul*, FS Records (2022). | p. 119 |
| Audio Recording 6 | 'Dido's Lament'. Track 13 from Fatima Lahham, *bulbul*, FS Records (2022). | p. 147 |

# Introduction

*Improvisation: how we live now; the way creativity seeks freedom; an alternative way to imagine the world. The way I relate to you over an ocean of difference. A mode of listening; a rhythm of breathing. The song of the nightingale, the buzz of the bee, the opening of a flower. How I read texts, and how you write my thoughts. The communities we dream to find, the cities and sonicities we dream to inhabit.*

This book started with a PhD project in 2018, and was led by my desire to research my practice as a recorder player trained in historical performance with a particular love of improvisation. My readings of early modern English texts naturally seeped into all the other parts of me: my interests in feminism and decolonial theory, my love of Arabic music, my practice and identity as a Muslim, my experiences as a British and Shami woman who has always lived in the UK.

Many of the ideas and relationships in this book—as a scripted improvisation of sorts—stretch the boundaries of theory, music, academic discipline and temporality. At these stretching points, I have laid some of my fears to rest: are the connections I have made across historical texts, personal reflections and decolonial feminist theory meaningful outside my own thoughts? Have I adopted some of the coloniality of the historical texts I read in my own 'decolonial' analysis? Will this book, with its many shortcomings, offer anyone the inspiration to improvise otherwise, or to revisit histories differently?

I voice these fears and release this imperfect text with Foluke Taylor's beautiful words resonating: 'writing is a practice of forgiveness made into a habit; the habit of laying down words while forgiving all the loose threads and dropped stitches; every frayed uneven edge'.[1] May you, the

---

[1] Foluke Taylor, *Unruly Therapeutic: Black Feminist Writings and Practices in Living Room* (New York: Norton 2023), p. 23.

©2025 Fatima Lahham, CC BY 4.0

reader, forgive me for the loose stitches and rough edges, and may this book offer you something that benefits you.

Making space for the dropped stitches, this book has been shaped by the need to leave 'spaces' for improvisation—both aural, in the audio tracks of my own playing that are interspersed throughout, and practical, in the four creative prompts that are entirely inspired by Audre Lorde's 'questionnaire to one-self', compiled from questions she poses in her essay *The Transformation of Silence into Language and Action* (1977). These prompts, which are marked out using italic typeface, and the sonic parts of the book, invite you to take my ideas off the page into your world, perhaps encouraging you to read *otherwise*.[2]

Throughout the course of researching and writing *Improvising Otherwise*, I have been asked some of the same questions many times. I therefore decided to start this introduction with some frequently asked questions.

1. How can you research improvisation that happened in the past if no audio recordings were made of them?

This question was constantly asked of me as I navigated my PhD. I would always struggle through responses, trying to pretend it was not a problem—when in fact, not having access to any audio recordings of early modern people improvising is a huge and fundamental problem, a beautiful dilemma that challenges traditional historiography and the role of imagination in this work. It has encouraged me to listen and look more deeply into any existing texts and scores that discuss or mention improvisation practices, to try and piece together an aural picture. This 'problem' has also led me to think of recordings as not only aural/sonic but also written, drawn, hinted at, scribbled down in a margin...

2. What does decolonial feminism have to do with early modern improvisation?

I have been encouraged not to name my work 'feminist'. I have considered the reasons why it is important for me to do so. Feminist texts, particularly those that deploy a decolonial framework, are often about re-imagining words and worlds: what is improvisation? What could it be?

---

2   Maya Caspari and Ruth Daly, 'Reading Otherwise: Decolonial Feminisms', *Parallax* 29.2 (2023), 139–53.

Anchoring myself in some of these authors' words and worlds has also allowed me to think critically about constructions of coloniality in the texts I read.

Toni Morrison writes about the *spaces between* in historical study, those abandoned interstices between what is written and unwritten, where she locates what is important to her:

> It is in the interstices of recorded history that I frequently find the 'nothing' or the 'not enough' or the 'indistinct' or 'incomplete' or 'discredited' or 'buried' information important to me.[3]

I have embraced this idea of attending to indistinct or buried historical information, using my ears to try to listen between the lines, or between the slipped stitches, where the fabric lets in some light: listening through the layers, listening to the spaces between—as a methodology—chimes with Sara Ahmed's notion of a feminist ear: how you hear what is not being heard.[4] This feminist ear has been central to my research: how could we use feminist ears to listen to early modern texts, to all those sounds that are not being heard, the voices that are concealed, the narratives that are not considered?

Naming my work a 'decolonial feminist approach' is intended to honour the feminist ears and citational bricks that have contributed to the structure and shape of this book.

3. What does 'otherwise' mean?

The 'otherwise' has a deep history of radical imagination, rooted in Black feminist thought, writing and creativity and the intellectual and artistic production of Black women. It is of huge importance for me to acknowledge this as a non-Black person attempting to listen beyond white colonial historiographies in the Anglo-Ottoman contexts I consider in this book. *Therapist and writer Foluke Taylor writes of the 'OtherWise' in relation to liberatory therapeutic writing, drawing from Saidiya Hartman's description of 'wayward' and the 'social otherwise'.[5] For Taylor:

---

[3] Toni Morrison, *Mouth Full of Blood* (London: Chatto and Windus, 2019), p. 280.
[4] Sara Ahmed, *Living a Feminist Life* (Durham: Duke University Press, 2017), p. 203.
[5] Taylor uses an asterisk before the word 'therapist' as both a placeholder and wildcard, signalling Black feminist modes of creation, space-making and care.

> OtherWise evokes particular modes of experiencing, relating, and knowing as they emerge through and as Black life, as it survives a world predicated on antiblackness… Black life is positioned here as a space of possibility—the edge of exclusion that is also threshold and gateway; an entry point to possibly the only space through which we might genuinely consider a world in which all life matters. The relevance of writing OtherWise (as liberatory practice), extends beyond Black life and—in its challenge to an anthropocentric, white supremist framing of life—beyond the human.[6]

This book draws on some of the richness of the idea of the 'otherwise' to investigate what improvisation could mean as a tool for understanding some of the imperialism and proto-colonialism between England and the Ottoman empire in the early modern period, as well as asking how improvisation as a musical practice can question or even destabilise some of these constructions. For me, 'improvising otherwise' is a way to use improvisation as a practice, a way of reading, and a way of writing, in order to ask: how could this be imagined, sounded and heard differently?

4. What historical sources and methods are used in the book?

One of the key aims of this book is to show how non-musical sources can be used alongside musical ones to reimagine historical musical attitudes and theories. My intention has been to think with music about some of the connections between early modern embodiment, conceptions of the natural world, encounter and nascent coloniality.

In my book I read a variety of early modern English texts, both musical and non-musical. I have tried to engage these texts 'contrapuntally', to borrow from the Palestinian academic and theorist Edward Saïd, who wrote: 'we must […] read the great canonical texts with an effort to draw out, extend, give emphasis and voice to what is silent or marginally present or ideologically represented in such works. The contrapuntal reading must take account of both processes—that of imperialism and that of resistance to it, which can be done by extending our reading of the texts to include what was once forcibly excluded'.[7]

---

6 Foluke Taylor, 'OtherWise: Writing Unbearable Encounters through the Register of Black Life', *LIRIC Journal* 2.1 (2022), 120–41 (p. 123), https://liric.lapidus.org.uk/index.php/lirj/article/view/40/27

7 Edward Saïd, *Culture and Imperialism* (London: Random House, 1994), pp. 78–9.

Transferring Saïd's approach to musical historiography of the early modern period is not a new phenomenon, as David R. M. Irving explores in his study on music in early modern Manila in the Philippines. Irving writes that he is inspired by Saïd to mobilise the term 'counterpoint' as a social analogy of how colonial society combined several voices according to 'a strict, uncompromising set of rules wielded by a manipulating power', as well as a way to understand 'cultural relationships between parent states and their overseas colonies'.[8]

In the context of my project, I draw loosely on the concept of contrapuntal analysis to situate England and English people in constant dialogue with Islam, Muslims and countries falling under the jurisdiction of the Ottoman empire, giving 'emphasis and voice to what is silent or marginally present', and attempting to weave a narrative that is alert to processes of imperialism, coloniality and resistance to them—both in the early modern period and in historical processes of understanding today.

This latter approach of considering present contexts in historical research is also informed by my engagement with pre-modern critical race studies. This is exemplified by much recent public scholarship on early modern literature undertaken by a collective of scholars and activists mainly concentrated in North America, who cultivate anti-racist perspectives and pedagogies in their approaches to William Shakespeare and other early modern English playwrights. This movement often considers how the reading and study of Shakespeare is important for the present socio-political moment, as well as reflecting on how scholars who study race can avoid replicating the racism in the texts and contexts they address, and instead mobilise the space of early modern studies as a liberatory and anti-oppressive movement.[9]

Finally, my book approaches questions of different creativities and how they can draw on and be inspired by different histories. The album[10] that accompanies this book offers an example of how my own

---

8   D. R. M. Irving, *Colonial Counterpoint: Music in Early Modern Manila* (Oxford: Oxford University Press, 2010), pp. 3–4.
9   See Kim F. Hall, *Things of Darkness: Economies of Gender and Race in Early Modern England* (Ithaca. Cornell University Press, 1995) for the book that arguably launched the field, as well as the Twitter hashtag #ShakeRace.
10  Alongside this book, I offer my solo album, *bulbul*, which was imagined and recorded alongside researching and writing the thesis that became this book. To the reader: you are invited to listen to this album in any order and fashion that appeals—as a playlist while you read the book, away from the book, at home, in

creativities as a musician have been informed and shaped by historical research and texts, as well as how they collide simultaneously with my own contexts, backgrounds and locations. As I argue through various modes in my book, I believe that improvisation can facilitate and offer a space for these historical processes of creativity that are still grounded in contemporary concerns.

My project draws on several different disciplines, bringing together various concepts and methodologies. As I have reflected and drawn together the threads of the authors and voices that have inspired me or shaped my work, I have enjoyed dancer and scholar Tara Aisha Willis's idea of citation itself as a form of improvisation and a constant dialogue of gathering:

> Citation is not unlike dance improvisation, and dance improvisation is always citational: they have in common a multi-directional time–space organization. We spin something old–new (nothing new under the sun or in our bodies; nothing that once was can ever be again). They have in common a process of *gathering* experience (Goldman 2010; Coan et al. 2018)—in real-time/space—and evidencing it in the world, sometimes even on one's own terms, not needing to be proved to be believed. Improvisational/citational practices push us to work with what we have: to gather experience into and beyond the present moment; to gather others and our relations to their work into ourselves and out again anew.[11]

## Between the Critical and the Historical: On Improvisation Studies

This gathering must start with some consideration of historical musicology's contribution to historical improvisation studies, and in particular with scholars who in recent times have sought to bring together theory and practice in the domain of historical performance studies.

In 2017, Massimiliano Guido edited a collection of essays intended to establish the existence of 'historical improvisation' as a discipline in itself, building on cumulative work at universities and institutions across

---

the company of nightingales and bees... Fatima Lahham, *bulbul*, FS Records (2022), https://www.naxosdirect.co.uk/items/bulbul-593683

11   Tara Aisha Willis, 'A Litany on An/notations', *Performance Research* 23.4–5 (2018), 85–7 (p. 85).

Europe and North America over the past five years.[12] Guido describes this discipline as a concerted attempt by musicologists and theorists to enable the 'reconstruction of improvisational practices of the past, through the study of primary and secondary sources'.[13] However, Guido notes that the exploration of historical improvisation is not simply a reconstruction of an old-fashioned practice but rather, 'it is […] adding some fresh spring water to the river. This closes the circle: from improvisation to theory, and from theory back to improvisation. And the water goes […] into the ocean'.[14] Alongside the possibility of bringing historical sources into conversation with present-day experience and improvisation as a current practice, there is also a hint of the danger and excitement of being aware of the bigger picture—the metaphorical ocean beyond musicology's reach.

Guido's collection is not unprecedented. Musicologists such as Rob Wegman,[15] Jessie Ann Owens,[16] Peter Schubert,[17] and Julie E. Cumming[18] among others have contributed studies that pave the way to the new discipline that Guido describes, crucially by problematising modern notions of 'composer' and compositional process, and expanding our understanding of musical pedagogies. Alongside Guido's volume, the edited volume by Rebecca Herissone and Alan Howard on creativities in early modern England offers further frameworks within which we can understand ideas of imagination, composition, rhetoric and memory in this period, problematising the anachronistic idea of 'improvisation' understood in opposition to composition.[19] Additionally, Rebecca

---

12   Massimilano Guido, 'Introduction, Studies in Historical Improvisation: A New Path for Performance, Theory and Pedagogy of Music', in *Studies in Historical Improvisation: From Cantare super Librum to Partimenti*, ed. by Massimiliano Guido (Abingdon: Routledge, 2017), pp. 1–6 (p. 1).
13   Guido, 'Introduction', p. 1.
14   Guido, 'Introduction', p. 2.
15   Rob C. Wegman, 'From Maker to Composer: Improvisation and Musical Authorship in the Low Countries, 1450–1500', *Journal of the American Musicological Society* 49 (1996), 409–79.
16   Jessie Ann Owens, *Composers at Work: The Craft of Musical Composition, 1450–1600* (New York: Oxford University Press, 1997).
17   Peter Schubert, 'Counterpoint Pedagogy in the Renaissance', in *The Cambridge History of Western Music Theory*, ed. by Thomas Christensen (Cambridge: Cambridge University Press, 2002), pp. 503–33.
18   Julie E. Cumming, 'Renaissance Improvisation and Musicology', *Journal of the Society for Music Theory* 19.2 (2013), https://mtosmt.org/issues/mto.13.19.2/mto.13.19.2.cumming.php
19   Rebecca Herissone and Alan Howard (eds), *Concepts of Creativity in Seventeenth-*

Herissone's work on notions of communal authorship and music-making productively destabilises the fixity of later concepts of 'composer' and 'text', refocussing our attention on oral improvisatory processes.[20]

Improvisation practices have also been considered within studies of the early music and historical performance movements. Bruce Haynes considers improvisation to be central to historical performance practice, writing in 2007 that

> the separation between composing and performing hasn't always existed. Before the rise of Romanticism, improvisation and composition were normal activities for any musician. In a time when new pieces were in constant demand, being a composer was nothing special, just part of the process of producing music. But even if a musician didn't always write their improvisations down, they had to know how to make up music on the spot. Without that ability, they couldn't play the music of the time.[21]

Nick Wilson also considers improvisation to be central to 'early music', not only as a practice but even as an ethos or aesthetic: '"Playing" early music with its distinctive approach to authentic historical performance looks like such a case in point [that of play as identity]. Under the "imaginary" rhetoric of play we find an interest with improvisation, imagination and "creativity" of the animal and human play worlds'.[22]

While much of this scholarship paves the way for work on historical improvisation practices, the focus has tended to be primarily musical and historical, with the ostensible aim of reconstruction. Yet the phrase 'historical improvisation' is itself an oxymoron; simply put, one word is in the past and the other can only exist in the present. How can such a study ever be truly historical, and how does historical work address the present nature of improvisation? Motivated by this question, my work brings research exploring historical improvisation into conversation with critical improvisation studies to dwell on these uncomfortable interstices between 'historical' and 'improvisation'.

As a discipline, critical improvisation studies grew around a few pivotal

---

    *century England* (Woodbridge: The Boydell Press, 2013).
20  Rebecca Herissone, *Musical Creativity in Restoration England* (New York: Cambridge University Press, 2013).
21  Bruce Haynes, *The End of Early Music: A Period Performer's History of Music for the Twenty-First Century* (Oxford: Oxford University Press, 2007), p. 4.
22  Nick Wilson, *The Art of Re-enchantment: Making Early Music in The Modern Age* (New York: Oxford University Press, 2013), p. 170.

conferences, and led to an important two-volume handbook published in 2016.²³ In their introduction to this handbook, George Lewis and Benjamin Piekut describe critical improvisation studies as creating an agenda where 'the arts become part of a larger network tracing the entire human condition of improvisation'.²⁴ In another recent work in this field, Daniel Fischlin and Eric Porter define their work as falling into a trajectory of critical improvisation studies that 'is committed to understanding the possibilities, and limitations, of musical improvisation as a model for cultural, and ethical dialogue in action—for imaging and creating alternative ways of knowing and being known in the world even as it interrogates the ways in which aesthetic practices impact other forms of social practice'.²⁵ In other words, critical improvisation studies aims to examine 'how improvisation mediates cross-cultural, transnational, and cyberspatial (inter) artistic exchanges that produce new conceptions of identity, history, and the body'.²⁶

These descriptions of critical improvisation studies suggest a potential framework for studying historical improvisation in a contextual manner that reaches beyond the purely musical to create a dialogue between present and past human practices more broadly. By integrating the model of critical improvisation studies into existing paradigms of historical improvisation studies, I propose that we can offer not only better historical insights by considering wider (and non-musical) contexts, but also productively relate this work back to present-day improvisations and improvisers in the historical performance movement, and to wider contexts of music-making today.

As a result, my approach integrates musical and non-musical forms of historical improvisation. It also allows the methods and processes of improvisation themselves to inform my historical approach, and to interrogate the practice's present ramifications. For example, in Chapter 1, I argue that studying extemporary prayer practices can tell us about issues of temporality and authority in the improvisation of music, and in Chapter 2, I propose that ways of reading and performing travelogues are not fully separate from the actual instances of musical

---

23  George Lewis and Benjamin Piekut (eds), *Oxford Handbook to Critical Improvisation Studies*, Vols 1–2 (New York: Oxford University Press, 2016).
24  Lewis and Piekut (eds), *Oxford Handbook*, p. 2.
25  Daniel Fischlin and Eric Porter (eds), *Playing for Keeps: Improvisation in the Aftermath* (Durham: Duke University Press, 2020), p. 3.
26  Lewis and Piekut (eds), *Oxford Handbook*, p. 1.

improvisation found in the pages of these books.

However, in contrast to a central tenet of critical improvisation studies (and in acknowledgment of the specific contexts I explore) I do not claim that the examples of improvisation presented in this book were necessarily always a resistive or even liberatory practice. As I explore throughout, the historical materials point to improvisation as a mode of expression that could be mobilised for many different ends, rather than a practice that carried any inherent quality of liberation. Still, in my concluding explorations of the potential impact of my work on historical performance practices today, I do turn to improvisation as a way to seek creative and hermeneutic freedoms, and this endeavour links back to some of the central motivations of critical improvisation studies.

## Tell Me a Story: On Decoloniality and Historical Narrative

The way we tell stories, and the stories we tell, are inherently political. And, of course, in some ways, they reflect and reveal more about us and about our histories than about the events we try to narrate. In my book, I therefore actively question the kinds of events and figures who become historical anchor points to my project. The main contexts I draw on in this study of historical practices of (musical) improvisation are print culture/orality and English relations with the Ottoman empire, two areas which intersect and whose politics tangle with iterations of coloniality. However, the issue of coloniality in this context is one fraught with complications and subtleties.

As a historian approaching seventeenth-century Anglo-Ottoman relations, I must take into account the expansion of the Ottoman empire from Turkey to the so-called 'Ottoman Arab lands' (or *Bilād al-Shām*—present-day Syria, Lebanon, Jordan, Palestine) and the proto-colonial attitudes of English travellers in these lands, as well as our knowledge of the later English colonisation and occupation of so many West Asian and North African countries. Nabil Matar has observed that in the case of Palestine for example, European Renaissance mapping foreshadowed later colonial ideologies by presenting it as a land without inhabitants, and without a political or social identity.[27] Throughout my book I show that even though England had not yet formally colonised any South-West Asian and North African countries, there is still evidence of colonial ideology in the way that the subjects and lands of the Ottoman empire were discussed. In fact, the existence of Ottoman imperialism may have served to fuel England's imperial envy.

In response to the coloniality—a decolonial concept in itself[28]—that I have encountered in many of my sources, my approach draws on decolonial theory as a frame for my analysis and critique. In adopting this frame, I draw a crucial distinction between decoloniality and decolonisation, as defined by Walter Mignolo. Mignolo explains that decolonisation originally meant 'freeing a colony to allow it to become self-governing or independent; to build the former-colonized own nation-state'.[29] And in the infamous words of Eve Tuck and K. Wayne Yang, 'decolonisation is not a metaphor'—it is the material processes of land-back movements, restoration and reparations made to Indigenous peoples.[30]

However, Mignolo shows that many such liberation movements for decolonisation left coloniality (defined as a complex structure of domination and control) intact, at which point decoloniality emerges 'from the shortcomings of decolonization'.[31] For Mignolo then, decoloniality is the process of delinking from the 'colonial matrix of power', in order to imagine and engage in being decolonial subjects.[32] He builds on the work of Peruvian decolonial theorist Aníbal Quijano to encourage a critique of the European model of rationality/modernity that emerged in the early modern period, and argues that an epistemic mode of disengaging from coloniality must be paired with material decolonisation, to which it is central.[33]

---

27  Nabil I. Matar, 'Renaissance Cartography and the Question of Palestine', in *The Landscape of Palestine: Equivocal Poetry*, ed. by Ibrahim Abu-Lughod, Roger Heacock and Khaled Nashef (Birzeit: Birzeit University Publications, 1999), pp. 139–51 (p. 139).

28  Walter D. Mignolo and Catherine E. Walsh, *On Decoloniality: Concepts, Analytics, Praxis* (Durham: Duke University Press, 2018), p. 112.

29  Mignolo and Walsh, *On Decoloniality*, p. 121.

30  Eve Tuck and K. Wayne Yang, 'Decolonization Is Not a Metaphor', *Decolonization. Indigeneity, Education & Society* 1.1 (2012), 1–40.

31  Mignolo and Walsh, *On Decoloniality*, p. 124.

32  Mignolo and Walsh, *On Decoloniality*, p. 125.

33  Aníbal Quijano, 'Coloniality and Modernity/Rationality', *Cultural Studies* 21.2–3 (2007), 168–178.

While I draw on Walter Mignolo's work at several crucial moments in my book—including my title, which in part takes the 'otherwise' from his idea of 'thinking and doing otherwise' as a counter to paradigms of coloniality[34]—I would like to take note of the dangers of decolonial theory's possible proximity to narratives of nationalism and purity, especially when applied outside specific geographical and historical contexts. Furthermore, I believe the decentring of actual decolonisation, and reification of decolonial theory within the academy, is often seen to do the 'job' of decolonisation. In response to these potential pitfalls, and acknowledging the diminishing nature of decolonial thinking as a trend or buzzword, I do not describe my methodology as fundamentally 'decolonial', but instead draw some useful tools from decolonial theory to be applied in specific contexts in my work. I am mindful of Audre Lorde's powerful statement that 'the master's tools will never dismantle the master's house'. As such, I am not claiming to dismantle the house with this project so much as proposing how we might fashion tools that will de-stabilise it.[35]

Throughout my work I strive to imagine how—as musicologists in general and historical musicologists in particular—we can produce work that is socially responsible and politically engaged, fundamentally challenging the value systems that uphold certain knowledges over others, and certain ways of knowing over others. As such, acts of improvisation seem a particularly potent starting point, posing a foundational challenge to the dominant method of conducting historical research through the study of printed sources, as well as complicating the idea of a purely historical/historicised study, given that the act of improvisation is one that must happen in the present moment.

In defining the historical and methodological anchor points for my project, I have been indebted to Nabil Matar's extensive scholarship on cross-cultural historiographies between (broadly speaking) Europe and the Arabic-speaking world, and his proposal of alternative centres and peripheries in the making of these histories. My project has been particularly inspired by the approaches in *Europe through Arab Eyes*

---

34   Mignolo and Walsh, *On Decoloniality*, p. 113.
35   Audre Lorde, 'The Master's Tools Will Never Dismantle the Master's House', in *Your Silence Will Not Protect You*, (London: Silver Press, 2017), p. 89.

(2008)³⁶ and *Britain and the Islamic World* (2011).³⁷ In the former, Matar discusses the multiplicity of narratives available in this period, writing that 'in the early modern period [...] and in the Arab-Islamic West, there was less of a monolithic construction of otherness and more of a diversity of perspectives'. He continues, 'the study of the early modern period is important because it redirects today's East-West and colonized-colonizer discourse to the specificity of historical antecedents'.³⁸ My research builds on Matar's meticulous studies of relationships between early modern Britain and the Islamic(ate) world, seeking alternative stories of Anglo-Ottoman engagement that challenge the mono-cultural/lithic construction of 'British' history, and propose instead several ways of making history *otherwise*.

In light of my above discussion of modes of writing history, I present this timeline of nineteen dates as an amalgam of some specific points of reference in my book combined with more 'canonic' moments in early modern English and Ottoman histories. Running from the Ottoman capture of Palestine and Syria in 1516 to the publication of Henry Maundrell's *A Journey from Aleppo to Jerusalem* in 1697, this collection of dates is meant to highlight certain temporal anchor points for the reader, rather than to orient them within a linear time-sphere. I intend to demonstrate in my book that while events such as Elizabeth I's excommunication by the Catholic Church is undeniably a significant moment in early modern English history, so is the moment when she sent an organ to Topkapi Palace.

## Timeline

| | |
|---|---|
| 1516 | Selim I captures Palestine and Syria |
| 1517 | Selim I captures Cairo |
| 1534 | Henry VIII establishes Anglican Church, with him as its head |
| 1570 | Elizabeth I is excommunicated by the Catholic Church |

---

36  Nabil Matar, *Europe through Arab Eyes, 1578–1727* (New York: Columbia University Press, 2008).
37  Nabil Matar and Gerald MacLean, *Britain and the Islamic World, 1558–1713* (Oxford: Oxford University Press, 2011).
38  Matar, *Europe through Arab Eyes*, p. 5.

| | |
|---|---|
| **1581** | Turkey Company established (renamed Levant Company in 1592) |
| **1594** | Elizabeth I receives a letter from the Ottoman empress Safiye |
| **1599** | Elizabeth I sends an automated organ via Thomas Dallam to Sultan Mehmed III (Safiye's son) |
| **1603** | End of Elizabeth's reign |
| **1609** | The first edition of Charles Butler's bee-keeping manual *The Feminine Monarchie* is published, the first English text to gender the queen bee as female |
| **1636** | Henry Blount's *Voyage into the Levant* is published |
| **1638** | Francis Godwin's *The Man in the Moone* is published, believed to be the first work of science fiction in English |
| **1644** | Jacob van Eyck's *Der Fluyten Lusthof* is published in Amsterdam |
| **1659** | Publication of first edition of Christopher Simpson's *The Division-Viol or The Art of Playing Extempore upon a Ground* |
| **1661** | Ireneus Freeman's *Non-Conformity to Common Prayer* is published |
| **1665–6** | Great Plague of London |
| **2–6 September 1666** | Great Fire of London |
| **1676** | Thomas Mace's *Musick's Monument* is published |
| **1697** | Henry Maundrell's *A Journey from Aleppo to Jerusalem* is published |

In the conclusion to his study of Islam in Britain from 1558 to 1685, Nabil Matar reflects on the contradictory relationships between England and Islam/Muslims, writing that 'throughout the seventeenth century, England experienced simultaneously a centripetal and a centrifugal relationship with Islam, either embracing elements in the civilization of the Arabs and the Ottomans or vilifying that civilization'.[39]

In response to this, he claims that:

---

[39] Nabil Matar, *Islam in Britain, 1558–1685* (Cambridge: Cambridge University Press, 1998), p. 188.

studies of early modern Britain have uniformly focused on its internal history and its links with Christian Europe—both Protestant and Catholic. The confrontation with Spain in the 1580s and 90s and with Catholicism throughout the Elizabethan and Stuart periods; the parliamentary and financial transformations that gave rise to the Civil Wars; the ascendancy of the gentry and the emigration to the New World; the alliance and/or confrontation with Scotland and Ireland; the regicide and the expansion of the navy; the Interregnum and the diffusion of sects; the Restoration of Charles II and the persecution of Nonconformity; the Dutch wars, the Popish plot, the rivalry with France and the Glorious Revolution—all these are factors that transformed England and the rest of the British Isles. But [...] there was, parallel and sometimes intertwined with these factors, the cultural legacy of Arabic Islam and the military might of the Turkish Empire which made the 'Renaissance' for England not only an inter-Britannic and inter-European experience, but an inter-Mediterranean and inter-religious one too.[40]

It is within this in-between moment of relation between England/ English people and the Islamicate world that I situate this musical study of improvisation. Not only is this moment of relation inter-Britannic, inter-European, inter-Mediterranean and inter-religious, but also inter-colonial. As Matar notes,

> the period under study witnessed the beginnings of British colonial ideology, in which the key to domination lay in the religious conversion and the cultural subordination of the 'natives'—as occurred in North America and West Africa. This colonial ideology was not possible in the Muslim Levant. From the eighteenth century on, however, Britain's relationship with the domains of Islam, both in the Levant and in the Far East, was transformed into a relationship of power and empire.[41]

Poised at these junctures, my project challenges the historiographical conventions of what is deemed central and what is deemed peripheral in early modern histories, asking why are battles in the English Civil War considered an essential backdrop to histories of prayer in early modern England, but not ideas about memory palaces? What happens to histories of nature when we pay attention to the moment when the queen bee's gender is identified correctly? Why is the first English story about moon travel not generally deemed as significant as other 'real' travelogues to distant lands?

---

40  Matar, *Islam in Britain*, pp. 184–5.
41  Matar, *Islam in Britain*, pp. 190–1.

# 1. Improvising the Human: Extemporary Practice and the Body in Early Modern England

> Asking how we became improvisers is almost the same as asking how we became feminists. It is the story of how we became who we are today.
> —'Feministing Free Improvisation'[1]

## Towards the 'Extemporary'

In 2018, when I first started researching the topic of historical improvisation practices in early modern England, I became fixated on naming. How we name things carries histories and layers of woven meaning. While etymology is not the only meaning-making process through which words evolve, it was my starting point here: the story of how we became who we are today.

As an English-speaking musician in the twenty-first century, I am accustomed to and familiar with the word 'improvisation', a word that Leo Treitler has described as the alternative to a historically-imposed silence.[2] This silence and the lack of naming around historical improvised and oral practices is part of what has made this project simultaneously challenging and infused with creativity. Most of my struggles at the start of my research were around naming, and the lack of explicit references to improvisation. In fact, as my etymological searches soon revealed, the first use of the word 'improvisation' in English was not in fact recorded

---

1   Hannah Reardon-Smith, Louise Denson and Vanessa Tomlinson, 'Feministing Free Improvisation', *TEMPO* 74.292 (2020), 10–20 (p. 13).
2   Leo Treitler, 'Speaking of the I-Word', *Archiv für Musikwissenschaft* 72.1 (2015), 1–18.

©2025 Fatima Lahham, CC BY 4.0    https://doi.org/10.11647/OBP.0451.01

until 1777 by the OED. The earliest closest reference I could find was John Florio's inclusion of the Italian 'improvisare' in his *World of Words, or, Most Copious, and Exact Dictionarie in Italian and English* (1598), which he translated using the more common way of describing improvisation: 'to sing or speak extempore'.³ While the word 'improvisation' may have been known through Italian in seventeenth-century England, it was not commonly used in the vernacular to describe improvisatory practice. Instead, the Latin word 'extempore' or the anglicised 'extemporary' is frequently found to describe improvised practice, with the earliest recorded example (dating from c.1556) by the schoolmaster and playwright Nicholas Udall, who used the word to describe how 'ditties' were improvised—'*extempore* will he dities [sic] compose'.⁴

In my preoccupation with how meanings get woven into names, I traced the word improvisation to the Latin *improvisus*, indicating something unexpected, while the word 'extemporary' comes from the Latin phrase *ex tempore*, which literally translates as 'out of (the/this) time'. This temporal aspect of extempore spoke to me: indicating a type of time travel that I was attempting as a musician or historian. There are several different interpretations one could make of the phrase 'out of this/the time': does it mean *out of time? Timeless?* Arising from *this particular moment in time?* Existing *outside the bounds of time?* When referring to different types of improvised behaviour, the term was rarely evoked solely in opposition to writing, but rather to *premeditation*. For example, on his trip to Italy in 1673, John Ray noted 'academies or societies of Virtuosi' who met to discourse on various topics in a manner 'sometimes extemporany [sic], sometimes premeditated'.⁵ Likewise, *unpremeditated* became directly synonymous with the extemporary, and the two adjectives were paired together to describe (and cast aspersion on) extemporary praying practices in numerous texts, including works by the rector Richard Lewthwat,⁶ Lancashire preacher Zachary

---

3   John Florio, *A Worlde of Wordes, or Dictionarie of the Italian and English tongues* (London: Arnold Hatfield, 1598), p. 17, https://archive.org/details/worldeofwordesor00flor

4   *OED Online*, 'Extempore, adv., adj., and n.', https://www.oed.com/view/Entry/66917

5   John Ray, *Travels through the Low Countries: Germany, Italy and France, with Curious Observations* (London: J. Walthoe et al., 1673), p. 341, https://archive.org/details/travelsthroughlo02rayj/page/n5/mode/2up

6   Richard Lewthwat, *A Justification of Set Forms of Prayer and in Special of the Liturgy of the Church of England; in Answer to, and Confutation of Vavasor Powel's Fourteen*

Taylor,⁷ and Somerset vicar Matthew Hole.⁸ The extemporary was not defined only by a lack of writing or text, but rather through a departure from temporal bounds, and a sense of revelling in the chance and unpremeditated nature of that activity.

The majority of my research for this book was done during the Covid-19 lockdowns. Subsequently, I became increasingly reliant on digital open access databases of historical materials, such as Early English Books online. I would search the word 'extemporary' and the variety of spellings and forms that existed for this word in the sixteenth and seventeenth centuries according to the OED, including: extempore (adv. adj. c.1556), extemporal (adj. 1570), extemporate (adj. 1590), extemporanean (adj. 1621), extempory (adv. 1623), extemporean (adj. 1624), extemporize (v.1644), extemporality (n. 1656), extemporaneous (adj. 1656), extemporany (adj. 1673). This plurality in terms is also reflected in the different ways each term could be used.

The OED definitions for 'extempore', for example, are numerous:

A. *adv.*

    a. At the moment, without premeditation or preparation; at first sight; off-hand. Now usually with reference to speech, composition, or musical performance. *to speak extempore* in present use often merely means to speak without notes, or without reading from manuscript. *to pray extempore* is opposed to using a set form of prayer.

    b. On the instant; at once; immediately.

    c. *To live extempore*: to live 'from hand to mouth'

---

    *Considerations, against All Composed and Imposed Forms of Prayer. By Richard Lewthwat, M.A. and Rector of Wethersdale in Suffolk* (London: Printed by A. Godbid and J. Playford, for Robert Clavel, 1679), p. 31, http://hdl.handle.net/20.500.14106/A48298

7  Zachary Taylor, *A Disswasive from Contention Being a Sermon Preached and Designed for the Last Itineration of the King's Preachers in the County Palatine of Lancaster / by Zachary Taylor* (London: Printed by John Gain for William Cadman, 1683), p. 3, http://hdl.handle.net/20.500.14106/A64270

8  M. Hole, *The Expediency of a Publick Liturgy, to Preserve the Reverence of Publick Worship a Sermon Preach'd at Bridgewater, for the Satisfaction of an Eminent Dissenter / by Matthew Hole* (London: Printed for Matt. Wotton, 1697), p. 10, https://quod.lib.umich.edu/e/eebo2/A44142.0001.001?view=toc

B. *adj.*

    a. Arising out of the moment; casual, occasional; sudden, unprepared for. Now only of personal actions

        i. Of a discourse, etc.: Composed, spoken, performed, or acted at the moment, without premeditation or preparation. Now usually understood to mean: Without the assistance of notes, or without reading.

        ii. Of speakers, performers.

    b. Contrived for the occasion, makeshift

C. *n.* Extempore composition, speech, or performance; an impromptu, improvisation

Notably, the term is not restricted to music-making, but also found when discussing improvised poetry, theatre, and prayer, indicating a historical network of improvised living across different parameters, and recalling critical improvisation studies in the breadth of capturing human experience. As a result, the historical texts I have read in the course of writing this book have spanned theological tracts, poetry, books about nature, bee-keeping treatises, and more. The stories of 'how we became improvisers' and 'who we are' have merged closer in the process of my research, as I have experienced extemporary ways of being (whether named or not) come to life through my reading and listening. In this chapter, I introduce some of the musical contexts of improvising 'divisions on a ground' (see discussion below) in early modern England, and the physical and psychological processes that underly it, such as the 'memory storehouse'. I then immediately complicate the picture by drawing a sharp contrast with texts on extemporary prayer, which hint at how the 'extemporary' was a space in which early modern colonial thought expressed constructions of 'others'. I discuss these contexts here as a way to deconstruct and dismantle some of the violent ideologies implicated in the musical histories I originally set out to examine—the woven meanings carried in 'extemporary'—that my work uncovered. I present them here not to replicate their violence, but to make the colonial contexts of these histories clear, as well as the imperative to improvise *otherwise*.

## Christopher Simpson's *Division Viol* (1659)

The first musical text that I considered in my research and that uses the term 'ex tempore' is by the English musician Christopher Simpson, who wrote a treatise on how to play and improvise divisions on a ground on the viola da gamba. As a recorder player, I was already familiar with this treatise, which offered printed instructions on the musical practice of improvising divisions on a ground and was printed in London in 1659 by William Godbid and sold by John Playford. Simpson's book *The Division-Viol or The Art of Playing Extempore upon a Ground* is one of the most comprehensive texts on this practice, appearing a year after the death of Oliver Cromwell and a year before the accession to the throne of King Charles II. The second revised edition (with the addition of a Latin translation) was planned to come out in 1665 but most copies exist in a later state from 1667, due to delays caused by the Plague and the Fire of London. A third edition appeared in 1712, a testament to the huge success the volume enjoyed—Sir Roger L'Estrange, who licensed the second edition, dubbed it 'one of the best Tutors in the world' and 'a work of exceeding use in all sorts of Musick whatsoever'.[9]

In this treatise, Simpson uses the phrase 'extemporary musick' to describe two viols improvising together 'on a ground' (or repeating bass line), and comments:

> I have known this kind of *Extemporary Musick*, sometimes (when it was performed by *Hands* accustomed to Play together) pass off, with greater *Applause*, than those *Divisions*, which had been the most Studiously Composed.[10]

By contrast to some of the non-musical references to the extemporary that describe something unplanned, Simpson's 'extemporary music' leaves little to chance, since the improvisation of such divisions is covered carefully in his book, offering detailed instructions and examples to anyone wishing to try their hand. His treatise offers examples of the kind of diminutions or divisions a musician could make on particular intervals, as shown below in Figure 1:

---

9   Christopher D. S. Field, 'Christopher Simpson [Sympson]', *Grove Music Online* (2001), https://www.oxfordmusiconline.com/grovemusic/view/10.1093/gmo/9781561592630.001.0001/omo-9781561592630-e-0000025844
10  *The Division-Viol, or The Art of Playing Ex Tempore upon a Ground by Christopher Simpson*, A Lithographic Facsimile of the Second Edition, 1677 (Faber Music: Curwen Edition, 1965), p. 59.

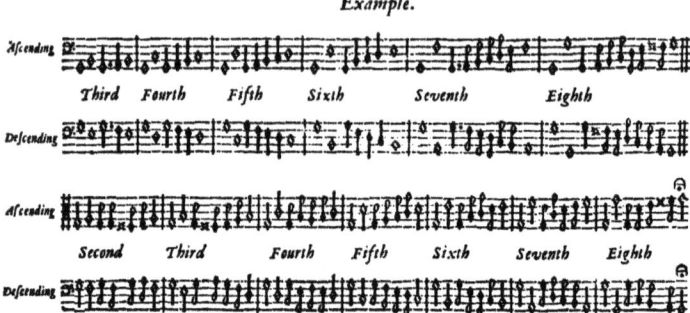

Fig. 1 Christopher Simpson, *The Division Viol* (London: Printed by Mr Godbid, and sold by John Playford, 1659), p. 22, public domain.

Simpson's book also includes fully written out 'divisions' on a ground, a genre also represented by *The Division Violin* (1684) and *The Division Flute* (1706). These prints are, in a sense, the closest we can get to hearing someone improvise in seventeenth-century England, but they also highlight print's intermediary role between orality and literacy.

The solo divisions I recorded illustrate this on a more practical level (see Figure 2): printed in *The Division Flute* (1706), the score maps out a set of divisions that lies somewhere in between Simpson's examples and a fully-composed piece of music.

Audio Recording 1 'Division for Flute'. Track 2 from Fatima Lahham, *bulbul*, FS Records (2022). https://hdl.handle.net/20.500.12434/21649b70

> *When I play the solo divisions from The Division Flute, they feel more like an example of how one should improvise; playing out the movements of someone else's body before you. I wonder, how do you re-inhabit this space, once it's already been mapped out in the text? For me it's a matter of timing, articulation, playfulness—trying to put the extemporary back in, imagining the improvisation that inspired someone to write it down…*
> (creative reflection, December 2021)

What can you not improvise yet? [Or, 'for what do you not have the tools to improvise, yet?']

# 1. Improvising the Human

Fig. 2 John Walsh, *The Division Flute* (London: Playford, 1706), Part 2, p. 11, public domain.

However, the existence of solo divisions somewhat destabilises and challenges the premise of 'divisions on a ground'. The ground bass's notable absence makes us question what it is that we are making divisions 'over' (or 'of'). It suggests some freedom and fluidity around what divisions were, and how they should sound—prompting me to wonder what is not there, and what is there that is not being heard?

Simpson also categorises divisions into three types:

> In playing to a Ground we exercise the whole compass of the Viol, acting therein sometimes the part of a Bass, sometimes a Treble or some other Part. From hence proceed Two kinds of Division, viz. a Breaking of the Ground, and a Descanting upon it: Out of which two, is generated a Third sort of Division; to wit a Mixture of Those, one with the other; which Third or last sort, is expressed in a two fold Manner; that is, either in Single or in Double notes. These several sorts of Division are used upon the Bass-Viol, very promiscuously, according to the Fancy of the Player or Composer…[11]

According to Simpson's model, there are two main modes of improvising—one where the musician makes divisions *out of* the bass line, one where they make divisions *over* it. A third mode consists of a combination of the former two. However, in popular understanding and discussion today by both performers and musicologists (largely promoted by the modern publishing of treble divisions over a static repeated bass), this second type of division is taken to represent the whole practice and genre.

'Breaking the Ground', as Simpson calls it, is 'the dividing [of] its Notes into more diminute Notes'.[12] He writes that this practice 'admits divers ways of expression, according to the divers ordering and disposing the Minute parts thereof' and offers five ways of 'breaking a note'. The first is a simple rhythmical alteration of the same pitch, the second consists of decoration around the note being 'broken', the third uses passing notes to connect the bass note in question to the next note in the ground bass, the fourth 'breaks' the bass notes into other 'concords' or notes that are consonant with those notes being broken, and the fifth consists of running notes around the main bass notes.[13]

According to Simpson, the third main mode of improvising is 'more excellent' than the other two. He writes:

> I call that Mixt Division which mixeth Descant and Breaking the Ground, one with the other; under which name I comprehend all Division which presents to our Ears the Sounds of Two or more Parts moving together: And, this is expressed either in single Notes, by hitting first upon One String and then upon an Other; or in double Notes, by touching two or more Strings at once with the Bow. This, as it is more excellent than

---

11   *The Division-Viol*, p. 28.
12   *The Division-Viol*, p. 28.
13   *The Division-Viol*, pp. 28–31.

the single ways of Breaking the Ground, or Descanting upon it, so it is more intricate, and requires more of judgement and skill in Composition; by reason of the Bindings and intermixtures of Discords, which are as frequent in This as in any other Figurate Musick. and requires also a greater level of skill both due to the playing of chords (only possible on some instruments) and to the addition of suspensions and discords.[14]

Figure 3 shows an example of a ground bass being improvised upon in all three of these modes: first the bass itself is 'broken', then Simpson gives us a descant voice that improvises over the bass, and finally we get a mixture of the broken bass and descant diminution. The intention of this print is not only to provide the musician with music to perform from, but primarily as a tool to initiate the musician into the extemporary practice of making divisions on a ground.

Fig. 3 Christopher Simpson, *The Division Viol* (London: Printed by Mr Godbid, and sold by John Playford, 1659), p. 32, public domain.

---

14   *The Division-Viol*, p. 29.

## A Musical Memory House

Simpson's manual provides detailed musical instructions on how to extemporise upon a ground, but his text does not seem to go much further into describing the mental, psychological and bodily processes that musicians developed their extemporary imaginations. The English music theorist Roger North (1653–1734) offers a different dimension to the common practice of learning to improvise through sample passages that show different ways to improvise a particular interval or bass line (in the tradition of Italian *passaggi*, for example). North describes the practice of improvising a voluntary as something that is located in the different parts of the body, likening the process to preparing to give a speech through the 'gathering' of 'materialls' in one's memory. Not only should the orator's mind be 'filled with the materiall' but 'the proper formes' should also be at their 'tongue's end, always ready on occasion'.[15] North describes how the musician's body should be 'filled' with different passages and parts of music that they hear:

> Even so a musitian, to become a good voluntier, must know the art of musick and have the knack of composition and full comand of his instruments (which here I have presumed to be the organ). And as for ayre of all sorts, he must be filled with it by a constant exercise, as well in the performing part, as in the imploy of perusing, wrighting, comparing, and transposing from key to key the best musick (of many parts in score and with as much variety as) he can procure; and all this so continuall that (as in the institution of an orator formerly used to be required) it may be accounted to have bin the great buisness of his life.[16]

Through the process of collecting these musical extracts, North asserts, the musician's memory will be filled with:

> ...numberless passages of approved ayre, and have...all the cursory graces of cadences and semi-cadences, and comon descants and break-ings, as well as the ordinary ornaments of accord, or touch. And all these in a manner as may be termed memoriter, in like manner as persons that deal in tunes and lessons have them by heart and can performe

---

15  John Wilson (ed.), *Roger North on Music; Being a Selection from His Essays Written during the Years c. 1695–1728* (London: Novello, 1959), p. 140.
16  Wilson (ed.), *Roger North on Music*, pp. 140–1.

without thinking, and even as sometimes camon fidlers will play when fast asleep; which I mention to shew what exactness and perfection of memoriall habit a master ought to be armed with, to enable him to be a perfect voluntier.[17]

The cultivation of so-called artificial memory was present across many different sectors of society across Europe up into the early eighteenth century, revived from a set of techniques employed primarily in classical oration. Orators in ancient Greece and Rome were trained to imagine 'memory houses' in order to memorise speeches, placing key pieces of information in specific rooms or *loci* that could then be accessed by conjuring up a visual image of the 'house' and visiting various rooms to recall parts of the speech. The practice was used across many different activities and disciplines including music, as scholars such as Gregory Butler,[18] Leo Treitler[19] and Massimiliano Guido have shown.[20] The art of memory was often called upon in the composition or improvisation of certain genres, with musicians memorising certain melodic formulae, contrapuntal modules or harmonic paradigms that would act as aural *loci* or rooms that could be visited in order to facilitate the creation of a particular genre of music.

The notion of creating a 'memory house' in the imagination comes from the Aristotelian principle that we are 'imprinted' by the things we perceive through our senses. This idea was adopted in early modern England by several figures including the physician Helkiah Crooke (1576–1648), who in his *Mikroksomographia* (published in 1615) proposed a reading of the Aristotelian model where sensing was an active way of engaging with and being imprinted by the sensory environment.[21] The

---

17   Wilson (ed.), *Roger North on Music*, p. 141.
18   Gregory G. Butler, 'The Fantasia as Musical Image', *The Musical Quarterly* 60.4 (1974), 602–15.
19   Leo Treitler, 'Speaking of the I-Word', in *The Oxford Handbook of Critical Improvisation Studies, Vol. 2*, ed. by Benjamin Piekut and George E. Lewis (n.p.: Oxford Handbooks Online, 2014), https://doi.org/10.1093/oxfordhb/9780199892921.013.19
20   Massimiliano Guido, 'Climbing the Stairs of the Memory Palace: Gestures at the Keyboard for a Flexible Mind', in *Studies in Historical Improvisation: From Cantare super Librum to Partimenti*, ed. by Massimiliano Guido (Abingdon: Routledge, 2017), pp. 41–52.
21   Elizabeth L. Swann, 'Anatomizing Taste: Practice, Subjectivity, and Sense in *Mikroksomographia*', in Elizabeth L. Swann, *Taste and Knowledge in Early Modern England* (Cambridge: Cambridge University Press, 2020), pp. 71–100 (p. 93).

memory house was thus filled with both purposely placed/memorised things, and those environmental sounds, sights, tastes, and touches that the individual had encountered more passively.

Classical sources on this topic were continuously revived and adopted in early modern England. For example, in 1634, English politician and author Miles Sandys (1601–36) wrote a tract on 'Prudence', the sixth chapter of which treats memory as the first of three parts of prudence (the others being understanding and providence). Sandys describes this type of sensory encounter filling the memory storehouse:

> Memory keeps and hides, sayeth Aristotle, as it were a thing deposited, all sensible species judged, and thought one; that she may use them, when need requires. [...] As light and all colours and shapes of bodies are discerned by the eyes; by the ears all kinds of sounds; all odours by the passage of the nose; all tastes by that of the mouth, and by the sense of the whole body, what is hard, what soft, what warm or cold, gentle or sharp, heavy or light, either extrinsically or intrinsically: so all these things doth that grand receptacle of the memory receive; yea she restores and calls them back to mind at pleasure.[22]

Across the various sources on extemporary practice consulted for this chapter, this basic concept of memory as a bodily storehouse of past sensory experiences that are 'printed' on the body or brain remains constant. Rather than relying on a printed text, improvised activity was thus understood as a practice by which these 'prints' on the body might be read and performed—in some sense, the body becomes a text. This theory of memory and improvisation centres not only the physical bodies of historical personages and musicians, but also their personal experiences and identities. According to this theory, it seems logical to conclude that an English man who had travelled to Syria in the seventeenth century would produce different improvisations to a woman who stayed her whole life in rural Hampshire. The sounds, sights, and smells that they each imbibed during their lifetimes would be present in their improvisations, which become a bodily script of their personal histories.

---

22  William Engel, Rory Loughnane and Grant Williams (eds), *The Memory Arts in Renaissance England: A Critical Anthology* (Cambridge: Cambridge University Press, 2016), p. 133.

*Asking how we became improvisers is the story of who we are today.*

The idea of memorisation as a commitment of musical material *into* the body, which would then be able to improvise with this material almost of its own accord is a transhistorical phenomenon. For example, in a study of improvisation processes in jazz, Martin Norgaard relates a violinist telling him: 'the hand is gonna crawl around and the brain is gonna like try to pick out something that the hand is doing'.[23] Norgaard elaborates on this: 'in all cases, it appears that the process the improvisers described is separate from the conscious control of physical movements. When the violinist describes the hand as "crawling around" and "the brain" as picking out material, he gives the impression that the brain is monitoring what the hand is doing and the hand is not under conscious control'.[24]

In fact, in early modern music texts, the hand is often used to stand metonymically for the musician. Thomas Mace, for example, offers this brief description of a ground:

> The Ground is a set Number of Slow Notes, very Grave, and Stately; which, (after It is expres'd Once, or Twice, very Plainly) then He that hath Good Brains, and a Good Hand, undertakes to Play several Divisions upon It, Time after Time, till he has shew'd his Bravery, both of Invention and Hand.[25]

Simpson also uses the same language when describing how to make divisions: '…in this manner of Play, which is the perfection of the Viol, or any other Instrument, if it be exactly performed, a man may shew the Excellency both of his Hand and Invention, to the delight and admiration of those that hear him'.[26]

He continues:

> But this you will say is a perfection which some excellent Hands have not attained unto… True that is, that Invention is a gift of Nature, but much improved by Exercise and Practice. He that hath it not in so high

---

23 Martin Norgaard, 'Descriptions of Improvisational Thinking by Artist-Level Jazz Musicians', *Journal of Research in Music Education* 59.2 (2011), 109–27 (p. 117).
24 Norgaard, 'Descriptions of Improvisational Thinking', p. 117.
25 Thomas Mace, *Musick's Monument*, Reproduction en fac-similé (Éditions du Centre National de la Recherche Scientifique: Paris, 1958), p.129.
26 *The Division-Viol*, p. 27.

a measure as to play *ex tempore* to a Ground, may, notwithstanding give both himself and hearers sufficient satisfaction in playing such Divisions as himself or others have made for that purpose; in the performance whereof he may deserve the Name of an excellent Artist; for here the excellency of the Hand may be shewed as well as in the Other...[27]

Having an excellent 'Hand' or technical/physical skill does not equate to excellence in 'invention' or improvisational ability, which while it can be improved through application, is fundamentally 'a gift of Nature' that nevertheless must be exercised and improved upon. For these people who have not been blessed by nature with the gift of invention, they should play written divisions pre-composed either by themselves or someone else, which they might still be able to play with excellence since it is the hand not the invention that is responsible for this.

Unsurprisingly, another part of the body that appears in discussions of extemporary music-making is the ear. In a passage that echoes Simpson's notion of invention as a 'natural' gift, Roger North names the ear as an essential attribute for the improviser, writing that a 'good voluntiere' (or improviser) must be: 'a genius capable of musick, or what they call an ear, for divers persons have not that; and tho' application and industry will conquer some ineptitudes, yet others that proceed from naturall defect, of which musicall incapacity is one, are never to be remedied'.[28] According to North then, the ear could be trained to a certain extent yet ultimately was largely dependent on nature for its success.

The ear is also discussed as an autonomous entity by the Italian violinist Nicola Matteis, who came to London in the 1670s. In Book 2 of his collection of *Ayrs* for example, he presents a *Corrente da Orecchia* (Corrente for the ears) and *Corrente da piedi* (Corrente for the feet) alongside one another, where one is for 'listening' and one for 'dancing'.[29] Instead of denoting the activities for which they are intended, he names

---

27 *The Division-Viol*, p. 27.
28 Wilson (ed.), *Roger North on Music*, p.136.
29 *Other Ayrs Preludes Allmands Sarabands with Full Stops for the Violin by Nicola Matteis, The Second Part* (n.p.: n.d.), pp. 24–5, https://s9.imslp.org/files/imglnks/usimg/5/5e/IMSLP99060-PMLP203526-Matteis_Nicola_2._Other_ayrs_preludes_allmands_sarabands.pdf

instead the body parts that they engage. In the two versions of this piece, shown in Figure 4, a very similar melody is presented differently to accommodate the ear and the feet respectively: the ear's version contains violin stopping for its delectation and running quavers to display the violinist's virtuosity (and no doubt, their ornamentation on the repeats); the version for the feet, on the other hand, starts with the same motif an octave higher (perhaps to be heard better by dancers), and presents a much simpler melodic contour to highlight the Corrente's rhythms.

Fig. 4 Nicola Matteis, *Ayrs*, Book 2 (n.d.: n.p.), p. 24, public domain.

Like Simpson, Matteis also discusses the hand, notating some pieces in the same collection as 'per far la mano'—to 'make the hand'.[30] As Figure 5 displays, the passage over which this phrase is written shows a very simple falling sequence, quite different to the preceding material. Matteis does not elaborate on what he means by the phrase or why it is related to this musical passage, yet its scalic and sequential nature suggests it may have been a way to train the violinist in the performance of similar falling sequences, perhaps similarly to Simpson's exemplar passages on how to make divisions over particular intervals.

---

30 *Ayres For the Violin to Wit...The Third and Fourth Parts Composed by Nicola Matteis* (n.p.: n.d.), p. 2, https://s9.imslp.org/files/imglnks/usimg/7/75/IMSLP99061-PMLP203526-Matteis_Nicola_3._Ayres_for_the_violin.pdf

Fig. 5 Nicola Matteis, *Ayrs*, Book 3 (n.d.: n.p.), p. 2, public domain.

Matteis's well-known reputation as an improviser adds a further dimension to his embodied markings. A diary entry by John Evelyn on 19 November 1674 describes the extraordinary powers of the violin in Matteis's hand, using the word 'spiritato', in seventeenth-century English most commonly used to refer to a religious enthusiast, to describe his 'ravishing' improvisations on a ground bass:

> I heard that stupendious Violin Signor Nicholao (with other rare Musitians) whom certainly never mortal man exceeded on that instrument: he had a stroak so sweete, & made it speake like the Voice of a man; & when he pleased, like a Consort of severall Instruments: he did wonders upon a note: was an excellent Composer also: here was also that rare Lutinist Dr. Wallgrave: but nothing approch'd the Violin in Nicholas hand: he seem'd to be spiritato'd & plaid such ravishing things on a ground as astonish'd us all.[31]

Evelyn's use of religious vocabulary to describe Matteis's 'spiritato'd' state and almost mystical abilities is particularly striking given my later discussion of practices of extemporary prayer and their resonances with extemporary music-making. In fact, they also exist side-by-side in Evelyn's diary. An entry just four days earlier on 15 November had described his visit to hear Gilbert Burnet (1643–1715), 'the most celebrated extempore preacher of his day'.[32]

---

31  E. S. de Beer (ed.), *Diary of John Evelyn, Volume IV: Kalendarium, 1673–1689* (Oxford: Oxford University Press, 1955), p. 48.

32  de Beer (ed.), *Diary of John Evelyn*, pp. 47–8 (see footnote 5).

Of this occasion, Eveyln writes:

> The Anniversary of my Baptisme I first heard that famous and Excellent Preacher Dr. Burnet [...] explicating the nature and Dignity of the human Soule, & new-man: how to be made conformable to the Image of God; with such a floud of Eloquence, & fullnesse of matter as shew'd him to be a person of extraordinary parts.[33]

Whether in music or prayer, successful improvisation could be achieved by training different parts of the body and mind. Simpson and Matteis's texts show the hand and ear being 'cultivated' from their natural state, becoming useful tools for extemporisation. However, this 'making' of the ear and hand occurs here through the musical entrainment of bodies via print, somewhat complicating the relationship between improvisation and a printed text.

While printed music and improvised music are frequently imagined as polar opposites, Simpson's text in particular challenges this binary understanding of the two: at which point does an improviser stop following Simpson's printed examples and trust their own storehouse of material, and is it ever possible to make a clear distinction between them?

## Print, Orality and Literacy

The position of print between orality and literacy was perhaps symptomatic of the role of popular print in English society at this moment more broadly. The history of printing in England had started two centuries earlier in 1473/4, when William Caxton famously printed *The Recuyell of the Historyes of Troye*, closely followed in 1477 by the publication of Geoffrey Chaucer's *Canterbury Tales*, and in 1495, the first music print—eight notes in Chester monk Ranulf Higden's *Policronicon*, printed by Wynkyn de Worde in Westminster. However, it was not until the century following the Reformation that print became widely accessible and an important part of the dissemination and performance of early modern English culture, as epitomised by genres such as the broadside ballad, the woodcut picture, and the chapbook.[34] After Ottaviano Petrucci produced his first musical

---

33   de Beer (ed.), *Diary of John Evelyn*, pp. 47–8.
34   See Tessa Watt, *Cheap Print and Popular Piety, 1550–1640* (Cambridge: Cambridge University Press, 1991).

print in Venice in 1501 (a collection of ninety-six secular pieces in three/four parts), the course of music printing everywhere (including England) was to change, and in 1530 the first known print of English secular music appeared, a collection titled *XX Songes*.

Between the 1530s and the mid-seventeenth century, the printing and dissemination of secular and 'popular' music went from being a rarity to becoming an established practice in England, and had become a standard way for music to be written down and shared across different contexts and by different musicians. However, the way that print (both musical and non-musical) was used, and the way it functioned within the entrenched, pre-existing oral culture of seventeenth-century England, meant that the popular printing of these texts did not immediately herald the end of an oral society and the start of a literate one. Rather, they shaped a society in which print became part of oral culture, and oral culture became part of print.

Within this wider context, Simpson's treatise functions as a key example of how print and improvisation were not considered as opposites but became blurred in calling upon print to train the improvising body. However, Simpson's text goes beyond merely training the body to improvise; his understanding of music in/and the world suggests that such a practice is connected to a wider conception of the harmony of body, soul and universe. In the earlier part of his text where he discusses how to play the viol, Simpson elaborates on his theory of cosmic harmony, explaining how the seven notes of a scale and their potential consonances lead him to reflect on 'the Mysterious Number of Seven' and encourage a 'Contemplation of the Universe'.[35] He continues:

> When with these I compare my Seven Graduall Sounds, I cannot but also admire the Resemblance of Their Harmonies: the Concords of the One so exactly answering the Aspects of the other; as a Unison, to a Conjunction; an Octave, to an Opposition; the Middle Consonant in a Diapason, to the Middle Aspects in an Orb; as a Third, Fifth, Sixth in Musick, to a Trine, Quartile, Sextile in the Zodiack. And as These by moving into Such and Such Concords, Transmit into the Eare an Influence of Sound, which doth not only strike the Sense, but even affects the very Soule, stirring it up to a devout Contemplation of the Divine Principle, from whence all Harmony proceeds; and therefore very fitly applied to Sing and Sound forth his Glory and Praise.[36]

---

35  *The Division-Viol*, p. 23.
36  *The Division-Viol*, pp. 23–4.

This conception of musical harmony as a way for the musician to reach 'devout Contemplation of the Divine Principle, from whence all Harmony proceeds', is configured as a process that progressed from the ear to the striking of the senses and the stirring of the soul. In fact, musical harmony and the making of such harmonies by the musician, becomes an analogue for the perfection of the universe and God's creation:

> ...when I further consider, that taking any One Sound, if you joyn thereto Another, a Third above it; and then place Another, a Third above that also; these Three thus conjoined and Sounding together, do Constitute One entire Harmony, which Governs and Comprises all the Sounds, which by Art, or Imagination, can at once be joined together in Musicall Concordance: This I cannot but think a Significant Embleme of that Supreme, and Incomprehensible Three in One, Governing, Comprising, and Disposing the whole Machine of the World, with all its included Parts in a Perfect Harmony.

Since Simpson heard the Holy Trinity and its ordinance over the 'whole machine of the world' reflected in the harmony of the musical triad, his concept of the seven notes of a scale as comprised of three superimposed triads place the musician in a role of great responsibility, where their treatment of the triad should mirror divine perfection and harmony. Playing a 'wrong' note or disharmonious chord in this context is not just jarring to the ear, but could be detrimental to the musician's soul and to the world's order. In this light, the stakes of musical improvisation are high: who would be willing to risk causing such disharmony through unskilful improvisation?

Simpson concludes, 'what I have already mentioned, is enough to persuade me, that in the Harmony of Sounds, there is some great and hidden Mystery above what I find delivered'.[37] This tone of mysticism frames the study of harmony and of making divisions as an arcane practice. Later in the book, Simpson refers explicitly to the 'chief Mysterie of Division to a Ground', splitting this mystery into three parts: firstly that the division be harmonious to the holding note, secondly that the division leads to the next note of the bass line in a 'smooth and natural passage' and thirdly that if the division passes into discords, that 'they should be such as are aptly used in Composition'.[38]

---

37  *The Division-Viol*, p. 24.
38  *The Division-Viol*, p. 30.

In light of Simpson's theory of cosmic harmony, which reflects widely-held beliefs at the time, the importance of improvising correctly, and ironically of *not* leaving anything to chance, becomes more apparent.[39] But what, then, was the relationship between improvisation, the musician's body, and print? And what possible dangers did improvisation entail, given its deeply embodied location?

## Extemporary Prayer

As I followed the 'extemporary' through the digital early modern English archive, I became drawn into reading texts on extemporary prayer, looking there for a fuller understanding of the 'extemporary' in early modern England—how it affected early modern bodies and conceptions of being human, and how it related to the memory storehouse model that North and others describe.

'Extemporary' or 'unpremeditated' prayer had become a site of significant and heated debate throughout seventeenth-century England, a time of great tumult in liturgical practice following first the Reformation in 1517, Elizabeth I's excommunication from the Catholic Church in 1570, and the Civil War and so-called 'Glorious Revolution' through the 1640s–80s. The English historian Judith Maltby situates liturgical practice in revolutionary England between two main events: the collection of laws governing religious practice introduced between 1558–63 by Elizabeth I (known as the Elizabethan Religious Settlement), and the rise of a seventeenth-century reform movement within the Church of England started by the Archbishop William Laud (known as 'Laudianism').[40]

One of the central debates within the church in this period of upheaval concerned the *Book of Common Prayer* (1559). While many preachers urged worshippers to follow its set forms, others rejected both the notion of having 'stage directions' for worship, and the idea

---

39 It is worth noting that this cosmic connection between musical notes, celestial bodies and human souls and bodies was a philosophy shared entirely with the Eurasian Islamicate world.

40 Judith Maltby, '"Extravagencies and Impertinencies": Set Forms, Conceived and Extempore Prayer in Revolutionary England', in *Worship and the Parish Church in Early Modern Britain*, ed. by Alec Ryrie and Natalie Mears (Farnham: Ashgate, 2013), pp. 221–43.

of repeating the same text day after day and month. These preachers claimed both that the text of the liturgy needed reform, and that the 'creative workings' of the Holy Spirit were being stifled by the *Book of Common Prayer*'s repetitive nature. On this latter point, for example, the Ipswich town preacher Samuel Ward wrote in 1635: 'there was not that life to quicken either hearer or speaker in the reading of an homily or prayer, though penned never soe elegantly, as there was by prayer and preaching by the Spirit, and that a Parrett might be taught to repeat forms without affection'.[41]

Since 'all the [Protestant] reformers agreed that true prayer was created by the workings of the Holy Spirit—in other words, true prayer could never be a "work"', this created some major issues around the use of the *Book of Common Prayer* and in 1645 a new worship book was approved by an ordinance of Parliament to replace the *Book of Common Prayer*. This new manual was titled: a 'Directory for the Public Worship of God'.[42] As Maltby observes,

> the Directory was a revolutionary solution to the Prayer Book 'problem'. To those more familiar with the latter, the Directory reads like a set of stage directions with very few speaking parts. The noted mid-twentieth century liturgist, E.C. Ratcliff put it succinctly by remarking that the Directory was 'not so much a prayer book as a rubric book'.[43]

The unique relationship between orality and written text in the Directory framed the book as a set of structures for extemporisation, operating as a kind of halfway house between the set forms of the *Book of Common Prayer* and the complete freedom of extemporary prayer, in a similar fashion to how Simpson's text mediated between printed music and free improvisation.

While Simpson concedes that consecutive fifths and eights created when playing divisions to a ground may '...scandalize a young Composer, and perhaps give offence to some old Critick', he does not describe forms of transgressive extempory music-making in too much further detail.[44] In the domain of extemporary prayer however, we find a

---

[41]  Maltby, '"Extravagencies and Impertinencies"', p. 181.
[42]  Maltby, '"Extravagencies and Impertinencies"', p. 222.
[43]  Maltby, '"Extravagencies and Impertinencies"', p. 225.
[44]  *The Division Viol*, p. 42.

number of written refutations against the practice, in the form of printed books and pamphlets explaining how harmful it could be.

In the preface to his English translation of bishop Lancelot Andrews's Greek prayer book in 1648, parish priest and Laudian ceremonialist Richard Drake writes that readers should learn of '...His [Andrews's] *Judgement* concerning Extempo|re Conceptions, and undigested Praiers'.[45] It is worth noting the bodily language used even here, with the womb-like associations of 'conception' and connotations of the gut evoked by 'undigested'. Drake continues:

> I am confident He had as great abilities of expressing himself to purpose *without pre|meditation*, as anie Rabbie that pretends to the highest pitch of In|spiration. But his *De|votion* had not taught Him to cast off his *Humilitie*; nor was He so little aquainted with *His God* and *Him|self*, as not to know His distance and to keep it. It had been a sin to Him to appear before *His God* emptie, or with that which cost Him no|thing.[46]

In other words, Drake sees extemporary prayer almost as disrespectful, arguing that even in the case of Andrews, who had 'great abilities of expressing himself to purpose *without pre|meditation*', to improvise prayer would be to overstep the boundaries of divine intimacy and represent a cheap or 'emptie' manner in which to address God. Drake goes on:

> There is too much of a Pharisee in him that dares to trust to his Mem|orie, his Phancie, or Invention before the Majestie of Heaven; when even his most premeditated and weigh|ed thoughts, though clothed in the best at|tire of language, would be esteemed by himself too unworthie to be offered to his Prince. And yet such is the ir|religion of this Age, the most High God must take up and be content with that homelie en|tertainment, which my Lord or Ladie, forsooth, would not receive from their most faithfull ser|vant without great scorn and indignation.[47]

Drake reaches his fever pitch of indignation as his text continues, and actually invokes music: 'But it is the highest pitch of sacrilege to make the Scripture pa|tronize Impietie. They abuse the Text and the Apostle,

---

45 John Walter, 'Affronts and Insolencies: The Voices of Radwinter and Popular Opposition to Laudianism', *English Historical Review* 122.495 (2007), 35–60.

46 *A Manual of the Private Devotions and Meditations of The Right Reverend Father in God Lancelot Andrews, Late Lord Bishop of Winchester Translated out of a Fair Greek MS. of His Amanuensis by R.D., B.D.* (London: Printed for W.D. by Humphrey Moseley, 1648), n.p., https://quod.lib.umich.edu/e/eebo2/A25391.0001.001?view=toc

47 *Devotions and Meditations*, n.p.

that urge His, *I will praie with the spirit*, to justifie *En|thusiasm in Praijing*, unless they will, what never anie brainsick Novelist attempted, in|terpret to us, *I will sing with the spirit*, with their *extempora|rie Music*'.[48] Here Drake is referring to a passage in *Corinthians* which discusses modes of prayer and the importance of praying both with 'the spirit' and with 'the understanding': 'What is it then? I will pray with the spirit, and I will pray with the understanding also: I will sing with the spirit, and I will sing with the understanding also'.[49]

Drake seems to be suggesting that extemporary prayer—and by extension extemporary music—uses the idea of praying/singing with the spirit as a way to justify the lack of understanding inherent in improvised acts. Finally, lest the reader should be left in any doubt as to the salvific nature of the written word and its superior status to the extemporary in not permitting 'fruitless matter' or 'idle words', he explains that Andrews did not use this passage in Corinthians to draw such 'wild conclusions' about the permissibility of extemporary prayer and song:

> His Reading had not taught this learned Father to make such wild conclusions; Nor would his *Pietie* per|mit Him to licence them to others, or Him|self. Hence it is that, in His addresses to His God, His *Heart* was kindled, first, with *ho|lie fire*; nor would He then present His *Thoughts* upon the *Altar*, til He had weigh'd them in the balance of the Sanc|tuarie, and by commit|ting them to *Faithful writing* left no room for fruitless *matter* or idle *words*.[50]

Drake's characterisation of the extemporary is as a wild, disrespectful mode of expression that ignores the rational 'understanding' in favour of 'spirit'—an unbalanced reflection of the 'holie fire' that kindled the speaker's heart. Its unpremeditated nature represents goes against any notion of planning ahead, and against the ultimate pre-planned nature of text. In this characterisation, the extemporary is othered in opposition to the *Book of Common Prayer*—the author's extreme position on how a person is to communicate with God precludes any kind of spontaneity in expression.

The construction of the extemporary as a space of alterity also

---

48   *Devotions and Meditations*, n.p.
49   Corinthians 14:15, King James Bible (1611), https://www.kingjamesbibleonline.org/1611_1-Corinthians-14-15/
50   *Devotions and Meditations*, n.p.

extended to religious and racial othering. As a result, Islam and Muslims were often evoked in these texts. An embedded and complex example of this occurs in a polemical work of 1661, in which Ireneus Freeman (potentially an alias for the clergyman John Sedgwick) responded to the nonconformist Henry Daubney's earlier defence of extempore prayer over prescribed forms of public worship.[51]

Freeman argues that even if extemporary prayer is what seems naturally right to us, it is still wrong if we are commanded to pray by the book. He uses illustrative examples to explicate his point that are not directly relevant to the topic at hand yet deeply telling of some of the unspoken connections between extemporary prayer, authority and notions of otherness. Freeman claims that to strengthen his point, he will 'prove' that 'lawful Authority' in the church has the power to impose 'significative Ceremonies'—in other words, ceremonies or practices that show reverence through what they signify rather than what they inherently mean.[52]

By way of example, he describes how a Magistrate has the power to command that people should uncover their heads when they pray to God, not because it is indecent in itself to uncover one's head, but because the command entails a level of respect and reverence. Freeman continues '…we are not to understand by it, the absolute nature of man universally, but the conditional nature and Idiopathy of such Countrey-men…many times signifying Birth and Breeding. Otherwise nature would teach the Turks the same manners, who yet signify their respects by keeping on their Turbans'.[53]

This passing reference reveals a fascinating logic by which discussions of the extemporary might actually shape understandings of human nature. Here, 'Turks' (a term that stood for racial and religious otherness, denoting both Muslims and Turkish/Arab people) are somewhat distanced from conceptions of nature by reason of their 'birth and breeding', and are thus not to be included within English

---

51 Ireneus Freeman, *Logikē latreia the Reasonablenesse of Divine Service: Or Non-Conformity to Common-Prayer, Proved not Conformable to Common Reason: In Answer to the Contrary Pretensions of H. D. in a Late Discourse Concerning the Interest of Words in Prayer and Liturgies/by Ireneus Freeman* (London: Printed and sold by Tho. Basset, 1661), https://ota.bodleian.ox.ac.uk/repository/xmlui/handle/20.500.12024/A48963
52 Freeman, *Logikē latreia*, p. 3.
53 *Logikē latreia*, p. 4.

Christian assumptions of what is 'natural'. Furthermore, a mistrust of human nature as a guide to correct behaviour means that we must look to authority (whether religious or political) to tell us what to do. By evoking the example of the 'Turk', Freeman implicitly sets up a scale of 'human nature' that some measure up to and others fall short of through his enunciation of human-ness.

The Scottish Protestant minister George Gillespie also implicated Muslims in his writing on extempory prayers, although this time in support of the practice. In a pamphlet entitled *Reasons for Which the Service Booke, Urged upon Scotland Ought to Be Refused* (1638), he argues that prayers should be spontaneous, rather than pre-planned, so that the Holy Spirit may influence the speaker. He lists many reasons supporting extemporary prayer, arguing that 'it is not lawfull for a man to tie himselfe, or bee tyed by others, to a prescript forme of vvords in prayer and exhortation'.[54] He lists ten reasons why this is the case, including: '*Eyghtly*, It may all be done by a *Boy of 7 yeares olde,* and so every private man that can read, yea, a Turcke if he can read, may be such a Minister'. By Gillespie's argument, since the text does not require spontaneous engagement, anyone could be a minister, even someone who is a heretic or who is clearly (to him and his reader) not suited for this role. A fixed liturgy cannot discover whether the person reading it and praying has a suitable nature.

In both Freeman and Gillespie's texts, the figure of the Turk functions as an undefined figure of alterity, serving to re-affirm each author's position on extemporary prayer. By situating arguments for or against extemporary prayer in relation to this undefined figure, both authors actually write Muslims into a spectrum of humanity and nature. The extemporary either illuminates how far away 'English nature' is from that of the Turks, or shows how, under the cover of the printed word, that nature can be disguised. Either way, it is often in relation to the Turk that the extemporary is discussed, constructing ideas of both Christian and Muslim humanity in the process.

---

54 George Gillespie, *Reasons for Which the Service Booke, Urged upon Scotland Ought to Be Refused* (Edinburgh: Printed by G. Anderson, 1638), n.p., https://quod.lib.umich.edu/cgi/t/text/text-idx?c=eebo2;idno=A11744.0001.001

## Reading the Body's Prints

In other anti-extempore texts, the process of extemporising prayer was intimately connected to transgressions of the body, notions of self-love and a concomitant dangerous, individualistic passion for freedom. Elsewhere in his tract, Freeman explains that when a schoolboy uses his 'invention' to make up his own poetic verses, he will experience a certain 'intention and heat' (perhaps similar to Drake's 'holie fire'—in fact the language of heat is pervasive in many of these texts) which 'reading an Author' will simply not yield, since 'invention takes up the soul, be it in what subject it will.'[55]

This 'invention' that supposedly lay at the heart of extemporising one's own words derived its 'heat' from love of the self: 'men are naturally more affected with their own inventions, then with those of others; and therefore extempore Prayers may more affect them then prescribed forms, upon no better an ac|count then [sic] that of self-love'.[56] The heat of this exertion is represented as a dangerous and intensely bodily practice: 'when a man doth strongly bend his wit in study (most of all in *invention*) he feels a sensible heat in his body, insomuch that I have known some to put a napkin dipped in cold water on their heads'.[57] English literature scholar Joseph Pappa describes further the early modern belief that bodily heat could be caused by an extreme passion that stimulated the imagination, and explains how such passions could also imprint the memory/brain.[58]

In addition to this heat, the invention associated with extemporary prayer affects the breath too:

> Any man (I think) may experience, that in such an employment he doth not breath so freely and frequently as ordinarily he doth; which will be most apparent to such as take Tobacco; even as a man holds his breath when he is about with all his might to strike a blow. And this obstruction of the breath alone is sufficient to effect an extraordinary fervency in the blood and spirits.[59]

---

55 *Logikē latreia*, p. 27.
56 *Logikē latreia*, p. 27.
57 *Logikē latreia*, pp. 28–9.
58 Joseph Pappa, *Carnal Reading: Early Modern Language and Bodies* (Newark: University of Delaware Press, 2011), p.16.
59 *Logikē latreia*, p. 29.

Moreover, Freeman seems to suggest that the unpremeditated nature of the extemporary and its need for quick invention could exhaust and strain the body: 'Besides, when a man is not only to invent, but to invent as fast as the Auditors expect he should utter: in case matter comes not fast enough, he will be apt to draw out his last words to the great straining of his body, and to make up the defect of matter with more then ordinary earnestnesse in the delivery'.[60]

To overcome this extemporary passion and its negative effects on the body, it is necessary to be restrained by 'forms'. Freeman quotes the Bishop of Norwich who likens these composed forms to physical ropes and bondage (echoing Gillespie, who used such language negatively): 'Now men using their own liberty in extempore Prayers, but being limited and tyed up by Forms, they may be more intent and fervent in the former then in the latter, upon no better principle then that which is most predominant in the most corrupt men, which are the most independent, and say, Let us break their bonds asunder, and cast their cords from us'.[61] This image of 'breaking bonds asunder' is striking; the claim is that people who extemporise prayer are 'corrupt' and 'independent', breaking free of printed text that becomes a *cord* to prevent freedom and a person's own inventions.[62] In this context, the practice of reading prayers takes on a controlling and oppressive role, restraining not only the person's freedom but also their invention.

According to Freeman, the advantage of reading 'prints and characters in a book' lies in the 'easie bringing of the Idea's into the head'.[63] He argues that:

> every man that is an expert reader (especially in reading that, which he hath read often, in a fair print) doth probably find, that he heeds the characters little, or not at all, but minds the sense, or something else. Nor is the Soul necessarily more abstracted from all created objects in extempore Prayers, then it may be in reading a Prayer out of a Book. The created objects, which are met with in a Book, are the Prints and Characters in the Book: But he that prayes without book (especially with vocal prayer) must needs look upon the like prints and stamps made in the Brain: or whatsoever things the species are, without which a man

---

60  *Logikē latreia*, p. 29.
61  *Logikē latreia*, p. 28.
62  *Logikē latreia*, p. 28.
63  *Logikē latreia*, p. 30.

can neither speak nor think, they must needs be created objects...[64]

This passage starts as a direct rebuttal of Henry Daubney's suggestion that the worshipper's soul is 'abstracted' during extemporary prayer since it is focussed solely on the action of praying and not on the material object of the book. On the contrary, Freeman argues, if the worshipper's attention is not on the printed text in a book, it will be redirected to the 'prints and stamps made in the Brain', recalling my earlier discussion of early modern beliefs around the brain-printing capacities of sensory impressions. Freeman's argument is that it is better to read from a book of scripture than your own brain, since prayer must depend on reading one or the other. This assertion goes back to a belief that the human mind is the product of a bodily text, written through a person's sensory engagements with the world. Following this model, the practice of improvisation is thus a process of reading and reanimating the stamps and imprints formed on the brain through these sensations.

Freeman's arguments against extemporary prayer are based on an assumption that the practice physically affects the body negatively and results in overheating and exhaustion, as well as the conviction that reading from a book is necessarily better than reading the 'brain's prints'. In this context, then, there is less of an opposition between body and text than a convergence, where the body becomes a type of text that can be read, perhaps as a memory book of that person's histories. The separation between body and text results in a type of bondage, restraining that person's imagination and inventions, and curtailing their body and its memories to a certain extent. As we shall see, this view of the extemporary affecting the body and leading the person to damage themselves in some way could take even more striking forms, with text positioned almost as a means of self-preservation.

One extreme example of the belief that improvisation could negatively imprint itself on the body is found in sectarian literature. George Spinola's book of 1646 falls into this category, in which the author proposes ways in which those separatists from the Church of England who participate in the un-orthodoxies of extemporary prayer might engage in 'face-mending' to 'correct' the facial differences that

---

64   *Logikē latreia*, p. 30.

their practices had supposedly caused.⁶⁵ The text tells us of his extremely racist and ableist beliefs about what extemporising could do to the body, and also intimates how the practices of these people (including those of extemporary prayer) were heard as acts of non-conformity and transgression that (here at least) could be countered by a type of eugenicist bodily 'correction'.⁶⁶

Spinola writes about the 'exotick, forrain' appearance of separatists, for whom he presents exercises of the 'imagination' for 'facemending', since he notes that their imagination is greater than their 'reason' and a 'clear intellectual minde.'⁶⁷ The possession of reason and a clear intellectual mind are thus set in opposition to the lack of rationality and imagination of the 'exotick' and 'forrain', ascribing a racist and exoticised otherness to those who engage in extemporary prayer—in fact, in another passage, Spinola explicitly states: 'your companies are full, and of shapes, strange and exotick [...] if you chance to mingle your loves promiscuously [...] as you interweave opinions, and beget monsters, in reason, your church may well vie with Africk for monstrous shapes'.⁶⁸

The key to changing physiognomies lay in reading 'corrective' texts—sometimes as much for their visual characteristics as for what they actually say, since Spinola believed that if people were to look at certain images or words, these images would affect the appearance of their children, making them resemble what they had looked at and read.⁶⁹ Spinola asserts that print could physically effect changes on people's physiognomies, mobilising ableist and racist ideologies to curtail extemporary practice. In this way, the 'otherness' of the extemporary becomes racialised and sexualised; it is a way to compromise 'human nature', which is constructed in the process.⁷⁰

---

65  *Rules to Get Children by with Handsome-faces: Or, Precepts for the Paptists, that Get Children by Book and for the Extemporary Sectaries, that Get Children without Book, to Consider What They Have to Doe, and Look Well before They Leape* [...] *Composed by George Spinola. Published According to Order* (London: Printed for T.S., 1646), http://hdl.handle.net/20.500.14106/A93684

66  While it is beyond the scope of my chapter to explore this further, it is worth noting that sects that embraced extemporary prayer were often not in favour of musical expression in devotional practice, while those sects that embraced music as part of worship frequently reviled extemporary prayer practices.

67  *Rules*, p. 2.

68  *Rules*, p. 6.

69  *Rules*, p. 5.

70  Walter Mignolo's 'local and self-promoted emergence of *the model/human* in

The association of the extemporary with a 'deviant' sexuality recall Freeman's notion of the extemporary as a type of transgressive self-love—a self-reflexive category that destabilises the normative separation between self and text, as though the extemporiser has transgressed the boundaries of divine authority and textual authorship by taking themselves as that authority and *becoming* their own text. The entanglement with temporality (signalled by *ex tempore*) thus seems to reach beyond the 'unpremeditated' and become associated with an 'unnatural' reflexivity of self, one in which the extemporiser subverts the proper separation between reader and text by inscribing themselves with the improvisations they imagine.

These writings about extemporary prayer show that, whatever the writer's stance, they often became a space to discuss and construct ideas of human nature. By problematising a clear-cut distinction between print and extemporary practice, improvisation become a space of making and remaking the human body through mediating between the body's prints and printed texts. And in the spaces between these two, perhaps we can start to sense something of the 'mystery' of improvisation that Simpson evokes. The extreme beliefs about extemporary prayer leading to physical disfigurements or racialised otherness also serve to inscribe and put limits on 'human-ness', a limitation that is more easily conveyed and fixed through text than through the fluidity and flux of improvisation. In this light, Simpson's instructions for improvisation, and the status of his printed text, transcend the purely musical and may take on a role of social and spiritual regulation.

## Law and Order: Policing the Extemporary Body

The extemporary's reach extended not only to bodies in prayer, but also to the early modern state and its laws. Freeman theorises extemporary prayer as a break with law and (natural) order, arguing rather obtusely that while it is unlawful to impose the Common Prayer over other forms

---

the European Renaissance' comes to mind—what he describes as a 'fictional' reconceptualization and reinvention of the human, achieved through 'the (epistemic) invention of imperial and colonial differences'. See Walter D. Mignolo and Catherine E. Walsh, *On Decoloniality: Concepts, Analytics, Praxis* (Durham: Duke University Press, 2018), p. 153.

(including extempore ones), this does not mean that it is unlawful to use the Common Prayer in itself, and furthermore that it should be used when commanded. The idea that the Common Prayer is not to be used, he argues, is 'absurd', 'since I could instance in hundreds of things, which ought not to be commanded; and yet ought to be done, when commanded'.[71] Yet despite the unlawfulness of the imposition, Freeman argues that the upholding of these 'commands', regardless of whether they are reasonable or should be made, is essential to maintenance of personal and public 'order': 'Suppose the Magistrate command me to go three miles to Church, when there is as good a Minister in every re|spect within a mile: This command hinders the exercise of my devotion not a little, and therefore it ought not to have been imposed: Yet for all that, it must be obeyed'.[72]

He continues:

> If it be re|plyed, that every man is bound to take the course which tends most to his edification in it self, though it be forbidden by Au|thority: and consequently that in such a case I should go to the nearest Church, and make use of extempore prayers, rather then prescribed ones: I answer, that by this Rule every houshold-servant should leave all attendance on his Master on Sun|days, and go into his Closet; that way tending most directly in it self to his edification.[73]

In other words, extemporary practice can call obedience and authority into question, since it offers the possibility of following one's own will rather than that of an external authority—here, for example, it might stop the hypothetical servant doing as the master says, in order to further their own 'edification'. Freeman counters this with an argument of expediency:

> the servant should wisely con|sider, If I disobey my Master, that I may have a better opportu|nity and help for my devotion now; I shall be outed of his fami|ly, and put into a condition attended with far more distractions at other times. And the wise Christian subject will argue in like manner. If I disobey the Magistrate in going to the next Church, or not using the Common Prayer; and many others do as I do: the Laws being exposed to contempt, wars and confusions will arise in the Kingdom: or, if the Laws

---

71   *Logikē latreia*, p. 2.
72   *Logikē latreia*, p. 2.
73   *Logikē latreia*, p. 2.

are vindicated, I who break them must be under restraint: and both these
wayes I shall have worse advantages of edification afterward, for using
those which I thought absolutely best; against the will of my Rulers.[74]

Extemporary prayer is thus not only portrayed as 'better' for individuals outside the ruling class, but also highly dangerous. If practised, it could either lead to 'laws being exposed to contempt, wars and confusions' or necessitate that the person engaging in it be placed 'under restraint'. In order to preserve the authority of the church and the ruling classes and avoid anything resembling anarchy, the servant must obey the will of their rulers regardless of what they command. The importance of obeying order is thus crucial to personal and public safety, but also a way of reflecting the macrocosm of universal order and perfection through the microcosm of social behaviours and interactions.

The relationship of writing and extemporisation to law and legal practice was further commented on some thirty years later by the English philosopher and physician John Locke (1632–1704), who wrote in a political tract of 1690:

> The legislative, or supreme authority, cannot assume to its self a power to rule by extemporary arbitrary decrees, but is bound to dispense justice, and decide the rights of the subject by promulgated standing laws, and known authorized judges: for the law of nature being unwritten, and so no where to be found but in the minds of men, they who through passion or interest shall miscite, or misapply it, cannot so easily be convinced of their mistake where there is no established judge...[75]

Locke argues here that laws must be written and not extemporised, since natural law is unwritten and any person can misrepresent and misapply its true nature through an extemporary approach that is not fixed through writing. Through this process of writing and relinquishing extemporary freedom, he argues, society may escape the 'state of nature': 'to this end it is that men give up all their natural power to the society which they enter into, and the community put the legislative power into such hands as they think fit, with this trust, that they shall be governed by declared laws, or else their peace, quiet, and property will still be at the same

---

74 *Logikē latreia*, p. 2.
75 John Locke, *Second Treatise of Government and A Letter Concerning Toleration*, ed. by Mark Goldie (Oxford: Oxford World's Classics, 2016), p. 69.

uncertainty, as it was in the state of nature'.[76]

In a subsequent passage, Locke goes on to assert that by following extemporary laws, society will actually be in a worse state than its 'natural' one, since people will abuse the power it necessarily gives to their improvisatory choices:

> whatever form the common-wealth is under, the ruling power ought to govern by declared and received laws, and not by extemporary dictates and undetermined resolutions: for then mankind will be in a far worse condition than in the state of nature, if they shall have armed one, or a few men with the joint power of a multitude, to force them to obey at pleasure the exorbitant and unlimited decrees of their sudden thoughts, or unrestrained, and till that moment unknown wills, without having any measures set down which may guide and justify their actions: for all the power the government has, being only for the good of the society, as it ought not to be arbitrary and at pleasure, so it ought to be exercised by established and promulgated laws; that both the people may know their duty, and be safe and secure within the limits of the law; and the rulers too kept within their bounds, and not be tempted, by the power they have in their hands, to employ it to such purposes, and by such measures, as they would not have known, and own not willingly.[77]

These passages are particularly significant given that Britain's constitution remained 'unwritten' despite the Civil War and Revolution, and the fact that one of the most significant documents that make up this uncodified constitution was the Bill of Rights in 1689, which established the supremacy of Parliament over the Crown. While it is beyond the scope of this chapter to discuss English constitutional change in any detail, Locke's association of 'extemporary' activity with a state of nature, as well as his proposal that writing should codify this true extemporary natural law, adds another element to the nexus of improvisation, freedom and nature. Further, it shows that beliefs around the extemporary included not only music-making and prayer, but extended to broader questions of governance and statehood.

---

76   Locke, *Second Treatise*, p. 65.
77   Locke, *Second Treatise*, p. 70.

## 'Held by the Ears': Conclusion

What, then, did it mean to play extemporary music in seventeenth-century England? Was it a dubious practice of freedom? A source of transgression and danger? Was it to follow your nature, perhaps to read the prints on your brain and body? In the latter case, would extemporary forms thus constitute a way of revealing one's nature, and conversely, did texts that placed conditions and bounds on the extemporary seek to define and limit certain types of human nature?

Against this backdrop of extemporary prayer practices and what they entailed, we can now gain a better understanding of Simpson's project. The potential negative impact of extemporary prayer on the body suggests that perhaps Simpson's careful instructions on how to make extemporary music were a way to avoid such transgressions; and, also, that perhaps extemporary music was the closest one could get to the kind of divine or cosmic 'mystery' he describes. The power of improvisation derived from the autonomy of following one's own authority instead of that of a text, which could be seen as a freedom, or as a dangerous mis-configuration of both somatic and world orders. And yet Simpson's text restricts the authority of the self to the textual in ways that complicate more binary debates around extemporary prayer. By following his instructions for making extemporary prayer, the early modern improviser existed in a liminal state between following text completely and relying exclusively on their own fancy.

Descriptions of contemporaneous improvisation, however, suggest that in practice musicians overstepped such boundaries between text and body. In a well-known account of the violinist Nicola Matteis improvising, Roger North recalls: 'I have knowne him hold a roomfull of gentlemen and ladys by the ears for hours, and not a whisper scarce to be perceived among them…'[78] A silent audience was largely not characteristic of early modern English audiences, evidenced by North hyperbolically declaring he had never experienced this before nor since. Also striking is this metaphor of 'holding the audience by the ears'. The phrase recalls a Latin proverb of 'holding a wolf by the ears', with which classically-educated readers of

---

78  John Alexander Stinson, 'Roger North's Essay of Musicall Ayre: An Edition from the Autograph with Introduction and Commentary' (master's thesis, Australian National University, 1977), p. 331, https://openresearch-repository.anu.edu.au/handle/1885/133223

North would most probably have been familiar.

The proverb is exemplified through the character Antipho who, in the words of Roman playwright Terentius, says: *Auribus teneo lupum, nam neque quomodo a me amittam invenio neque uti retineam scio*[79]—'I hold a wolf by the ears, for I can't find either a way of getting rid of her nor do I know how to keep her'. According to Suetonius, this proverb was also used by the emperor Tiberius to describe his precarious and unstable position, exemplified by the dangers of the she-wolf.[80]

This linguistic background hints at a real sense of *mutual* danger between improviser and audience—Matteis might have seized control by holding them by the ears, but will he get bitten if he lets go? Here improvisation is framed as wild and dangerous, perhaps travelling from the invention of Matteis's ear and hands to the ears and bodies of the audience members. If extemporary practices trade in performances of human nature and revelations of each person's 'brain prints', perhaps what we are witnessing here is Matteis improvising *himself*. With no separation between body and text, the extemporary could become a space where human nature could be made and remade, heard and reheard, and where the potential for its expression was limitless.

---

[79] Terence, *Phormio*, ed. by Robert Maltby (Oxford: Oxbow Books, 2012), pp. 171–2.

[80] C. Suetonius Tranquillus, *Tiberius*, 25, ed. by Alexander Thomson. Perseus Digital Library, http://data.perseus.org/citations/urn:cts:latinLit:phi1348.abo013.perseus-eng1:25

# 2. Improvising Encounter: Travelogue Reading as World-Making

> For something to be a 'world' in my sense it has to be inhabited at present by some flesh and blood people [...] It may also be inhabited by some imaginary people.
>
> —María Lugones[1]

## Improvising 'Otherness'

In the years following the Protestant Reformations, England expanded its travel networks outside Europe. Elizabeth I had been officially excommunicated by Pope Pius V in 1570, which freed her of papal edicts that forbade Christian trade with Muslims. As a result, she started to send diplomats and merchants into the lands of the Ottoman empire. In this period, we therefore find reports of Christians 'turning Turk' (embracing Islam), as well as examples of Muslims who embraced Christianity, records of Muslims settling in England, and several visits from Ottoman and Moroccan diplomats. In literature and on the stage, Muslim characters cast as 'Turks' and 'Moors' entered the popular imagination, while countless travel accounts started to be published by English travellers in Turkey and the Ottoman Arab provinces, Morocco and Iran.

The role of print was crucial in disseminating these accounts, creating an English identity forged both in opposition to and alongside some of these cultural and geographical 'others'. As a result, early modern travel literature,

---

1 María Lugones, 'Playfullness, "World"-Travelling, and Loving Perception', *Hypatia* 2.2 (1987), 3–20 (p. 9).

both real and speculative, are significant texts for understanding this historical moment. In this chapter, I read some early modern English and Arabic travel texts that provoke questions around music, improvisation, listening and power.

As I have read and listened to these travel texts, I have tried to think with Argentine feminist writer María Lugones's concept of 'world-travelling': the sense of entering someone else's world, being changed by it, and seeing and hearing the world through their eyes. I have noticed this in myself as I have tried to enter the world of the texts, and I have also perceived what Lugones writes of as 'arrogant perception' in the imperialist attitudes found in some of these texts. When she writes about cultivating 'loving perception', I have located this as an attitude to traversing worlds that is accepting, curious and relational. Although Lugones' context of work (and life) is very different to mine here, I have found her thinking very helpful in my readings of these historical texts. When she considers 'playfulness' in this travel process, I have seen it as akin to a type of improvisation. I feel that the way I have drawn on and been inspired by Lugones's terms and ideas is improvisatory and playful in itself: an experiment in wondering, in improvising with ideas and texts across different times and places.

Before starting this world-travelling, it is important for me to highlight that the travelogues I read in this chapter were written at a time when England had not formally colonised any countries in the Ottoman empire. And so, when I occasionally refer to English writing as 'pre-/proto-colonial/imperialist', it is in relation to the countries under consideration: Egypt, Syria, Lebanon and Palestine. However, it is crucial to recognise that England's first colony was on the land of the Powhatan people (Jamestown, Virginia) in 1607, and that the seventeenth century is when the East India Company created colonies in India, as well as being the century of Royal prerogative in the African-Atlantic slave trade. These histories of colonialism, violence and brutality cannot and *should not* be set apart from England's contemporaneous relationships with inhabitants of South West Asia and North Africa, nor indeed from the imperialism of the Ottoman empire and the ways in which people of different religions and ethnicities lived under its jurisdiction.

These histories of 'pre'-colonisation are also deeply intertwined with stories of trade: by the time Elizabeth I's reign came to an end in 1603, several major trade companies had been established, including the Turkey Company in 1581, renamed the Levant Company in 1592. The seventeenth century would continue to see and hear major changes in England's relations to Istanbul and the so-called Ottoman Arab lands, moving from what historian Gerald Maclean calls 'imperial envy' to the formation of England's own 'Eastern empire'.[2] Moreover, as Maclean observes, despite England's lack of political power at this 'pre-Orientalist' moment, English depictions of the Ottoman East 'developed certain representational themes that would feed directly into the Orientalist mind set: these include such notions as backwardness, licentious eroticism, "different sexualities", barbaric cruelty, despotic absolutism'.[3] These discourses grew from and around the trade companies that maintained a double function as both economic and diplomatic bodies.

At the same time, as part of this culture of 'imperial envy', Elizabeth's renown and power as monarch were reinforced by her knowledge of and proximity to Ottoman/Islamic(ate) cultures and languages. In a poem of 1612 by the musician Richard Johnson (c.1583–1633) for example, her purported skill in speaking Turkish and Arabic resounds alongside her 'wonderfull' music-making, showing the elevated status of these languages alongside other skilled arts in early modern England, as well as her sonic excellence conveyed both through the sound of music and of these foreign tongues:[4]

> None like *Elizabeth* was found,/in learning so deuine:
> She had the perfect skilfull arts,/of all the muses nine.
> In Latten Gréeke and Hebrew shée,
> most excellent was knowne:
> To forraine Kings Ambassadors,
> the same was daily showne,
>
> The Itallian French and Spannish tongue,
> she well could speake and read.
> The Turkish and Arabian spéech,
> grew perfect at her need.

---

2   Gerald Maclean, *Looking East: English Writing and the Ottoman Empire Before 1800* (Basingstoke: Palgrave Macmillan, 2007), p. 20.
3   Maclean, *Looking East*, p. 19.
4   While I am not aware of any clear evidence that Queen Elizabeth I did indeed speak Arabic and Turkish, here the significance is more around the perceived importance and value of her fluency in these languages.

> Her musicke made her wonderfull,
> so cunning therein found:
> The fame whereof about the world,
> in Princes eares did sound.[5]

These contexts all form an important backdrop to my explorations of Anglo-Ottoman relations and constructions of identity through improvisatory practices in contemporary travelogues. As a metaphor for encounter and travel, I propose musical improvisation as an important lens through which to understand the complicated relationship between England and the Ottoman empire at this moment of imperial envy, colonial aspirations, and developing orientalist discourse: a way to travel worlds.[6]

## Sensory Encounter in Henry Blount's *Voyage into the Levant* (1636)

Early modern English travelogues of this period often included examples of improvisation, including but not limited to written depictions of 'improvising' Ottoman subjects by English travellers, and the scripted improvisations of the English travellers themselves.[7] These travelogues are fascinating locations for the study of imperialist (auto-)ethnography, and often became a site for extemporary processes of imagination and invention.[8]

---

5   Richard Johnson, *A Most Royall Song of the Life and Death of Our Late Renowned Princesse Queene Elizabeth* (London: Printed by G. Eld for Iohn Wright, 1612), n.p., https://name.umdl.umich.edu/A04551.0001.001
6   For a discussion of how eighteenth-century travel and travelogues were often treated as a space to explore wider socio-political issues, see Vanessa Agnew, *Enlightenment Orpheus: The Power of Music in Other Worlds* (Oxford: Oxford University Press, 2008), pp. 12–70.
7   This sense of improvisation as a self-interested imperial tool of simulation wielded by English travellers is discussed by Stephen Greenblatt in his book *Renaissance Self-Fashioning: From More to Shakespeare* (Chicago: The University of Chicago Press, 1980), pp. 222–54. Greenblatt frames improvisation as 'a central Renaissance mode of behaviour' defined by an ability to 'empathise' in a disinterested and manipulative manner.
8   See also Katherine Brown's article on representations of Indian music in seventeenth-century travel writing, which analyses topoi used to describe and understand 'Eastern' music in India: 'Reading Indian Music: The Interpretation of Seventeenth-Century European Travel-Writing in the (Re)construction of Indian Music History',

One such travelogue is that of Henry Blount (1602–82), an English landowner, traveller and author. Blount is known for publishing an account of his travels to Turkey and the Ottoman Arab lands in 1636, and for being a keen advocate of coffee, which he had encountered in Turkey and which he helped bring to England.[9] It is possible that Blount was on an official journey financed by Charles I (who knighted him in 1639); but regardless, as Sabine Schülting argues, the text holds great value in showing England's political, military and economic interests in the 'East'.[10]

Blount opens his journal with a consideration of sensory perception and cultural difference in the travelogue, framed by what might be described as 'imperial envy.' He writes of his desire to visit this part of the world, since the Turks are 'the only moderne people, great in action, and whose Empire hath so suddenly invaded the World, and fixt it selfe such firme foundations as no other ever did'.[11] Blount explains the cultural differences between England and 'Turkey' by appealing to climate: 'seeing the customes of men are much swayed by their natural dispositions, which are originally inspired and composed by the Climate whose ayre, and influence, they receive, it seems naturall, that to our North-West parts of the World, no people should be more averse, and strange of behaviour, than those of the South-East'.[12] This notion that people were affected by the 'ayres' of their country (a term that could be used both of the gaseous substance called 'air' and of a piece of music) is grounded in the ideas explored in my previous chapter—the notion that sensory perception could imprint the body in a particular way, which would affect that person's 'nature', and thus inform how they would draw on their bodily memories in order to improvise.

---

    *Ethnomusicology Forum* 9.2 (2000), 1–34.

9  *A Voyage into the Levant: A Breife Relation of a Journey, Lately Performed by Master H.B. Gentleman, from England by the Way of Venice, into Dalmatia, Sclavonia, Bosnah, Hungary, Macedonia, Thessaly, Thrace, Rhodes and Egypt, unto Gran Cairo: with Particular Observations Concerning the Moderne Condition of the Turkes, and Other People under that Empire* (London: Printed by I. L. for Andrew Crooke, 1636), https://archive.org/details/avoyageintoleva00blougoog

10  Sabine Schülting, 'Strategic Improvisation: Henry Blount and the Ottoman Empire', in *Early Modern Encounters with the Islamic East: Performing Cultures*, ed. by Sabine Schülting, Sabine Lucia Müller and Ralf Hertel (Farnham: Ashgate, 2012), pp. 67–84 (p. 67).

11  *A Voyage into the Levant*, p. 2.

12  *A Voyage into the Levant*, pp. 1–2.

Climate or natural environment was considered a significant factor in the formation of the early modern memory storehouse. In his memory treatise of 1661, John Willis (d. 1625) names a long list of 'things that debilitate memory', citing different kinds of air such as 'unwholesome air that is infected with vapor of standing-waters, Marshes, Woods, Prisons, Dunghills, Common Sewers, & co.', 'Windie aire, that is agitated with violent winds', and 'aire infected with smoke of strong sented combustible things'.[13] Since memory was central to the improvisatory process, and air was perceived to affect memory, this theory is particularly significant in considering travellers and improvisers in the Ottoman lands. Moreover, according to these contemporary beliefs, surely Blount's own memory and creativity would have been affected by his travels in these 'ayres and influences'.

Blount continues that 'above all other senses, the eye having the most immediate, and quicker commerce with the soule, gives it a more smart touch than the rest, leaving in the fancy somewhat unutterable; so that an eye witnesse of things conceives them with an imagination more compleat, strong, and intuitive, then he can either apprehend, or deliver by way of relation...'[14] Positioned at the start of his narrative, this passage explains the eye's closer relationship to the soul but ascribes to it the sense of touch too, noting that it has a 'quicker touch' than the other senses. This superior ability of the eye to 'touch' what it perceives means that an eyewitness is able to 'conceive' the people and places they have witnessed for themselves 'with an imagination more compleat, strong, and intuitive' than had someone related these details to them second-hand. Further on, Blount acknowledges the ear when stating that 'the reader is like one feasted with dishes fitter for another mans stomacke, than his owne: but a traveller takes with his eye, and eare, only such occurencies into observation, as his owne apprehension affects, and through that sympathy, can digest them into an experience more

---

13 *Mnemonica, or, the Art of Memory Drained Out of the Pure Fountains of Art & Nature, Digested into Three Books : Also A Physical Treatise of Cherishing Natural Memory, Diligently Collected out of Divers Learned Mens Writings / by John Willis* (London: Printed and to be sold by Leonard Sowersby, 1661), p. 137, http://hdl.handle.net/20.500.14106/A66483

14 *A Voyage into the Levant*, p. 3.

naturall for himself, than he could have done the notes[15] of another...'[16]

In this context, Blount is explaining the merits of visiting a place oneself rather than simply reading about it (hence justifying the publication of his own travelogue); yet the intersensory language he uses tells us more. The reader who feasts on travel accounts will become gorged on food that was intended for 'another mans stomacke', since they are not travelling themselves and thus only able to take in only so much as they can withstand and 'digest'. The metaphor of reading as eating was a common one in the early modern period, and perhaps most famously used by the philosopher and essayist Francis Bacon (1561–1626), who claimed that 'some books are to be tasted, others to be swallowed, and some few to be chewed and digested'.[17] In the context of Blount's book, the metaphor positions eye and ear as organs that quite literally imbibe the sounds and sights of abroad into the body and digest them. The sensory experiences of travel and new environments were thus taken *into* the body, *worked on* the body, and *were worked on by* the body, in the process of transforming them into something new.[18] These discussions of reading as digestion also evoke Richard Drake's description of extemporary prayer as 'undigested' in the last chapter, placing reading as digestion, reading as travel, travel as digestion, and improvisation as indigestion, into a series of complex and shifting relationships.

While Blount seems to accord the ear a somewhat secondary role here, I wonder whether the eye and ear's shared mode of imbibing material into the body and digesting it renders the exact organ unimportant: eye and ear are simply two entry points. In this light, I ask how we could hear

---

15  It is interesting to reflect on this word choice—'the notes of another' might in another context refer to notated music, bringing to mind debates about the authenticity of improvised or self-dictated prayers, or about musical divisions that were printed versus those that were entirely extemporised.

16  *A Voyage into the Levant*, p. 3.

17  Francis Bacon, 'Of Studies', *Essays or Counsels, Civil and Moral* (1627), http://fountainheadpress.com/expandingthearc/assets/francisbaconstudies.pdf

18  Perhaps unsurprisingly, since early modern meanings of the word 'travel' are inextricably connected to the word 'travail', indicating the 'work' of travelling. See Dyani Johns Taff, 'Precarious Travail, Gender and Narration in Shakespeare's *Pericles, Prince of Tyre* and Margaret Cavendish's *The Blazing World*', in *Travel and Travail: Early Modern Women, English Drama and the Wider World* ed. by Patricia Akhimie and Bernadette Andrea (Lincoln: University of Nebraska Press, 2018), pp. 273–91(p. 273).

Blount's text as a collection of sensory experiences imbibed by the ear as well as the eye (and perhaps the stomach), relating to the same organs in the reader 'gorging' themselves back home. Perhaps Blount's resulting memory house could be filled not just with aural but also visual and gastronomic experiences, to be performed in an extemporary fashion that made use of the body's storehouse of memories, experiences, and airs.

In addition to describing his own sensory experiences and nature (and thereby shaping those of the reader), Blount's volume recounts several encounters that include various instances of improvisatory behaviour, which to him reveal the 'nature' of Ottoman subjects improvising. One of these encounters is described in an anecdote on his way to Constantinople, which the literary historian Sabine Schülting has analysed as an instance of 'strategic' improvisation.[19] Blount has met some Ottoman soldiers en route, and relates how on seeing him, the soldiers recognised him as a Christian and called to him. Blount did not understand their words, so he stood still until 'they menacing their weapons, rose, and came to me, with lookes very ugly'.[20]

He continues:

> I smiling met them, and taking him who seemed of most port, by the hand, layed it to my forehead, which with them is the greatest signe of *love*, and *honour*, then often calling him *Sultanum*, spoke *English*, which though none of the kindest, yet gave I it such a sound, as to them who understood no further, might seeme affectionate, humble, and hearty; which so appeased them, as they made me sit, and eate together, and parted loving...[21]

Through this combination of speech and bodily acts, Blount's 'improvisation' of friendliness is 'successful'—the soldiers invite him to share a meal with them. According to Schülting, this kind of simulated behaviour is born out of inadequacy and the inability to communicate with the Turks whom he meets, thus falling back on this type of 'play-acting' to convince both himself and the reader that he is somehow able to get the better of them despite his lack of understanding and knowledge. Here, improvisation is a type of trickery, it is Iago's 'I am

---

19 Schülting, 'Strategic Improvisation', p. 69.
20 *A Voyage into the Levant*, p. 98.
21 *A Voyage into the Levant*, p. 98.

not what I am', relayed by Stephen Greenblatt as 'the motto of the improviser, the manipulator of signs that bear no resemblance to what they profess to signify'.[22]

The continuation of the passage reveals that an Italian merchant passed through just after Blount, also on his way to Constantinople. In contrast to Blount, however, this traveller was not able to perform correctly—'he not yet considering, how the place had changed his condition, stood upon his termes, till they with their Axes, and iron Maces (the weapons of that Country,) broke two of his ribs, in which case, we left him behind, halfe dead, either to get backe as he could, or be devoured of beasts'.[23] Blount's callous abandonment of this man to his likely death is matter-of-fact; he was not able to survive because he had not considered how his new surroundings had 'changed his condition', and thus 'stood upon his termes' inflexibly, rather than responding to the change and to his new environment by taking in all its stimuli and acting accordingly.

Blount's success in befriending those Turks who intended violence towards him on the road is 'daily', and he boasts: 'I grew so confident of the Turkish nature, as when Lances, or Knives, were often set against me, I doubted not my selfe, unlesse it were by a Drunkard [...] for drinke makes the fancy of the one uncertaine...'[24] Blount's purportedly skilled imitations of the 'nature' of the Turks is achieved through these on-the-spot encounters, suggesting that his behaviour is somewhat improvisatory. And in similar fashion, the 'nature' of the Turks whom he has grown so adept in imitating is presumably revealed (if we follow contemporaneous theories of memory and the extemporary) through improvisatory behaviours too. After all, the reason Blount is still wary of a drunkard is that alcohol makes for an 'uncertain' fancy; in other words, he cannot trust that the person will act in accordance with their nature, of which he has grown so confident. Blount is thus in a constant state of flux, observing the nature and behaviours of the Turks in order to imitate them, while also experiencing some change in his condition through his travels in new countries, climates, and sensory stimuli. When viewed through such a lens, these scenes of encounter in

---

22  Greenblatt, *Renaissance Self-Fashioning*, p. 238.
23  *A Voyage into the Levant*, p. 98.
24  *A Voyage into the Levant*, p. 99.

his travelogue show improvisation to be a complex and shared activity: behaviours overlap, scripts and improvisations collide, climates and cultures act on and are acted upon by the people engaging with them. Furthermore, improvisation is mobilised here to cast the travelogue as a stage for such encounters, a space in which the reader could almost enter the scene vicariously and imagine themselves acting out Blount's part. While the reader back home had not been saturated in the same sensory experiences that Blount describes in his introduction (and which perhaps played a role in influencing his improvisatory behaviours as he gained familiarity in his new surroundings), the travelogue might become a way to experience them second-hand.

This sense of improvisation hinted at grows sharper in the accounts of musical 'airs' that Blount experienced and made during his travels through the atmospheric airs abroad. Musical performance can present a complicated and nuanced picture of reciprocal improvisation, and a striking example in Blount's text occurs in his disparaging description of Ottoman music, itself containing yet another example of his own experimental 'improvisation'. Blount introduces the topic of music in 'Turkey' (used often by travellers in this period to denote any Ottoman land), in the context of a discussion of coffee and the proliferation of coffee houses: 'there upon scaffolds, halfe a yard high, and covered with Mats...[the Turks] sit crosse-legged after the Turkish manner, many times two or three hundred together, talking, and likely with some poore Musicke passing up and downe'.[25]

The association of music with coffee houses in the Ottoman world was extremely common in this period, with the French traveller Monsieur de Thévenot even likening the sound of sipping coffee to a kind of music: 'They all drink it sipping, for fear of scalding themselves; so that being in a *Coffee-hane* (so they call the place where they sell it ready made) one hears a pretty pleasant kind of sippling musick'[26] ('on le boit tout à petits traits de peur de se brusler, de sorte qu'estant dans un cafehane, (ainsi nomment les lieux où on le vend tout prepare,) on entend une

---

25  *A Voyage into the Levant*, pp. 105–6.
26  Jean de Thévenot, *The Travels of Monsieur de Thevenot into the Levant in Three Parts, viz. into I. Turkey, II. Persia, III. the East-Indies / Newly Done out of French* (London: Printed by H. Clark, for H. Faithorne, J. Adamson, C. Skegnes, and T. Newborough, 1687), p. 33, https://archive.org/details/travelsofmonsieu00thev/page/n7/mode/2up

affez plaisante musique de humerie...').²⁷ The OED gives 'sippling' as a derivative of the verb 'sipple',²⁸ while Cotgrave's French-English dictionary of 1611 gives the original French word used, 'humerie', as 'a supping, sipping; sucking up'.²⁹ Once again, we encounter an entanglement of imbibing food/drink with hearing/making music, perhaps prompting us to wonder whether the music played in the 'coffee-hane' itself mimicked the physical motions of sipping a cup of coffee that in itself created this additional soundscape.

On the 'poore Musicke' that passes 'up and down' in these coffee houses (presumably this refers to the communal nature of the music-making, although it could also refer to an ensemble of strolling musicians), Blount comments:

> The Musicke of Turkey is worth consideration; through all those vaste Dominions, there runnes one tune, and for ought I heard, no more, nor can every man play that; yet scarce any but hath a fiddle, with two strings, and at Feasts, and other meetings, will confidently play upon it, but hee knows not to what tune, nor can play the same twice over...³⁰

This dense passage contains a wealth of observation and insight into Blount's listening experiences and perceptions. Firstly, he makes the bold claim that 'through all those vaste Dominions, there runnes one tune, and for ought I heard, no more'. While this may refer to a melody that Blount heard across all the Ottoman countries he visited, it seems more likely an indication of his lack of experience with this music and its *maqamat* (modes), leading his ear to collapse all the melodies he heard into one and the same homogenous 'tune'—perhaps an example of Lugones's 'arrogant perception'. Secondly, he comments that although

---

27  Jean de Thévenot, *Relation d'un voyage fait au Levant: dans laquelle il est curieusement traité des estats sujets au Grand Seigneur... et des singularitez particulières de l'Archipel, Constantinople, Terre-Sainte, Égypte, pyramides, mumies [«sic»], déserts d'Arabie, la Meque, et de plusieurs autres lieux de l'Asie et de l'Affrique... outre les choses mémorables arrivées au dernier siège de Bagdat, les cérémonies faites aux réceptions des ambassadeurs du Mogol et l'entretien de l'autheur avec celuy du Pretejan, où il est parlé des sources du Nil / par Monsieur Thevenot* (Paris: n.p., 1664), p. 63, https://gallica.bnf.fr/ark:/12148/bpt6k106525z/f83.item
28  *OED Online*, 'Sipple, v.', https://www.oed.com/view/Entry/180351?redirectedFrom=sippling#eid22617279
29  Randle Cotgrave, *A Dictionarie of the French and English Tongues* (London: Printed by Adam Islip, 1611), http://www.pbm.com/~lindahl/cotgrave/534small.html
30  *A Voyage into the Levant*, p. 106.

scarcely anyone he came across was able to play this tune, anyone who has a fiddle with two strings (presumably an instrument similar to the *rebab*—a small bowed instrument of 1–3 strings found since the eighth century in South West Asia and North Africa) will confidently play at 'feasts' and 'other meetings'. However, Blount comments that such a musician 'knows not to what tune, nor can play the same twice over'—the tunes are unpremeditated, in other words, almost arising unconsciously from the musician, and cannot be replicated since they are unfixed and improvised. The noted confidence with which these musicians play this 'tune' contrasts with Blount's inability to pin down or grasp what he is hearing, yearning for some kind of repetition that he can recognise.

The idea of not being able to play the same tune twice is common in European descriptions of Arab and Turkish music, and often functions as a signifier of improvisation. A particularly clear example of this appears a little later in Guillaume-André Villoteau's description of Egyptian music in 1799, following Napoleon's invasion of Egypt. Villoteau is also disparaging about the level of musical skill he encounters in the Egyptian musicians and describes how he would ask them to sing/play while he attempted a transcription. However, he narrates that his attempts to notate their music was thwarted by their ornamentation and improvisation: 'in the beginning, that which vexed us the most upon hearing the Egyptian musicians sing [...] was that we were unable to discern the modulations of the melodies from the numerous and bizarre ornaments with which they overload their singing'.[31]

Despite the discomfort caused by the improvisations of the musicians around him, Blount himself improvises in response to the improvisations he observes. To give his account more credence, he tells his readers of an 'experiment' he conducted to test the musicians:

> ...this I'm sure of; for to make experiment, I have ventured to play at divers meetings, pretending the ayers of my country, to note whether they had skill or no, and took so well as they have often made me play againe; then I found their skill and mine alike, for I never understood the least touch of any instrument...[32]

---

31 Ruth Rosenberg, *Music, Travel and Imperial Encounter in 19th-Century France* (London: Routledge, 2015), p. 38.
32 *A Voyage into the Levant*, p. 106.

In other words, Blount himself made music at several 'meetings', falsely telling the Turks that he was playing English airs. Since they received his playing well and even asked him to play again, he decided that their level of musical skill/education is the same as his, i.e. one of ignorance—'I never understood the least touch of any instrument'. The resonance of the word 'ayer' here, as an almost improvisatory variant of the 'ayre' of the climate, is striking. Blount is trying to 'pretend' the airs of his country in a Turkish coffee house as a point of cultural difference, but he ends up noting his similarities to the musicians there—'I found their skill and mine alike'. On the surface, this is an improvisation of simulation and 'strategy', to quote Sabine Schülting. Yet is it possible within an early modern framework to improvise without changing yourself? It is striking, and important to highlight that the music is never explicitly marked as 'improvised' or 'extemporary'—the clues that point to the improvised nature of the music-making are all in its descriptions, or lurking between the lines of his text.

The questions that this scene provokes in a reader today are seemingly endless, since we can only imagine how the story would have unfolded—is Blount in a coffee house, or a dedicated 'meeting' of musicians? And once there, what instrument did he play upon? Was he invited to play alone, or did he join in with the musicians around him, improvising the 'false airs' to such acclaim? If we conceive more practically of Blount improvising alongside these musicians, it is hard to think of him as untouched by the sounds around him, and much more likely to think of him responding to the scales, harmonies and phrases that entered his ears. Sound literally would have worked upon him, as the vibrations moved his body, bringing him and his fellow musicians into a type of proximate intimacy and reciprocity in that moment.

We should also take contemporaneous theories of extemporary practice as a reading of sensory prints into account—perhaps Blount would have been imprinted (quite literally) by the airs (both atmospheric and musical), sounds, smells, sights, touches and meals he had imbibed while travelling—how could these have not shaped and contributed to his improvisations? In fact, we might wonder whether Blount was so changed by the airs of Turkey that he could no longer sustain a plausible performance of English-ness. Perhaps, then, we need to question or listen between the lines of his cold and strategic account of calculated improvisation intended to fool those around him, an account that denies the sense of reciprocity that surely shaped this musical encounter.

Audio Recording 2 'Huseyni Semaii'. Track 3 from Fatima Lahham, *bulbul*, FS Records (2022). https://hdl.handle.net/20.500.12434/ad2791b2

> *When I recorded Ali Ufki's Huseyni Semaii, I wanted to imagine the effects of this music being brought to England from Turkey by English travellers in the seventeenth century, what it would have sounded like on an instrument like the recorder. This re-imagining also took me away from the score, free to take 'liberties' and create my own version of this music.* (creative reflection, December 2021)

It is difficult to know whether Blount and his contemporaries believed that those living in different 'climates' actually had distinctly different natures, or whether their natures were simply susceptible to the conditions under which they lived.[33] If the latter were true, then one might ask how Blount (as a traveller living for some time in these countries) conceived of himself as different from the inhabitants of that place. Other descriptions of Ottoman subjects improvising music in early modern travelogues seem to corroborate the notion that these people simply had different natures, and this difference (usually negative) came out in moments of improvisation that revealed their true natures.

A particularly striking example of this occurs in the travelogue of Jean Dumont, a French publisher who was named official historiographer to Charles VI of France. The book was originally written and published in French in 1694.[34] In the English translation of 1696, Dumont writes

---

33 It is also worth noting Charles de Secondat Montesquieu's *L'Esprit des Loix* (1752), which evidences similar beliefs about how climate affected cultural behaviours. See Michael R. Dove, 'Chapter 1, Historic Decentering of the Modern Discourse of Climate Change: The Long View from the Vedic Sages to Montesquieu', in *Climate Cultures: Anthropological Perspectives on Climate Change*, ed. by Jessica Barnes and Michael R. Dove (New Haven and London: Yale University Press, 2015), pp. 25–47 (pp. 29–30).

34 Jean Dumont, *Nouveau Voyage du Levant/par le sieur D.M. contenant ce qu'il a vû de plus remarquable en Allemagne, France, Italie, Malthe, & Turquie: où l'on voit aussiles Brigues secretes de Mr. de Chateau-neuf, Ambassadeur de France à la Cour ottoman, &*

that the music of the 'Turks' is '...rather a hideous Dinn than a regular Harmony, and resembles exactly the howling Shrieks of a tortur'd Wretch'[35] ('...la musique Turquesque, c'est une chose horrible; ce sont des cris si desagreables qu'il semble qu'on les échorche...')[36].

Dumont continues:

> The first time I heard a *Turk* sing, I cou'd not forbear stopping to look upon him, concluding that he was certainly Mad: For I cou'd not imagine that a Man who had the use of his Reason, wou'd take pleasure in distorting his Body, and rolling his Eyes in so odd and extravagant a manner; tho' they pretend that all those unusual Motions are only the Marks and Effects of a tender and violent Passion.[37]

> (La premiere fois que je vis chanter un Turc, je m'arêtai à le considerer, croyant qu'il fut fou, car ils accompagnent ce chant de contorsions & de roulemens d'yeux, qui ne permetent pas d'en juger autrement, ils disent que ces mouvements là ne proviennent que de la passion, & de l'atendrissement, dont ils se sentent touches.)[38]

This visceral analysis ascribes madness to the grotesque passion that Dumont observes, the 'howling shrieks of a tortur'd Wretch' adding to the idea of a tortured body emitting these haunted and horrible sounds. In fact, the original French word used is 'échorche', literally meaning 'flayed' or 'skinned', which adds even more to the grotesque image of bodily suffering. His claim that the Turks excuse the singer's 'unusual motions' as 'only the Marks and Effects of a tender and violent Passion' reflects an understanding of these motions as 'marks' or visible touches, as it were, from such a passion.

The embodied narrative of horror bleeds into his description of the instruments too, some of which are described with reference to the human body:

> Their *Musical Instruments* are extremely suitable to the Nature of their Harmony: For they have a kind of *Violin* with three Strings, a Neck as

---

*plusieurs histoires galantes* (La Haye: Chez Etienne Foulque, 1694).

35 *A New Voyage to the Levant Containing an Account of the Most Remarkable Curiosities in Germany, France, Italy, Malta, and Turkey: With Historical Observations Relating to the Present and Ancient State of Those Countries / by the Sieur du Mont, Done into English, and Adorn'd with Figures* (London: T. H., 1696), p. 275, https://quod.lib.umich.edu/e/eebo/A36827.0001.001?view=toc

36 *Nouveau Voyage du Levant*, p. 324.

37 *A New Voyage to the Levant*, p. 275.

38 *Nouveau Voyage du Levant*, p. 324.

long as a Man's Arm, and a great Belly like the Block of a Hat; some ill-contriv'd *Flutes;* little *Timbrels* about the bigness of one's Fist, a *Drum,* some paultry *Hautbois,* and several little Brazen *Targets,* which they hold in their Hands, and knock against one another. Judge, Sir, what a mad Consort they make with the confus'd jangling of so many inharmonious Instruments.[39]

(Les instrumens dont ils se servent ordinarement, respondent parfaitement bien à la nature de cette musique, ce sont un espece de violon à trois cordes, dont le manche est long comme le bras, & le corps gros, comme la forme d'un chapeau, des mechantes flûtes douces, des petites timbales, grosses chacune comme le poing, un Tambour de Basque, plusieurs petites Rondaches d'airain, qu'ils frapent l'une contre l'autre avec les deux mains, & quelque mechant haut bois. Jugés Monsieur, lors que tout cela est ensemble qu'elle musique enrage il doit faire; c'est une vray charivary…)[40]

Here the musical disharmony of the instruments is mirrored by the disharmony in the human forms that the instruments mimic; the result is 'confused', just like the singer who has lost all 'reason'. In fact, the only instrument about which Dumont has a good word to say is the psaltery, which according to him owes its pleasurable nature to its Classical Greek origins, thus confirming that the horrific music described so far derives its character from the people from whom it emanates:

The only tolerable Instrument they have is the *Psalterion,* which is cover'd with Latten Strings, stretcht as upon a *Harpsical;* and they strike upon 'em with little Sticks, which they hold betwixt their two Fingers. All the Women play admirably well on this Instrument, for 'tis their usual Diversion in their Chambers, especially the *Greeks,* whose Musick may be heard with Pleasure, since 'tis a great deal more agreeable than that of the *Turks.*[41]

(Le seul instrument qu'ils ayent qui soit supportable, est ce qu'ils apellent un Psalterion, il est couvert des cordes de Laton, tendues comme sur un Clavessin, & l'on frape dessus avec de petit baguettes qu'on tient entre les deux doits, toutes les femmes en sçavent jouër en perfection, & c'est à cela qu'elles se divertissent dans leurs chambres, les Grecques particulierement, qu'il y a du Plaisir d'entendre, parceque leur musique est beaucoup plus agreable que celle des Turcs.)[42]

---

39  *A New Voyage to the Levant,* p. 275.
40  *Nouveau Voyage du Levant,* p. 324.
41  *A New Voyage to the Levant,* p. 275.
42  *Nouveau Voyage du Levant,* pp. 324–5.

Dumont concludes: 'I shall only add on this Subject, that neither of 'em sing the Notes without the Words; and our way of singing Tunes seems so ridiculous to 'em, that they usually laugh at the *Franks,* and ask 'em what their *Tartara lera* signifies'[43] ('Au reste ni les uns, ni les autres ne chantant jamais qu'en recitant, & se moquent des Francs qui disent *Tartara lera* leur demandant ce que cela signifie').[44] What Dumont seems to be alluding to here is the fact the Turks do not vocalise using syllables like *tartara lera* (which perhaps is referring to rhythmic/articulation syllables—see for example Jacques Hotteterre's discussion of *tu* and *ru*).[45] As a sign of learning, perhaps the absence of these types of syllables contributes yet further to the picture of wild and unsophisticated music-making that Dumont paints. If the music is in fact improvised, then to Dumont it is not a practised or skilled improvisation, more an uncouth bodily expression that he can take little pleasure in. Such a locating of bodily horror in the process of improvisation chimes with my readings of extemporary prayer in the previous chapter, suggesting once again that these musicians may have been performing *themselves*—their horrific performances being heard as expressions of their nature.

Another account of musical improvisation that evokes this inextricable connection between improvisation and expressions of nature is found when Blount visits Egypt. He describes some music that he hears in Cairo, played on a cittern by a Frenchman who enthrals a nest of snakes with his improvised tunes:

> ...many rarities of living creatures I saw in Gran Cairo: but the most ingenious was a nest of foure-legg'd Serpents, of two foot long, blacke and ugly, kept by a Frenchman, who when he came to handle them, they would not endure him, but ranne, and hid in their hole; then would hee take his Citterne, and play upon it; they hearing the Musique, came all crawling to his feet, and began to climb up him, till he gave over playing, then away they ran...[46]

---

43  *A New Voyage to the Levant*, p. 276.
44  *Nouveau Voyage du Levant*, p. 325.
45  Jacques Hotteterre le Romain, *Principes de la flute traversiere, de la Flute a bec, et du Haut-bois*, Op. 1 (Amsterdam: Estienne Roger, n.d.), pp. 21–9, https://imslp.org/wiki/Principes_de_la_flute_traversiere,_de_la_Flute_a_Bec,_et_du_Haut-bois,_Op.1_(Hotteterre,_Jacques)
46  Blount, *A Voyage into the Levant*, p. 45.

Blount concludes: 'nor is this stranger in Nature, to see such creatures delight in sounds delightfull to us, then to see them relish such meats, as relish with us: the one argues a conformitie to our composition in one of our senses; the other in another'.[47]

While the image of snake-charming was to become a rather tired orientalist trope in both India and South West Asia and North Africa, here it functions as a way through which Blount improvises the soundscape and its actors—and to some extent also himself as a listening subject, and us as the readers of his text—through a written description of the improvised music. For Blount, the role of man-made music here is to control creatures and make them obedient; the otherwise dangerous and intractable snakes may be handled safely only through making them hear certain sounds. There are also implicit gendered resonances of a temptress serpent, who can somehow be silenced and made docile through 'sounds delightfull to us'.

Early modern English travellers did not only use the language of improvisation to describe the music they heard, but also drew upon these tropes to characterise the lands they visited as sites of improvised lives and activities. While still in Cairo, Blount relates that a family friend with whom he stayed—'his Excellence the Lord Ambassador of Holland at Constantinople, Sir Corenelius Haga'—passed on some 'insider knowledge' to his guest, describing the Cairene streets as follows: 'then the noted streets, foure, and twentie thousand, besides petty turnings, and divisions'.[48] Of particular note here is the use of 'divisions', and its potential musical connections—much like 'ground', the term has many lives, all of them spatially-inflected. But in this context, even the improvisatory turnings of the streets are 'petty'—perhaps even unnecessary.

There are also signs of the land itself being improvisatory in the account of English traveller Henry Maundrell (1665–1701). While still in Lebanon, he writes of a garden:

> it may perhaps be wonder'd, how this Emir should be able to contrive any thing so elegant and regular as this Garden; seeing the Turkish Gardens are usually nothing else but a confus'd miscellany of Trees,

---

47  *A Voyage into the Levant*, p. 45.
48  *A Voyage into the Levant*, p. 38.

jumbled together without either knots, walks, arbours, or any thing of art or design, so that they seem like thickets rather than Gardens. But Faccardine had been in Italy, where he had seen things of another nature, and knew well how to copy them in his own Country. For indeed it appears by these remains of him, that he must needs have been a man much above the ordinary level of a Turkish Genius.⁴⁹

Maundrell feels that Turkish gardens as usually so confused and haphazard that they seem like thickets rather than a garden—part of the natural world rather than part of what he considers to be the 'human' world. The lack of order is 'confused', 'jumbled', and hazardous, typical in fact of a 'Turkish Genius' which in Maundrell's view could not achieve a garden that is 'elegant and regular' except through European contact.⁵⁰

Throughout these examples, the depictions of improvisation are complex and varied. At first glance, we see Henry Blount styling himself through improvisatory processes (both musical and non-musical) and a performative text. Yet on closer reading, it seems difficult to detach him from his environment as a key shaping factor in his improvisations. Further, the sense of reciprocity that comes across in his descriptions of music-making make it difficult to separate his acts from those of the Ottoman musicians he sits amongst. However, descriptions of improvised Ottoman musics in Blount's text and other contemporaneous travelogues are rarely complimentary, instead following orientalist tropes and hearing the supposedly 'deviant' nature of the musicians in their music—and even sometimes in the layout of the countries and spaces in which they lived.

This negative connotation of improvisation as something unplanned and 'wild' contrasts with the kind of performative improvisations of the English traveller, recalling once more my discussion in Chapter 1 of improvisation as an activity that should only be undertaken by some people under certain conditions. What remains consistent across these examples of improvisation, however, is the key notions that the act of improvising reflects one's 'natural disposition' and is affected by the sensory experiences and climates one had experienced.

---

49  Henry Maundrell, *A Journey from Aleppo to Jerusalem at Easter, A.D. 1697* (Oxford: Printed at the Theatre, 1703), p. 40, https://archive.org/details/gri_journeyfroma00maun

50  Despite these descriptions, it is worth noting that Ottoman gardens were actually frequently modelled on Roman and Byzantine styles.

## Silence and Absence in Henry Maundrell's *Journey to Jerusalem* (1697)

Now she waits quiet
Because inside her body there is music,
Nomadic, ancient...[51]

As popular printed texts, many early modern travelogues allowed readers not only to passively read the words on the page, but to engage vicariously through the traveller's performative narrations. So far, I have primarily considered the authors of these travelogues and the subjects they depict. But what of the readers of these texts? I now turn to another function of improvisation and embodiment in the travelogue, and ask how the genre became a location for developing modes of vicarious travel by the reader, and a space in which to enact imperial—as well as other— modes of world-making and travelling. This is perhaps particularly relevant in the context of considering improvisation as encounter in the travelogue; in Blount's text, for example, the improvisations of the Turks are largely absent, yet we know they must be there, and this knowledge requires readers to elaborate somewhat on the printed text, perhaps even extemporising on the scenes they read. After all, any sonic phenomenon is not actually present in the text, and needs to be imagined by the reader.

In pursuing this notion of an 'improvisatory' reading of the early modern English travelogue, I move from instances of explicit musical improvisation to considering how the travelogue as a genre of printed text could become a vehicle of vicarious travel, imprinting and filling its readers with second-hand experiences of the countries and peoples of which they read. English chaplain Henry Maundrell's travelogue of 1697 stands out as a particularly influential example of the early modern English travelogue, becoming one of the most popular books written by a European about the 'East' throughout the next few centuries.[52] By 1749 there were seven editions in different European languages and sections of the book started to appear in travel writing anthologies in the eighteenth and nineteenth centuries. As late as 1844, John Kitto

---

51 Rafeef Ziadeh, 'Silence Still', *We Teach Life* (2015).
52 Issam Nassar, 'Review: Maundrell in Jerusalem: Reflections on the Writing of an Early European Tourist', *Jerusalem Quarterly* 9 (2000), https://www.palestine-studies.org/en/node/78133

described the book as 'an account so intelligent and perspicuous, that his still remains the standard description in the English language, and is scarcely rivalled in any other'.⁵³

Despite its popularity, Maundrell's travelogue resonates with silence. This was not particularly unusual: seventeenth-century England championed the biblical centricity of Jerusalem over its reality as a contemporaneous city, resulting in an overflowing of music and literature that referred to the city as an ancient Holy Land with little reference to its current inhabitants. Perhaps unsurprisingly then, many of the travel accounts by English travellers in this period did not relate many details about the inhabitants of Ottoman Palestine and of the so-called Ottoman Arab lands more widely, instead rooting their experiences in the textual knowledge of biblical tales and classical antiquity.⁵⁴ On the one hand, Palestine was the birthplace of Christianity and Jerusalem the centre of the Christian world; on the other, the people who actually lived there were scarcely depicted—visually or aurally—in Western Christendom. This is by no means a new observation—as Nabil Matar, one of the foremost scholars on early modern relationships between England and the Ottoman Arab lands, observed in a paper on Renaissance cartography, 'the question of Palestine was posed cartographically in Europe long before it was posed politically or colonially'.⁵⁵ Imperialism occurred ideologically long before it did physically, and Palestine was imagined and mapped as a territory empty of people and sounds long before the 'formal' coloniality of British occupation in 1916.⁵⁶

Matar also considers Maundrell's travelogue in a fascinating comparative study alongside that of Syrian mystic scholar Abd al-Ghani al-Nabulusi, concluding that for Maundrell, 'the holiness of the land could only be re-established after its English possession'.⁵⁷ This comes through in a sense

---

53  John Kitto, *The Pictorial History of Palestine and the Holy Land* (London: Charles Knight and Co., 1844), p. xv.
54  Vanita Neelakanta, *Retelling the Siege of Jerusalem in Early Modern England*, (University of Delaware Press 2019).
55  Nabil I. Matar, 'Renaissance Cartography and the Question of Palestine', in *The Landscape of Palestine: Equivocal Poetry*, ed. by Ibrahim Abu Lughod, Roger Heacock and Khaled Nashef (Birzeit: Birzeit University Publications, 1999), pp. 139–51 (p. 139).
56  Edward Saïd, *Orientalism* (London: Routledge and Kegan Paul, 1975), p. 205.
57  Nabil I. Matar, 'The Sufi and the Chaplain: Abd al-Ghani al-Nabulusi and Henry Maundrell', in *Through the Eyes of the Beholder: The Holy Land, 1517–1713*, ed. by Judy

of regret throughout, sometimes voiced with startling clarity—'who can expect to see these holy places rescued from the hands of Infidels? Or if they should be recover'd, what deplorable contests might be expected to follow about them? Seeing even in their present state of Captivity, they are made the occasion of such unchristian rage, and animosity'.[58]

How, then, would an early modern reader engage with such a text? While the book may well have been received as confirmation that Biblical histories were more significant than the current stories of the contemporary inhabitants, I attempt here an 'improvisatory' reading that could point to the silences/absences in a text, or even fill in some of the missing sounds, taking inspiration from the Haitian anthropologist and historian Michel-Rolph Trouillot (1949–2012). Trouillot suggests that identifying the moments where silences enter the process of historical construction can become 'conceptual tools' that help us understand the differences between silences, and how they should be approached: 'any historical narrative is a bundle of silences, the result of a unique process, and the operation required to deconstruct these silences will vary accordingly'.[59] In the context of the early modern travelogue, I ask how the (sometimes extemporary) performativity embedded in these texts can result in a type of improvisation enacted by the reader, allowing them to participate in the process of reconstructing and reimagining the experiences of travel.

I begin with the moment when Maundrell is in Tripoli, Lebanon. He describes how he and his companions encounter, explore, and map out a tower under which they find a network of rooms for burial. Through narrating his entry and exploration of the tomb, he also imagines and reconstructs his own living body in the space alongside the corpses of the inhabitants, mediated through his readers' bodies as participants in his account.

Maundrell starts the day on Monday, 8 March 1697:

> Having passed over a restless night, in a marshy and unwholesome ground, we got up very early; in order to take a nearer veiw [sic] of the two Towers last mention'd. We found them to be Sepulchral Monuments, erected over two ancient Burying places. They stood at about ten yards distance from each other [...] Each of these barbarous Monuments had

---

A. Hayden and Nabil Matar (Leiden: Brill, 2012), pp. 165–84 (p. 182).
58  Maundrell, *A Journey from Aleppo*, pp. 69–70.
59  Michel-Rolph Trouillot, *Silencing the Past: Power & the Production of History* (Boston: Beacon Press, 1995), p. 27.

under it several Sepulchers: the entrances into which were on the South side. It cost us some time and pains to get into them: the Avenues being obstructed, first with Briars, and Weeds, and then with Dirt.[60]

From the outset, the natural world is pitted against the travellers—the ground is 'marshy and unwholesome' and entry to the monuments is obstructed by 'Briars, and Weeds, and then [...] Dirt', which act as the ground's natural doorkeepers in the absence of human inhabitants. The designation of 'marshy and unwholesome' to describe the ground brings to mind John Willis's description of the conditions that impair the fully-functioning memory, while the reference to the 'ground' (clearly here referring to the actual ground upon which they tread), resonates with the notion of a ground bass. Just as 'air' was used interchangeably to discuss both atmosphere and a musical piece, perhaps 'ground' also could fuse the marsh underfoot with a soggy bass-line in the mind.

Crucially, the briars and weeds resist the travellers, who must force their entry into the 'ancient Burying places' by 'time and pains', according them a rapacious role of domination as they break through the privacy and sanctity of the tomb. Maundrell goes on to say that they 'removed' these obstacles, 'encouraging ourselves with the hopes, or rather making ourselves merry with the fancy of hidden treasure'.[61] The fantasy of forced domination in order to gain a 'hidden treasure' is a common trope of coloniality in travel literature, and also positions the expedition in general as an opportunity for gain, and the travelogue as a way of theorising and materialising that gain. I read Lugones's 'arrogant perception' into Maundrell's behaviour and the way he reports it.

Despite these promises of gain, disappointment comes next:

assoon [sic] as we were enter'd into the Vaults, we found that our golden Imaginations ended (as all worldly hopes and projects do at last) in dust, and putrefaction.[62]

The phrase 'golden Imaginations' is telling of the type of proto-coloniality at work here, powered by the ambitions of imagination and fixed in texts of golden promise. The entrance taken by way of the briars and weeds promised conquest and a fulfilled fantasy of gaining hidden

---

60 Maundrell, *A Journey from Aleppo*, p. 21.
61 Maundrell, *A Journey from Aleppo*, p. 22.
62 Maundrell, *A Journey from Aleppo*, p. 22.

treasure, yet it ends in 'dust and putrefaction'. Maundrell's comment that this is the way of all worldly hopes and projects sounds a tone of regret or recognition that their pursuit was vain and inglorious, yet he seems determined that the trouble of forcing his way in should be met with 'some reward for our pains'. Tellingly, the reward comes in the form of 'an exact survey' of 'these Chambers of darkness'—in the absence of striking gold, he finds another way to take ownership of the space and make their toils worthwhile. In this context, the table that follows in Figure 6 can be read as a visual representation of ownership and domination—a revelation of the hidden treasure within, a cartography of capture shared with the reader.

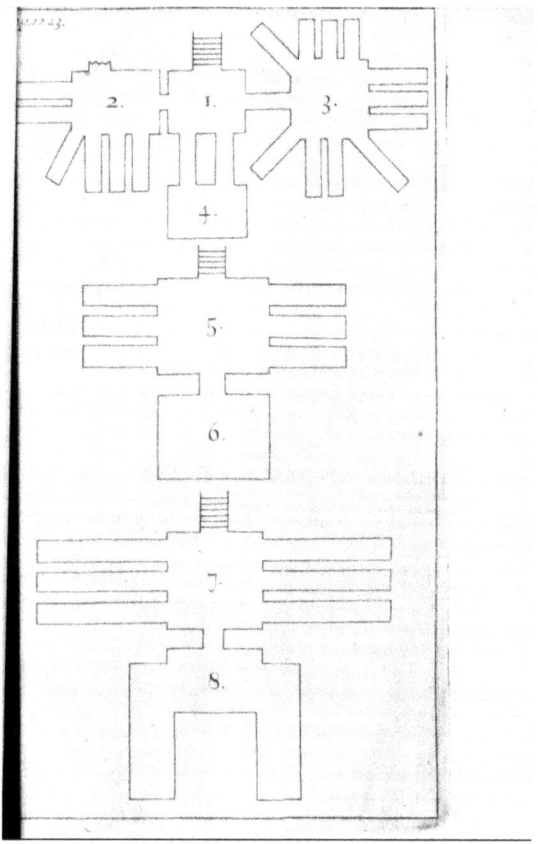

Fig. 6 Henry Maundrell, *A Journey from Aleppo to Jerusalem at Easter, A.D. 1697* (Oxford: Printed at the Theatre, 1703), https://archive.org/details/gri_journeyfroma00maun, p. 23, public domain.

The drawing comes accompanied with a text that explains its navigation:

> The Chambers under the Tower lay as is represented in the first figure. Going down seven or eight steps, you come to the mouth of the Sepulcher; where crawling in you arrive in the Chamber (1) which is nine foot two inches broad and eleven foot long. Turning to the right hand, and going through a narrow passage, you come to the Room (2) which is eight foot broad and ten long: in this chamber are seven cells for Corpses, *viz.* two over against the entrance, four on the left hand and one unfinished on the right. These cells were hewn directly into the firm Rock. We measured several of them, and found them eight foot and a half in length, and three foot three inches square. I would not infer from hence that the Corpses deposited here, were of such a Gigantick size, as to fill up such large Coffins: tho' at the same time, why should any men be so prodigal of their labour, as to cut these Caverns into so hard a Rock as this was, much farther than necessity requir'd?[63]

The bodily dimension of this description, and the nature of the diagram and directions, make this seem like a staging of a performance. The informal tone of 'going down seven or eight steps, you come to the mouth of the Sepulcher; where crawling in you arrive in the Chamber' coalesces the author's body with that of the reader, as does the later shift from second (you) to first (we and I) person pronouns. Maundrell invites his readers to live vicariously through his textually mediated experience, via a particular way of reading the text. The act of crawling also makes the body prone, and thus closer to the seven corpses for which there are carved cells of immense proportions, causing Maundrell to speculate on why such huge coffins would be made, and what sort of dead bodies they would house. Although the coffins should house corpses and thus already be occupied, his account makes no recognition of them either in life or death, replacing their bodies with the somatic silence and absence of death that makes the space open for occupation by his own body.

The possibilities of this reading of silence as presence of absence, or as a sound that has evaporated, also encourages us to examine the way in which the sepulchre is centred as an object of exploration.[64] As a house of silence, it affords a space for ownership and performativity quite literally because its occupants are dead. The lack of fear or trepidation

---

63  Maundrell, *A Journey from Aleppo*, p. 22.
64  The notion of silence as 'evaporated sound' is elaborated on by Palestinian poet Mahmoud Darwish, see Mahmoud Darwish, *A River Dies of Thirst: Journals*, translated by Catherine Cobham (New York: Archipelago Books, 2009), p. 33.

at being contained in a narrow space with these foreign corpses also signals Maundrell's erasure of the occupants—they are both silent and invisible in death, unable to resist the advances of the travellers. In fact, in this whole account, the only resistance offered to the sepulchre's invasion is from the weeds and briars. The stage is empty, ready for an imperial fantasy of conquest to be enacted in part by the reader.

The lack of engagement with the local inhabitants comes across not only in Maundrell's account of entering the sepulchre, but more generally in his strategy of detaching Arab antiquity from the contemporary people of these lands and seeing it instead as the root of Western civilisation.[65] Edward Saïd names this phenomenon as a common orientalist trope:

> The orient existed for the West, or so it seemed to countless Orientalists, whose attitude to what they worked on was either paternalistic or candidly condescending—unless, of course, they were antiquarians, in which case the 'classical' Orient was a credit to *them* and not to the lamentable modern Orient.[66]

Of Beirut, for example, Maundrell comments: 'at present, it retains nothing of its Ancient felicity, except the situation', mobilising the notion of past antiquity as the golden age of the so-called Middle East that English people can relate to, access and even own through the study and appropriation of classical civilisation.[67] Returning to the scene of the sepulchre in Tripoli, he comments on the rest of the day: 'we saw many Sepulchers, old foundations and other remains of Antiquity. From all which it may be assuredly concluded, that here must needs have been some famous Habitation in ancient times: but whether this might be the Ximyra, laid down by Strabo hereabouts [...] the same possibly which the Country of the Zemarites [...] I leave others to discuss'.[68] Strikingly, all his reference points in the area are to the classical authors and biblical study that formed his education in England, rather than to the contemporary experience of being in Lebanon, or to interaction with present inhabitants.

On his map of the sepulchre and in the accompanying description, too, the most striking absence is in fact of these present inhabitants. The map is empty, peopled only by numbers and the measurements given in feet. Again, one way

---

65 As we saw earlier, with Dumont's praise for the Greek psaltery.
66 Saïd, *Orientalism*, p. 204.
67 Maundrell, *A Journey from Aleppo*, p. 38.
68 Maundrell, *A Journey from Aleppo*, pp. 23–4.

to read this is through the lens of pre-colonial erasure and proto-orientalism, which clearly play a role in Maundrell's text. Moreover, the emptiness of the text and its potential as performative script presented the possibility of entraining the early modern English reader into modes of coloniality.

Despite this invitation to an interactive and improvisatory relationship with the text, in many respects Maundrell's travelogue seems almost anti-improvisatory. Replacing people with measurements is a strategy employed throughout the book, with a meticulous approach to calculating every hour of travel and how it is spent, resulting in an unfalteringly accurate set of hours for each day. Nothing is left to chance, in other words; Maundrell needs to account for every moment. This urge is also present in his desire to create a quantifiable 'account' of the city of Jerusalem from his own footsteps, as a way to capture or encapsulate something previously uncaptured and unchartered.

On Wednesday, 14 April 1697, he writes:

> I was willing before our departure to measure the Circuit of the City; so taking one of the Fryars with me, I went out in the afternoon, in order to pace the Walls round. We went out at Bethlehem Gate, and proceeding on the right hand came about to the same Gate again. I found the whole City 4630 paces in Circumference, which I computed thus.[69]

|  | Paces |
|---|---|
| From *Bethlehem* Gate to the corner on the right hand | 400 |
| From that corner to *Damascus* Gate | 680 |
| From *Damascus* Gate to *Herods* | 380 |
| From *Herod's* Gate to *Jeremiah's* Prison | 150 |
| From *Jeremiah's* Prison to the corner next the Valley of *Jehosaphat* | 225 |
| From that corner to St. *Stephen's* Gate | 385 |
| From St. *Stephen's* Gate to the *Golden* Gate | 240 |
| From the *Golden* Gate to the corner of the Wall | 380 |
| From that corner to the *Dung* Gate | 470 |
| From the *Dung* Gate to *Sion* Gate | 605 |
| From *Sion* Gate to the corner of the Wall | 215 |
| From that corner to *Bethlehem* Gate | 500 |
| In all, paces | 4630 |

Fig. 7 Henry Maundrell, *A Journey from Aleppo to Jerusalem at Easter, A.D. 1697* (Oxford: Printed at the Theatre, 1703), https://archive.org/details/gri_journeyfroma00maun, p. 108, public domain.

---

69  Maundrell, *A Journey from Aleppo*, p. 108.

As a cartographic source or score, this example of 'measurement' shown in Figure 7 seems to be intended to provide little more than arithmetic. The Biblical reference points erase the Palestinian names for those places; in a sense Maundrell creates a 'new Jerusalem' as he paces, dissolving the more recent history of the city into indisputable numbers that are also silent. This strategy of recreation is also evident in the accompanying pictures of his travels, which portray a completely empty landscape, devoid of any signs of habitation or life. These silences in the book thus represent the absence of certain people, and the possibility for the reader's 'golden imagination' to take flight, through the interactive and vicarious nature of the text. Yet when we consider the nature of the text in light of theories of improvisation and the histories of print at this moment, perhaps we can start to think of another mode of improvisation in the travelogue: as a way for the reader to almost go on a guided tour of 'the East', via a text that needed interaction and involved the reader in its performativity. In this way, print culture's investment in the travelogue played an important role in disseminating early iterations of coloniality to literate members of the English public who would never leave the British Isles.

By thinking with silence/absence, we might start conceiving forms of 'improvisatory' readings that add to our understanding of how the travelogue as a printed text may have functioned in early modern England. My analysis engages beyond the text to imagine how readers might have involved themselves and their bodies quite literally in the traveller's accounts, vicariously experiencing some of the sensory stimuli encountered by original authors. Returning to Blount's introductory statement about readers becoming gorged on the accounts of travels they had not personally experienced, I circle back to ask whether this means a reader could actually imbibe and be inscribed by the sensory experiences of which they read. Travelogues were not simply an account of someone else's travels to be read at home, but in a sense, a way to travel for oneself, or to transform oneself into a traveller, with all the concomitant dangers and pleasures of being bodily imprinted.

As a reader today loosely using Lugones' work to think through some of the travels and perceptions I navigate in these texts, it often makes makes for uncomfortable reading. How do we locate and name oppression and erasure in these texts where we see and hear it? But more than this reactive approach, how do we listen to what is not being heard? I am still asking these questions.

## Imagine: The Listening Cyclamen

This interlude invites you to pause.

How do we re-imagine Maundrell's world; how do we analyse his writing, and then see past him—to the land, the people, and the plants—with a loving perception?

How do we sound if we mobilise a different awareness, tuning into feminist ears to hear what is not being heard by him? Who else is listening? Can you hear them?

---

On Monday, 1 March Maundrell describes the party's entrance into 'a Woody Mountaineous Country, which ends the Bashalick of Aleppo, and begins that of Tripoli':[70]

> Our Road here was very Rocky, and uneven; but yet the variety, which it afforded, made some amends for that inconvenience. Sometimes it led us under the cool shade of thick trees: sometimes thro' narrow Vallys, water'd with fresh murmuring Torrents: and then for a good while together upon the brink of a Precipice. And in all places it treated us with the prospect of Plants, and Flowers of divers kinds: as Myrtles, Oleaders, Cyclamens, Anemonies, Tulips, Marygolds, and several other sorts of Aromatick Herbs.

Tripoli was a passing point for many travellers on their way to Palestine in this period, as is evidenced by the more sonorous description of the Mevlevi Sufi lodge at Tripoli penned by Abd al-Ghani al-Nabulusi of Damascus. In a poem penned in his travelogue, the *Haqiqa w-al-majaz*, he wrote:

> Have you not seen the rivers beneath it flowing
> And the birds singing melodies without rhyming?
> Syrian Tripoli grew proud and was boasting,
> How blessed is he in seclusion retiring

---

70   Maundrell, *A Journey from Aleppo*, p. 5.

> And the lights of the shaykhs in that place were shining
> And chanters the *Mathnawī*'s mysteries chanting![71]

In contrast to these sounds of rivers, birds and the Sufi shaykhs of the Mevlevi lodge chanting, Maundrell seems at first hearing to be surrounded only by plants that serve as silent witnesses to his travails, despite their 'aromatick' smell. Perhaps all that he hears are the 'fresh murmuring torrents'.

However, a closer listen can tell us more.

The very fact that Maundrell recognises the cyclamen (Lebanon's national flower) tells a story of travel and cross-cultural exchange between England and the Levant region, since the flower was only introduced into Europe in the early seventeenth century. Perhaps the earliest reference to it appears in 1629, in John Parkinson's garden book *Paradisus Terrestris*,[72] in which he describes it as '*Cyclamen Antiochenum autumnale, flore purpureo duplici*, the double, red, autumn flowering cyclamen of Antioch'.[73] This description of the plant's origins contradicts the official name of the plant, *cyclamen persicum* and relocates its origins in seventeenth-century Antioch, at that time under the governate of Aleppo. Maundrell's very recognition of this plant and its red flower reveals a tacit dialogue between England, Lebanon and Syria: one that invites us to travel to a plant-world where borders do not exist, and seeds fly on clouds.

Local indigenous knowledge about the cyclamen tells us that the plant was variously called *bukhoor Mariam* (Mariam's incense), *asa el ra'ai* (staff of the shepherd) and *arn el ghazal* (horn of the deer). Plant historian Layla K. Feghali writes that the name *bukhoor Mariam* originates from the use of the plant's tubers as a sweet-smelling incense used in Eastern churches, and comments that it has often been used as a medicine for menstruation issues, and to support the health of the cervix and birthing processes.[74]

---

71  Elizabeth Sirriyeh, *Sufi Visionary of Ottoman Damascus: 'Abd al-Ghani al-Nabulusi, 1641–1731* (Abingdon: Routledge, 2011), p. 113.
72  Walter C. Blasdale, 'The Early History of the Persian Cyclamen', *The National Horticultural Magazine* (October 1949), 156–61.
73  Blasdale, 'Early History', p. 156.
74  Layla K. Feghali, *The Land in Our Bones: Plantcestral Herbalism and Healing Cultures from Syria to the Sinai* (Berkeley: North Atlantic Books, 2024), pp. 240–1.

Another tacit dialogue is between the cyclamen and an (unmentioned) bee, since the existence of the former implies the latter. The phenomenon of floral sonication shows that some plant species have anthers that must be buzzed to release pollen, therefore showing that plants can detect and respond to sound vibrations emitted by bees. A study in 2016 found that bumblebees are able to modify the frequency and amplitude of their buzzes to manipulate buzz-pollinated plants, which each have optimal sonication characteristics for releasing pollen.[75]

A story related in a seventeenth-century Arabic text on music compiled by Baddradin ibn Salim al-Maliki corroborates this idea of plants being able to hear. The story takes place just fifty kilometres away from Maundrell's Tripoli cyclamen, in a village called Al-Rumana near Ba'albeck.[76] The author relates:

I passed through one of the villages of Baalbeck, called Al-Rumana.

And I saw a plant that resembled a *manthour* (matthiola or stock in common parlance) in its colour and shape and I stopped, amazed by it. A kindly local said to me, 'I will add to your amazement!' and I asked how. He said, 'if two verses of a well-known poem are sung to this plant, it will shake until its leaves fall off and wither—let me show you!'

And he began to sing the two verses and to clap with his hands and sing:

*Oh inhabitants of the land of Balq'aa*
*Oh home of the oppressed, listen!*
*These are not my ruins,*
*These are the homes of my loved ones—*
*So mourn with me* [...]

[...] and by God, we saw around us the plant shook as though hit by a strong wind, until its leaves scattered and its energy withered.

Here, the plant does not just listen—it feels and is able to sense and express

---

75 Tan Morgan et al., 'Floral Sonication is an Innate Behaviour in Bumblebees that Can Be Fine-Tuned with Experience in Manipulating Flowers', *J Insect Behaviour* 29 (2016), 233–41.
76 My translation from *Qūt al-arwāḥ fī aḥkām al-samāʿ al-mubāḥ*, written before 1685, accessed via Markus Schmidt-Relenberg, 'Horen, Tanz und Extase nach Badraddin ibn Salim al-Maliki: Text, Ubersetzung und Kommentar / Al-Maliki' (PhD thesis, Kiel University, 1986), pp. 17–18.

solidarity for the oppression that the man expresses. Paradoxically, an awareness of the natural world being able to listen is perhaps dependent on listening to nature in the first place; thus Maundrell may not have listened to the plants, nor been aware of any possibility of their listening capacities.

Perhaps it is this that María Lugones would call a loving perception, if she were to read these texts with me…

*What do you need to improvise? [List as many things as necessary]*

## Conclusion: Divisions in Aleppo

In September 2021, I visited the National Archives at Kew, looking for traces of improvisation in travel stories between early modern England and Syria. I knew that there was an inventory belonging to Rowland Sherman, a factor for the Levant Company, from Bryan White's research.[77] Sherman had set sail from London to Aleppo in the summer of 1688, and stayed there until his death in 1747/8. The National Archives contain his letters to friends and family back home, and it was there in a bundle of papers where I came across the inventory of his extensive music collection. As Figure 8 shows, in this inventory, Sherman is recorded as having in his music library a collection of 'Divisions for Violin'—a seemingly trivial entry that, I would argue, represents several untold (and largely untraceable) histories of improvisatory thought and practice.

What does the presence of these divisions in Sherman's library indicate about early modern English extemporary practices in Aleppo, and what would it mean for Sherman to improvise his own divisions in this environment where he had spent so much time? As musicians and music historians today, should we take this entry simply as evidence for a material object in the archive, or as a sign that Sherman invented, created and imagined around this text?

---

[77] Bryan White, '"Brothers of the String": Henry Purcell and the Letter Books of Rowland Sherman', *Music & Letters* 92.4 (2011), 519–81 (p. 521).

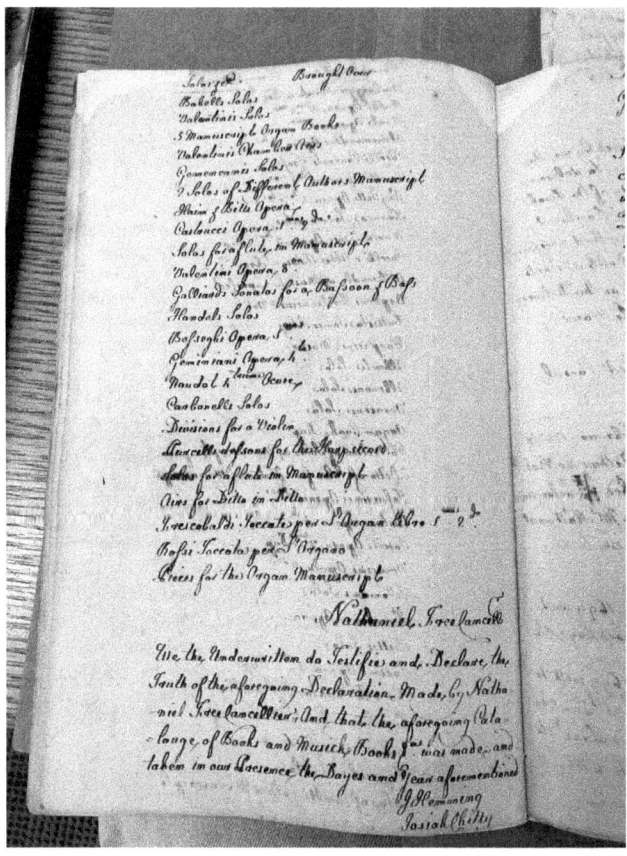

Fig. 8 SP 10/73, part 2, folio 73v, National Archives, Kew (reproduced with permission, all rights reserved).

My goal is not to answer these questions definitively; instead, by bringing theories of memory and improvisation to bear on travelogues and travel texts, I aim to open a portal to different creative readings and ways of conceiving of these texts that implicate the creativities of both the historical and contemporary readers' experiences and imaginations. In many ways, and as I explore more fully in the rest of the book, the historical project to understand early modern improvisation practices becomes a concern of the present, and the historical texts that tell us of such practices must be located within such imaginary worlds.

# Interlude: Bees on the Moon

## Colonial Pipes: A Song of Extemporary Queens

The early modern period in England was a significant time for the study and understanding of bees, reflecting contemporaneous issues of gender, coloniality and language. The first book in the English language to acknowledge that drone bees are male and that the queen bee is female was published in 1609, thus branding bee colonies as a system of 'feminine monarchie'. This bee-keeping manual by Charles Butler became the most popular text of its kind in seventeenth-century England, with revised editions appearing in 1623 and 1634.

As a child, Butler was a chorister at Magdalen College in Oxford, and he would later write a music treatise, *The Principles of Musik* (London: J. Haviland, 1636). His musical knowledge spilled into his perception of bees, whom he cast as musicians in this book, providing notations of their songs that ranged from transcriptions of their sounds in the 1609 edition (shown in Figure 9) to a madrigal composition in the editions of 1623 and 1634. The original piping sound is presented as a transcription of improvisatory sounds that are originally performed as a 'begging song' from the princess to queen bee, 'with more or fewer notes, as she [the princess bee] pleaseth' in her petition for the hive to swarm.

This piping sound is notated as a tone rising a second and pulsing eight times on that note, '&c'; or, in other words, repeating this pattern in like-fashion, and/or embellishing that second note at the will of the bee. Butler also notes that sometimes the bee will take a 'higher key', starting a note higher than in his previous notation and then sounding repeatedly a third higher.

©2025 Fatima Lahham, CC BY 4.0

Fig. 9 Charles Butler, *The Feminine Monarchie* (Oxford: Printed by Ioseph Barnes, 1609), p. 104, https://archive.org/details/bim_early-english-books-1475-1640_the-feminine-monarchie-_butler-charles_1609, public domain.

The Queen, however, sounds the bass, piping a third below the repeated sound of the princess bee's first example, and a fifth below the repeated sound of the princess's second example. Thus, as Butler notes, 'when they sing together, sometimes they agree on a perfect third, sometimes on a diapente, & (if you respect the terminology of the base), sometimes in a Diapase, With these tunes answering one another, and some pauses'.[1]

In Butler's transcription, the princess bee and queen bee naturally make harmony when they pipe together, instinctively sounding the notes in a triad. However, within this harmonic structure, the rest is improvised: the bees choose whether to pipe in thirds, in fifths or in

---

1   *The Feminine Monarchie or a Treatise Concerning Bees, and the Due Ordering of Them Wherein the Truth, Found out by Experience and Diligent Observation, Discovereth the Idle and Fondd Conceits, Which Many Haue Written anent this Subiect. By Char: Butler magd* (Oxford: Printed by Ioseph Barnes, 1609), p. 104, https://archive.org/details/bim_early-english-books-1475-1640_the-feminine-monarchie-_butler-charles_1609

unison; whether there are any passing notes; what rests or pauses they leave; what 'tunes' they sing that 'answer one another', and so on. More fancifully, we might hear the queen's 'bass' as a ground, with the other bees making divisions over it. In any case, these notations exist as some kind of transcription of an extemporised performance, and perhaps as it appears in Butler's book, as some kind of structure for extemporisation.

Later editions of this book departed from the simplicity of these transcriptions to present a fully-fledged four-part madrigal by Butler, along with expanded sections on the bee's music.[2] In the 1623 edition, Butler included a section titled 'In the Bees Song are the grounds of Musicke', commenting of the madrigals that were to follow, '...in this Melissomelos, or Bees Madrigall, Musicians may see the grounds of their Art'.[3] For Butler, the origins of human music-making thus seem to lie in the music of nature. Yet his language may hint at more. Could he even be suggesting that musicians can learn how to improvise over ground basses by listening to the bees improvising over the queen's drone? And how might an early modern musician have understood in practice that the bee's songs were the fundaments, perhaps even the ground bass of music?

Audio Recording 3 'The Bee'. Track 6 from Fatima Lahham, *bulbul*, FS Records (2022). https://hdl.handle.net/20.500.12434/610619fc

When I recorded this track, I wanted to offer a response to such a question from the perspective of a contemporary musician trained in 'historical performance'. I experimented with imitating the bee's piping alongside a repeated sample of this sound, before continuing alone into an extended improvisation premised (or grounded) on this

---

2 See Gerald Hayes, 'Charles Butler and the Music of Bees', *The Musical Times* 66.988 (1925), 512–15.

3 *The Feminine Monarchie: Or the Historie of Bees Shewing their Admirable Nature, and Properties, their Generation, and Colonies, their Gouernment, Loyaltie, Art, Industrie, Enemies, Warres, Magnanimitie, &c. together with the Right Ordering of Them from Time to Time: And the Sweet Profit Arising Thereof. Written out of Experience by Charles Butler. magd.* (London: Printed by Iohn Hauiland for Roger Iackson, 1623), p. 93, https://archive.org/details/RAM2023-1081

sound. My intention was to provoke exploration into the (historical and contemporary) boundaries drawn between 'natural' and 'unnatural' sound, as well as the boundaries of historical performance. How might we use historical texts such as Butler's as a way to creatively challenge these binaries, mobilising improvisation in response?

> ...we sample a recording of a bee piping (piping is the sound that bees make when it is time to swarm). The upwards melodic motion and repetition is identical to the notations of bee piping that Charles Butler notated, and my initial idea for this track was to improvise in the same vein as the piping, with the sample simply starting the track then fading out, leading into my own improvisation. But in the moment, I remember Butler's hints of bee-song as the ground bass of nature, and I find myself wanting to improvise with the bee. So that is what we record. It felt sacred and almost wrong to be inhabiting this space of bee language, of stepping into a bee's sonic world for a few moments, imagining their imagination in the moments before sounding, and then doing the same... (creative reflection, December 2021)

Butler's own response to the challenge of imagining musical responses to the bees' piping comes in this later edition of his text. The piping transcriptions that were included in the earlier versions of the book appear within a composed four-part madrigal in the 1623 edition. The text of the madrigal likens the bees' 'feminine monarchie' to that of the 'famous Amazons', and praises them for their aspirations: 'To seeke new Cities, for new habitation,/They send abroad their num'rous Colonies...' As Butler developed the bees' social model into a proto-colonial one that perhaps mirrored England's socio-political position and served (like the Ottoman empire) as an object of imperial envy, so their musical status rose from that of transcribed triadic improvisation to the sophistication of four-part harmony and the setting of a long text.[4] However, the extemporary 'piping' is still there in the Meane voice part, representing a rupture from text and notation.

Bruce R. Smith discusses the space between animal sounds and human sounds as a continuum, referencing Helkiah Crooke writing in 1616 that 'even in the tongue of man, sometimes it expresseth onelie

---

4   *The Feminine Monarchie* (1623), pp. 94–5.

those things that fall under the Sense, as when wee crie for paine, or for Foode and succour'.[5] The sound of the bee piping may fall into this category of 'sense' as in something that is 'sensed' and may only be felt rather than apprehended logically or through language, therefore also placing these sounds into a similar category to that of women, perceptions of foreigners/foreign languages, and of the natural world as non-verbal and overly 'sensual'. The piping also emphasises the lack of musical ordering in comparison to the carefully crafted madrigals that had come before. The cultivated harmony and ensemble of the four-part writing suddenly falls apart as the solo 'bee' abandons language, harmony and tonal melodic sense, instead vocalising on four pitches.

The second time the madrigal features piping, the text disappears again but the sound is no longer monophonic, instead involving all four voices but representing a much simpler and more repetitive type of four-voice interaction than the preceding polyphony. In fact, the notation itself is unfixed by Butler's earlier remark that 'they sing both in triple time the princess thus [...] with more or fewer notes, as she pleaseth. And sometime she taketh a higher key'. Thus the notation here operates as a kind of record of a live instance of 'performance', subject to change every time it is performed or heard.

Fig. 10 Charles Butler, *The Feminine Monarchie* (London: Printed by John Haviland, 1623), p. 96, https://archive.org/details/RAM2023-1081/page/n3/mode/2up, public domain.

The musical text in Figure 10 taken from the Meane part, thus has the character of a transcription, with Butler's role as transcriber rather than composer.

---

5   Bruce R. Smith, *The Acoustic World of Early Modern England: Attending to the O-Factor* (Chicago: University of Chicago Press, 1999), p. 45.

The musicologist Linda Austern describes the shift from the transcriptions in Butler's earlier editions of his book to the madrigal setting as follows: 'the entomologist-composer has transformed the simple sounds of his tiny winged females from the practical but barely comprehensible signals he had first notated into domestic decoration and witty wonder for human entertainment. No longer the natural philosopher observing the public customs of a manly state in miniature, he functions instead as the imperial explorer refashioning a simple effeminate product for consumption by his own culture'.[6] This re-imagining of Butler as an 'imperial explorer' who captures and 'refashions' the sounds of the female bees in print for the consumption of English people back home is striking, and shows how ways of interacting with the natural world can often mirror colonial ways of interacting with people from other cultures.

Early modern travelogues were not restricted to factual travels, and sometimes spilled into imaginary accounts of other-worldly voyages where sound and music were recreated in accordance with the authors' worldview. Austern's words similarly recall the notion of the travelogue as a text in which the traveller 'refashions' themselves and the places and peoples they encounter, in a way that allows readers to do the same back home. The transcription of languages and musics in travelogues was quite common, along with taxonomies of instruments played, and here Butler transposes some of these aspects of the travelogue genre into his beekeeping manual.

Although by the first edition in 1609 Elizabeth I had been dead for six years and been succeeded by James I (VI of Scotland), the madrigal text is clearly inspired by her 'feminine monarchie', sitting in the hive that is England and sending her worker bees—or diplomats and traders—abroad to create new colonies. Butler's revised text presented the 'feminine' rule of the bee as an impressive and well-ordered organisation, but contemporary views of the 'apiarchy' were not as tolerant or complimentary. Writing of John Milton's beehive, Nicole A. Jacobs traces the image of the hive in Milton's corpus, relating it to the English tradition of the bee as 'a divine symbol of monarchical and ecclesiastical power structures', and arguing that, for Milton, this imagery was used

---

6  Linda P. Austern, 'Nature, Culture, Myth, and the Musician in Early Modern England', *Journal of the American Musicological Society* 51.1 (1998), 1–47 (p. 11).

'to register harsh critiques of earthly monarchy, feminine influence, and Catholic superstition'.[7] Jacobs offers an important re-reading of a passage in Milton's *Eikonoklastes* of October 1649, a parliamentarian response to the *Eikon Basilike* promoted by royalists, in which they presented Charles I's final prayers and meditations before his January 1649 execution. In this passage Milton refers to the executed king as the 'Aegyptian Apis', a phrase that commentators had previously ascribed as referring to the sacred bull Apis who was the incarnation of the Egyptian god Osiris, overlooking the translation of the Latin *apis* or bee.

Images of the 'royalist bee and republican ant' became popular in mid-seventeenth century English political literature, linking the bee to the threat of female power and the need to dominate the natural world, as well as to the dangers of foreign Catholic popery.[8] Frederick R. Prete explains that the tradition of using bees as a way to discuss utopian visions of seventeenth-century English society came into conflict with beliefs around gender roles in this period. He writes: 'as the century wore on, an increasing number of seemingly anomalous discoveries about honey bees forced authors of beekeeping texts to deny or distort findings in order to continue to use the honey bee as a metaphor for the ideal English society'.[9] In this context, Butler's royalist agenda in writing his text is perhaps complicated by the radical nature of presenting an ideal image of a society run by female authority, producing the first text to admit that bee organisation was predicated on the supremacy of a queen bee, and gendering 'Princes' as female in this new model where female was the default mode of being.[10]

---

7   Nicole A. Jacobs, 'John Milton's Beehive, from Polemic to Epic', *Studies in Philology* 112.4 (2015), 798–816 (p. 798).

8   Here it is worth noting the spread of Catholicism in seventeenth-century Palestine, connecting foreign notions of Catholicism to the lands of the 'Turks' in the early modern British anxieties around these two threats. See Felicita Tramontana, 'The Spread of Catholicism in Seventeenth-Century Palestinian Villages', in *Space and Conversion in Global Perspective*, ed. by Giuseppe Marcocci, Aliocha Maldavsky, Wietse de Boer and Ilaria Pavan (Leiden: Brill, 2014), pp. 81–102.

9   Frederick R. Prete, 'Can Females Rule the Hive? The Controversy over Honey Bee Gender Roles in British Beekeeping Texts of the Sixteenth-Eighteenth Centuries', *Journal of the History of Biology* 24 1 (1991), 113–44 (p. 117); on the history of gendering bees, see Cyrus Abivardi, 'Honeybee Sexuality: An Historical Perspective', in *Encyclopedia of Historical Entomology*, ed. by John L. Capinera (Dordrecht: Springer, 2005), pp. 1103–04, https://doi.org/10.1007/0-306-48380-7_2057

10  Butler's interest in sound goes beyond bees; in 1633 he published a book on grammar in which he argued that words should be spelled how they sounded, and

In making his case for the 'feminine monarchie', Butler moves sonically from rustic improvised sounds to composed and more refined ones, taming the raw and natural piping into polished singing. The sanitisation of the original piping that he transcribed could have happened for many reasons: to impose order on the irrational sounds of nature, to add a selling point to his book, or to mollify the alien qualities of the bee—namely its proximity to Catholic popery, Charles's 'Egyptian bee' and to queenship as a model of rule.

Improvised sound as a default mode of language for creatures in the natural world was not unusual, as I explore later on with the nightingale's 'divisions'. However, more than that, improvised sound referred to a wider mode of describing the 'other' sounds of unchartered lands—and even planets. Early writings on the moon and its imagined exploration can illustrate this point, as well as indicating ideas about musical language. In 1641, the polymath John Wilkins described how a language could consist 'only of Tunes and Musicall Notes, without any articulate sound', since 'a man may frame a Language, consisting only of Tunes and such inarticulate sounds, as no Letters can expresse. Which kind of speech is fancied to bee usuall a|mongst the Lunary Inhabitants'.[11] The language that he describes is 'irrational', comprised of only musical sounds without verbal expression, and spoken by 'lunary inhabitants'.

Musical language is also present in the first piece of science fiction written in English, Francis Godwin's *The Man in the Moone* (1638), in which a man travels to the moon as part of a quasi-colonialist mission, and finds that the 'lunary inhabitants' all speak in musical tunes. In a very similar manner to Charles Butler's notations, Godwin makes some musical transcriptions of some of these phrases, shown in Figure 11:[12]

---

in his subsequent writings he trialled a new system of phonetic spelling.

11  John Wilkins, *Mercvry, or, the Secret and Svvift Messenger Shewing, How a Man May with Privacy and Speed Communicate his Thoughts to a Friend at Any Distance* (London: Printed by I. Norton, for Iohn Maynard and Timothy Wilkins, 1641), p. 141, http://hdl.handle.net/20.500.14106/A66051

12  Francis Godwin, *The Man in the Moone: Or, a Discovrse of a Voyage thither by Domingo Gonsales the Speedy Messenger* (London: Printed by John Norton, to be sold by Ioshua Kurton and Thomas Warren, 1657), pp. 94–5, https://archive.org/details/bim_early-english-books-1641-1700_the-man-in-the-moone_godwin-francis_1657/page/n1/mode/2up

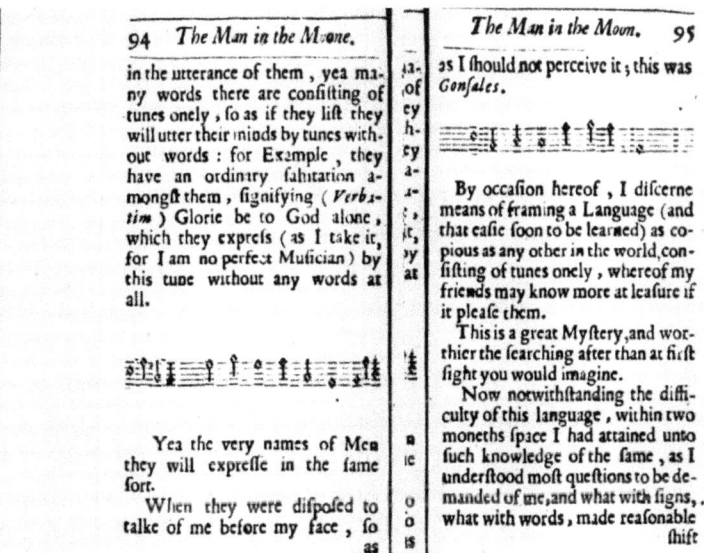

Fig. 11 Francis Godwin, *The Man in the Moone* (London: Printed by John Norton, to be sold by Ioshua Kurton and Thomas Warren, 1657), pp. 94–5, https://archive.org/details/bim_early-english-books-1641-1700_the-man-in-the-moone_godwin-francis_1657/page/n1/mode/2up, public domain.

As illustrated, Godwin imagines a world where phrases such as 'Glorie be to God' may be expressed by a melody 'without any words at all', or where the name 'Gonzales' may be communicated in a phrase of eight notes. As the protagonist of his story notes,

> by occasion hereof, I discerne meanes of framing a Language (and that easie soone to bee learned) as copious as any other in the world, consisting of tunes only, whereof my friends may know more at leisure if it pleases them. This is a great Mystery and worthier the searching after then at first sight you might imagine. Now notwithstanding the difficulty of this language, within two months space I had attained unto such knowledge of the same, as I could understand most questions to be demanded of mee.

The description of this musical language poses several questions about the role of invention and improvisation. John Wilkins continues:

> By this you may easily discern how two Musicians may discourse with one another, by playing upon their Instru|ments of *Musique,* as well as by talking with their instruments of *speech*. And (which is a singular curiosity) how the words of a Song may be contrived in the tune of it.

> I suppose that these letters and notes might be disposed to answer oneano|ther, with better advantage then here they are expressed. And this perhaps, would bee easie enough for those that are thoroughly versed in the grounds of Musique, unto whose further en|quiry, I doe here only propose this in|vention.[13]

For Wilkins, musicians already possess this ability to communicate without language through instrumental sounds. However, 'discourse' or conversation between people are by default improvised or made up in the moment without text to dictate how the sounds of letters and notes 'might be disposed to answer one another'. Wilkins goes on to say that such an exchange would be easy for one 'versed in the grounds of Musique'—which, according to Butler, could be learned from the bees—once again bringing us back to the domain of the extemporary as located in the natural world, which presented a spectrum of improvised and non-verbal sounds that 'explorers' could only grapple with through transcriptions.

Butler's bee-keeping treatise represents an important source for musicians and improvisers, as well as presenting a challenge to historians. How do we listen to such a text within the contexts I have explored here? In fact, I argue that ways of listening to this text are varied and fluid, but that they benefit from being underpinned by contemporaneous research into musical improvisation, which highlights ways in which to read this text contextually and to listen to what is not being heard. Furthermore, these texts offer musicians and improvisers a plethora of ways to engage creatively with different historical contexts and to mobilise a musical imagination that is grounded in historical spaces of imagining—for example, the imagination of sounds made by bees and lunary inhabitants. Improvisation here offers a space in which subjects may sound 'otherwise'—and where the notations of any such sounds in texts were always subject to change and took on an unfixed nature that the contemporary musician/music historian may engage creatively today.

---

13  *Mercvry*, pp. 142–3.

# 3. Improvising Nature: Transposable Tongues of the Nightingale

...birds seldome use any untruths to tell...
—English ballad writer Martin Parker (1632)[1]

Beasts and Birds their Stories tell
To One another Certainly,
And yet no Words they speak Plainly;
But by That Language which is giv'n
In Nature, (by Decree from Heav'n)
They Understand undoubtably
Each others Speech...
—Thomas Mace, *Musick's Monument* (1676)[2]

## The Extemporary Languages of Nature: On Bees and Birds

The speech of 'beasts and birds' preoccupied many philosophers, naturalists and musicians in early modern England. The unintelligible nature of this speech is referenced above by English music theorist Thomas Mace, who joined many contemporary writers in the belief that animals and the natural world lacked rational language and rhetoric.

---

1  *The Nightingale Vvarbling forth her Owne Disaster; or the Rape of Philomela. Newly Written in English Verse, by Martin Parker* (London: Printed by George Purslowe for William Cooke, 1632), p. 72, https://quod.lib.umich.edu/e/eebo2/A08974.0001.001?view=toc

2  Thomas Mace, *Musick's Monument*, Reproduction en fac-similé (Éditions du Centre National de la Recherche Scientifique: Paris, 1958), p. 37.

As musicologist Linda Phyllis Austern puts it, 'The world of nature, in which nightingales sang sweetly and bees produced their own form of esoteric discourse, lacked humanly comprehensible words. Bestial rhetoric often remained inaccessible to human ears'.[3]

This inaccessibility often fell in line with notions of nature as irrational, passionate, illiterate and unreasoned, but it could also point towards divine mystery. Mace continues, 'if you'l regard with stedfast Eyes,/ And dive into such Mysteries,/you'l find that Nothing's Plainer then/ That BRUTES have Speech as well as MEN'.[4] These 'mysteries' concerning the speech of creatures and the natural world were often entwined with matters of print and orality; the languages and sounds of nature emanated directly from their sources without recourse to a text or script, functioning as a set of extemporary behaviours, speeches and sounds that were created directly by and from the bodies of those who enacted them.

These early modern discourses on the language of animals often focussed on investigations into the study of birdsong (as well as bees and their sounds). Improvisation became located in the speech and sounds of animals as a 'natural' means of expression—one that presented a display of uncurbed nature and that could be improved upon through musical practice.

In this chapter, I discuss the role of improvisation in cultural understandings of the nightingale, building on narratives of embodied improvisation and improvisation as encounter, reading cross-cultural encounters through the bodies of improvising birds and identifying discourses of gender, coloniality and their intersections.

## Sweet Divisions: Paradoxes of the Nightingale

Discourses of improvisation surround the early modern nightingale. In their 2014 dictionary of Shakespeare and music, Michela Calore and Christopher R. Wilson note the idea that 'Elizabethan birds were accomplished in the art of division', citing Robert Nichol's description of the preparations made by the Nightingale for her singing contest with the Cuckoo, in *The Cuckow* (London: F[elix] K[ingston], 1607):

---

3   Linda P. Austern, 'Nature, Culture, Myth, and the Musician in Early Modern England', *Journal of the American Musicological Society* 51.1 (1998), 1–47 (p. 5).
4   Mace, *Musick's Monument*, p. 37.

> The little Philomel with curious care,
> Sitting alone her ditties did prepare,
> And many tunes...
> Dividing sweetly in division
> Now some sweet straine to mind she doth restore.⁵

This trope of the improvising nightingale was common in early modern poetry and depictions of the bird, which usually extolled her 'sweet strains'. In contrast to this sweetness, the origin of the nightingale's story in many popular English accounts lies in Ovid's tragic tale of Philomela and her rape by Tereus—the husband of her sister Procne—as related in Book 6 of the *Metamorphoses*, and, from the fifteenth century, through numerous English translations and retellings of Ovid's text. With some variations in content and narrative, the story relates not only that Tereus rapes Philomela, but also that he cuts out her tongue so that she is not able to tell anyone of his crime. Despite her lack of speech, Philomela reveals her fate to her sister through an embroidered tapestry, and the sisters take revenge by serving up a stew to Tereus that contains his son. When Tereus finds out what Philomela and Procne have done, he pursues them. The gods turn him into a hoopoe (in some versions the bird species varies), and Procne and Philomela become a swallow and a nightingale.

As a nightingale, Philomela gets a 'second' voice: despite Tereus cutting her tongue out when she was a woman, as a bird she is able to sing. However, her original voice is forever gone, as is her ability to verbalise the story of what happened to her. Instead, she sings sweetly—in the words of the English ballad-writer Martin Parker, who wrote in the first person to imagine her feelings:

> I *Philomel* (turn'd to a Nightingale)
> Fled to the woods, and 'gainst a bryer or thorne,
> I sit and warble out my mournfull tale:
> To sleepe I alwaies have with heed forborne,
> But sweetly sing at euening, noone, and morne.
> No time yeelds rest unto my dulcide throat,
> But still I ply my lachrimable note.⁶

---

5   Christopher R. Wilson and Michela Calore, *Music in Shakespeare: A Dictionary* (London: Bloomsbury Publishing, 2014), p. 143.
6   *The Nightingale Vvarbling forth her Owne Disaster*, p. 57.

The story of Philomela in this tradition is one of replaced voices, shifted identities and transposable tongues. The identity of the Common Nightingale (Luscinia megarhynchos) in England (both in the early modern period and now) is further complicated by the fact these are migrating birds, breeding in Europe, Northwest Africa and Southwest Asia, but spending the winter south of the Sahara from West Africa to Uganda, and coming to the UK from May onwards to spend the summer.

The absence of the nightingale for the remaining nine months of the year rendered her a travelling bird, perhaps going away to collect materials for the divisions she would come back to England to sing. Furthermore, her sojourn in those parts of the world that English travellers were starting to explore expands her songs to cross geographical and cultural borders that she easily flew over, further complicating the stories told about her, and causing her to feature in travelogues of the Ottoman empire as a consistently musical creature. In his travels into 'the Levant', for example, the French traveller Jean de Thévenot charted his journey at the River of Jordan, and noted that 'It is very full of Fish, and on both sides beset with little thick and pleasant Woods, among which, thousands of Nightingales warbling all together, make a most pleasant delightful and charming Consort'.[7]

The story of the nightingale that English travellers may have encountered in the traditions of countries in North Africa and the Mediterranean was quite different to the Philomela myth. In the Islamic Sufi tradition, the love story between nightingale and rose is a tale of divine love, where bird and flower are a metaphor for the lover and the beloved. Here, the nightingale falls in love with a white rose. He sings his sweet song to woo her, and she answers by opening her petals. Yet whenever the nightingale flies in to embrace her, thorns pierce his chest and stain the flower red with his blood.[8] The nightingale and the rose appeared frequently in varying formulations on this theme, across Arabic, Turkish, Persian and Urdu texts.

---

7   Jean de Thévenot, *The Travels of Monsieur de Thevenot into the Levant in Three Parts, viz. into I. Turkey, II. Persia, III. the East-Indies / Newly Done out of French* (London: Printed by H. Clark, for H. Faithorne, J. Adamson, C. Skegnes, and T. Newborough, 1687), p. 193, https://archive.org/details/travelsofmonsieu00thev/page/n7/mode/2up

8   Annemarie Schimmel, *A Two-Colored Brocade: The Imagery of Persian Poetry* (Chapel Hill: University of North Carolina Press, 1992), pp. 178–80.

While the English/Ottoman origin stories for the nightingale diverge, it is important to note the presence of the thorn in both traditions: in the passage I quoted above by Martin Parker, he describes how the bird warbles her sad song "'gainst a bryer or thorne', and in Shakespeare's narrative poem *The Rape of Lucrece* (1594), Lucrece also describes the nightingale as singing 'against a thorn'.[9] The reason for the bird's sorrow can thus be traced in both accounts to the pain caused by the thorn, perhaps resulting in a convergence of tragedy, both caused by different types of injury that the world can inflict.

Despite this cultural/geographical ambiguity, the nightingale was an important sonic symbol of early modern English culture. Perhaps most famously, Shakespeare uses her in *Romeo and Juliet* as a temporal indication of how much time the lovers still have together. In the exchange, Juliet tries to convince Romeo not to leave by telling him she can hear the sound of the nightingale, while he refutes her hearing and claims that the song they can hear is that of the lark (thus indicating dawn rather than night):

> JULIET
> Wilt thou be gone? It is not yet near day.
> It was the nightingale, and not the lark,
> That pierced the fearful hollow of thine ear.
> Nightly she sings on yon pomegranate tree.
> Believe me, love, it was the nightingale.
>
> ROMEO
> It was the lark, the herald of the morn,
> No nightingale.[10]

While it is the nightingale's song that pierces the 'fearful hollow' of Romeo's ear, the pomegranate tree here is also significant since it represents an 'exotic' fruit only recently brought to England from the Ottoman world. It is difficult to decide if the nightingale here is simply

---

9   Wilson and Calore, *Music in Shakespeare*, p. 56.
10  William Shakespeare, *Romeo and Juliet*, ed. by Barbara A. Mowat and Paul Werstine (The Folger Shakespeare), III.5, l.1–7, pp. 156–7, https://shakespeare.folger.edu/downloads/pdf/romeo-and-juliet_PDF_FolgerShakespeare.pdf

a familiar melancholy figure on the sonic English landscape, or in fact a further symbol of (Ottoman) danger, deception and otherness.

The paradoxes of the nightingale seem many—caught as she is between migrations, genders and cultural associations. Yet it is just this slippery quality that that make her such a promising point of focus for tracing the convergences of gender, animality, coloniality and otherness, forming in tandem the nightingale's 'transposable tongue', and perhaps aided and abetted by her extemporary skill.

The nightingale occupied a unique position between early modern English and Ottoman cultures. Since her stories, like her songs, were numerous, intricate and varying, I will now consider two case studies of the nightingale at moments of early modern Anglo-Ottoman encounter. In 1594, the Ottoman Empress Safiye (wife of Sultan Murad III who reigned from 1574 to 1595) wrote a letter to Queen Elizabeth I. This was not an isolated moment of contact, since Elizabeth corresponded with both Safiye and her husband. The two queens also exchanged gifts: Safiye received a golden coach from Elizabeth, and in return sent her the clothes of an Ottoman noblewoman. Her letters to Elizabeth were written in five colours of ink and sprinkled in gold dust. The 1594 letter is dated 'the first day of the Moone of Rabie Liuoll in the yere of the Prophet', and opens with an address eulogising Elizabeth. Safiye continues:

> I send you Majesty so honorable and sweet a salution of peace, that all the flocke o Nightingales with their melody cannot attaine to the like, much lesse this simple letter of mine. The singular loue which we haue conceiued one toward the other is like to a garden of pleasant birds: and the Lord God vouchsafe to saue and keepe you, and send your Maiesty an hap end both in this world and in the world to come...[11]

It is striking that Safiye heightens her 'honorable and sweet salutation of peace' by declaring that it excels not only her 'simple letter' but even the melody of a whole 'flocke' of nightingales. She goes on to describe the love and accord between her and Elizabeth as 'a garden of pleasant birds', extending the nightingale metaphor. Perhaps her reference point for the nightingale is that of a yearning lover singing to his rose, thus

---

11   Cited in Lamiya Mohamad Almas, 'The Women of the Early Modern Turk and Moor Plays' (PhD thesis, University of Minnesota, 2009), p. 3.

positioning her as an ardent admirer of the English queen. Yet the love between them is reciprocal—or at least, so Safiye would have us believe, and in this metaphor the two queens are likened to a garden of birds in their mutual affection. The aural image created is one of birdsong, with Safiye and Elizabeth warbling sweet divisions in imitation of the other.

But what is it about the nightingale that encourages Safiye to select her song for this gesture towards Elizabeth? The Persian mystic poet Farid ud-Din Attar's poem *The Conference of the Birds* (*Manteq at-Tair*, c.1177) is also of great importance to this discussion, since it was certainly known to Safiye and formed an important cultural touchstone for the nightingale's imagery in Sufi and Islamicate contexts. The poem narrates a story in which the birds of the world gather together, led by the hoopoe, to find their king, the Simorgh. In the course of the journey, each of the birds gives an excuse for why their quest is impossible the nightingale cannot leave his beloved, the finch is too scared to set off, and so on. The allegorical nature of the text allows the reader to see different facets of themselves and their failings on the spiritual path through the birds and their character traits.

The nightingale takes the character of the lover, yearning over the rose until he is sick. He claims to be unable to leave her side: 'My love is for the rose; I bow to her;/From her dear presence I could never stir./ If she should disappear the nightingale/Would lose his reason and his song would fail,/And though my grief is one that no bird knows,/One being understands my heart—the rose'.[12] The bird continues with his excuses for why he cannot undertake the journey:

> I am so drowned in love that I can find
> No thought of my existence in my mind.
> Her worship is sufficient life for me;
> The quest for her is my reality
> (And nightingales are not robust or strong;
> The path to find the Simorgh is too long).
> My love is here; the journey you propose
> Cannot beguile me from my life—the rose.
> It is for me she flowers; what greater bliss

---

12  Farid Attar, *The Conference of the Birds*, translated by Afkham Darbandi and Dick Davis (London: Penguin Books, 1984), pp. 41–2.

> Could life provide me—anywhere—than this?
> Her buds are mine; she blossoms in my sight—
> How could I leave her for a single night?[13]

The hoopoe responds to these excuses sharply, accusing the nightingale of a superficial love that must be overtaken by a less transient one:

> ...Dear nightingale,
>
> This superficial love which makes you quail
> Is only for the outward show of things.
> Renounce delusion and prepare your wings
> For our great quest; sharp thorns defend the rose
> And beauty such as hers too quickly goes.
> True love will see such empty transience
> For what it is—a fleeting turbulence
> That fills your sleepless nights with grief and blame—
> Forget the rose's blush and blush for shame![14]

The nightingale emerges here as a symbol of utmost devotion and love, although that love may also be in need of tempering and sublimating from a superficial passion to a more elevated love—in Somayeh Baeten's words, the nightingale here is 'a symbol of men interested in earthly unstable pleasures'.[15] Thus, in Safiye's evocation of the bird, perhaps the nightingale's paradoxical status that I outlined above leaves the exact nature of her devotion to Elizabeth in some ambiguity—is she simply stating her utmost adoration, or suggesting that this love should be curbed in some way?

Five years after Safiye sent her letter, in 1599, Elizabeth I sent an automated organ to Sultan Mehmed III (Safiye's son). It was the first organ sent to the Ottoman empire by an English trading company (although it is worth noting that in the Islamicate world organs had been gifted to Europe as early as the Abbasids, with the Caliph Harun al-Rashid presenting one to Charlemagne),[16] and was built by Thomas

---

13  Attar, *The Conference of the Birds*, p. 42.
14  *The Conference of the Birds*, p. 42.
15  Somayeh Baeten, *Birds, Birds, Birds: A Comparative Study of Medieval Persian and English Poetry, especially Attar's 'Conference of Birds', 'The Owl and the Nightingale', Chaucer's 'The Parliament of Fowls', and the Canterbury Tales* (Munich: Utzverlag, 2020), p. 40.
16  See Mika Natif, *Mughal Occidentalism: Artistic Encounters between Europe and Asia at*

Dallam, who accompanied the organ to repair it after damages on the sea voyage, and then to install it in the Topkapi Palace in Istanbul. Dallam kept a journal documenting his travels, in which he recorded his experiences installing and performing on this instrument, making it a well-documented journey.[17] In the words of Jennifer Linhart Wood, this organ was a 'necessary element in a complex set of diplomatic protocols that enabled the English Levant Company to maintain a commercial relationship with the Ottoman empire;'[18] according to Ian Woodfield, the organ was 'the most magnificent musical gift sent by any English company'.[19]

Dallam's mechanical organ was 'self-playing' and also featured a chiming clock and mechanical puppets including trumpet players and a nest of mechanical birds who sang and flapped their wings. His diary entry for 24 September 1599 reads as follows:

> The presente began to salute the grand sinyor; for when I lefte it I did alow a quarter of an houre for his cominge thether. Firste the clocke strouke 22; than The chime of 16 bels went of, & played a songe of 4 partes. That beinge done, tow personagis which stood upon to cornders of the seconde storie houldinge tow silver trumpetes in there hands did lifte them to theire heads, & sounded a tantarra. Than the mvsicke went of, and the orgon played a song of 5 partes twyse over. In the tope of the orgon, being 16 foute hie did stande a holly bushe full of blacke birds & thrushis, which at the end of the mvsick did singe & shake theire wynges. Divers other motions thare was which the grand sinyor wondered at. (55v)[20]

The song of the 'black birds and thrushis' (blackbirds and thrushes) was created through a special sound-effect stop called the 'Nightingale' in which the ends of the pipes were placed in a bowl of water or oil,

---

the Courts of India, 1580–1630 (Leiden: Brill, 2018), p. 139 and pp. 142–8 for a history of organs as gifts between Europe and the Mughal court.

17   Thomas Dallam, *A Brefe Relation of My Travell from the Royall Cittie of London towards The Straite of Mariemediterranum and What Happened by the Waye*. This manuscript account is in the British Library—BL Add MS 17480 and all references to it in my chapter are drawn from Jennifer Linhart Wood, *Sounding Otherness in Early Modern Drama and Travel: Uncanny Vibrations in the English Archive* (Cham: Palgrave Macmillan 2019).

18   Wood, *Sounding Otherness*, p. 168.

19   Ian Woodfield, *English Musicians in the Age of Exploration* (New York: Pendragon Press, 1995), p. 191.

20   Wood, *Sounding Otherness*, p. 184.

producing a sound imitating the warbling of birds.²¹ This technique dates from at least 1450, and is commonly referred to as a 'nightingale' stop, evoking Philomela's replaced tongue; her voice supplanted by that of the blackbird and thrush. Since Dallam's holly bush was full of birds that were native to England and other parts of Europe, he probably included many Nightingale stops to sonically represent multiple birds.²² Thus the mechanical birds that conclude the organ's concert were ostensibly sounds indicative of an English soundscape replicated for the Sultan: the nightingale was a sonic representative of England, sent to Istanbul.²³

While the organ was sent as an English gift that brought these English sounds to the Turkish court, the organ's materiality complicates the matter, and the instrument itself was 'transformed by its travels', as Wood argues compellingly.²⁴ Not only did the organ undergo repairs on site using Turkish materials, but the water, oil and air that went through the pipes to create this nightingale stop were indeed Turkish. The nightingale's identity is even more compromised by the fact that it is not actually her voice that is heard—she merely stands as a representative body for both blackbird and thrush. These two case studies show that the nightingale's accomplishment in the art of division was entangled with her cross-

---

21 *The Organ: An Encyclopedia*, ed. by Douglas E. Bush and Richard Kassel (London: Routledge, 2006), p. 371.

22 It is important to note that the nightingale stop was not a phenomenon restricted to England or Europe, see Wood, *Sounding Otherness*, pp. 189–90. There is also a striking mention of this feature in the Palestine travelogue (1693) of Damascene mystic and writer Abd al-Ghani al-Nabulusi. Nabulusi records that he heard the monks of Bethlehem making music with an organ, composing a poem in which he likened the organ's sounds to that of the blackbird (*shahrur*) and nightingale (*hizar, bulbul*). In 'Abd al-Ghanī al-Nābulusī, *Al-Haqīqa wa-l-majāz fī al-rihla ila Bilād al-Shām wa Miṣr wa-l-Hijāz*, ed. by Ahmad ʿAbd al-Majīd Harīdī (Cairo: Al-Hay'a al-Miṣriyya), p. 125, https://archive.org/details/hakika-majaz

23 It should be noted that the nightingale's 'sweet notes' would later be used as an English-sympathising counter to the sound of the Quran, which was likened to the sound of the cuckoo in the 'caveat' to the first English translation of the text made by Alexander Ross in 1649. See *The Alcoran of Mahomet, Translated out of Arabick into French, by the Sieur du Ryer, Lord of Malezair, and Resident for the French King, at Alexandria. And Newly Englished, for the Satisfaction of All that Desire to Look into the Turkish Vanities. To Which is Prefixed, the Life of Mahomet, the Prophet of the Turks, and Author of the Alcoran. With a Needful Caveat, or Admonition, for Them Who Desire to Know What Use May Be Made of, or if There Be Danger in Reading the Alcoran* (London: Printed and to be sold by Randal Taylor, 1688), n.p., https://archive.org/details/alcoranofmahomet00dury

24 Wood, *Sounding Otherness*, p. 170.

cultural transposability. From the divergences of her origin stories and the common thorn they share, to her slippage between women and bird/male and female/English and Ottoman, her improvising voice was perhaps a symbol of her unfixed identity and the flexibility she enjoyed in appearing in different contexts with different voices.

The nightingale also existed within another duality in early modern England: between the natural world and the musical one. As I noted above, the nightingale was frequently invoked in early modern English sources as an improvising bird who sang musical 'divisions', warbling her way through poems with a sweetness that belied her tragic origin story. One poet amongst many who found inspiration in the improvising nightingale was Joshua Sylvester (1563–1618). In a poetic transcription of the nightingale's songs, Sylvester describes a dialogue between nightingales, the first warbling 'sweetly, clear', the second repeating her strains, to which 'the first replyes, and descants there-upon;/With divine warbles of Division,/Redoubling Quavers; And so (turn by turn)/Alternately they sing away the Morn…'[25] The harmony of these songs, according to Sylvester, 'excels/Our Voyce, our Violls, and all Musick els.', and the improvisations of each nightingale on the other's melodies fill the morning's soundscapes.

The nightingale's divisions arise naturally from her surroundings; Sylvester recognises them as 'divine warbles of division', and 'descants', but she is of course entirely unschooled in the art of making division. In the context of both the recognised dangers of improvising freely, and the status of the nightingale as a gendered female songster, these improvisations were simultaneously acclaimed (as in Sylvester's poem) and potentially life-threatening, resulting in other poems that instead depict the nightingale's death. One such example of the latter story appears in retellings of the *Musical Duel* by Jesuit poet Famiano Strada (1572–1649), originally written in Latin in imitation of the Roman poet Claudian's tale, which stages a musical contest between a harpist and a nightingale. Strada's version was expanded upon in English by several writers, including an anonymous author who printed his version in London in 1671 by 'J.W.' for a 'William Gilbert, at the Half Moon in St. Paul's Churchyard'.

---

25  *The Penguin Book of Animal Verse*, ed. by George MacBeth (Harmondsworth: Penguin Books, 1965), pp. 218–19.

The story of the 'duel' was frequently retold throughout the seventeenth century, and, as the preface to this print notes, was 'first imitated in English by Mr. Crashaw, then by Mr. Hinton; and now by a third Hand so enlarg'd, and that the whole Frame of the Poem so alter'd, that little of Strada is preserv'd, save onely the Scene, and Issue of the Duel: All in a more familiar Style than that of Claudian imitated by Strada'.[26] From this preface then, we may surmise not only that the tale had been retold at least twice before in English print, but also that this version of the story is both a corruption of Claudian's original poem and also of Strada's. Rather than offering a comparison of the original Latin text and its subsequent retellings and translations, here I focus on the expanded and rewritten version as it was published in London in 1671 by this 'third hand'.

The story starts under a cool oak tree's shadow, where sits 'the Owner, and (what's more) the Master too/Of a sweet Harp; a Harp that might well go/ For Mistress of all Harps; his skilful Hand, As well as that his Thoughts, could understand;/And, what she understood, as well expound/In the sweet language of all Artful Sound'.[27] The harpist and harp are clearly depicted as 'Master and Mistress' from the start, and this union is given a telepathic quality: the harp is not merely a passive instrument, but a sentient being that is able to understand the harpist's thoughts and translate them into sound.

As we learn that the harpist has chosen 'This Instrument, This Time, This Place' so that he may 'give troubled thoughts some short repose', the nightingale is heard—described as a 'Wood-bred Syren', who is as harmless as the 'sea-breed' is harmful. The bird's comparison to a siren, a woman who lured sailors to their death by singing, is striking. But the author reassures us that while sirens are able to entrap a 'whole man' by simply singing into his ear, the nightingale herself can be captured by a man who takes *her* by the ear: 'A Man but by the Ear takes, those trapan,/And by the Ear alone take the Whole Man'.[28] Despite her reality as a small bird, the nightingale here is already set up as a threat, with the

---

26 *Strada's Musical Duel in Latine / Much Enlarg'd in English by the Addition of Several Traverses between the Harper and the Nightengale ; Together with a More Particular Account of the Issue of the Contest* (London: Printed by J.W. for William Gilbert, 1671), n.p., https://name.umdl.umich.edu/A61709.0001.001

27 *Strada's Musical Duel*, n.p.

28 *Strada's Musical Duel*, n.p.

danger directly linked to a sense of deviant womanhood; she is either a siren, luring men by the ear, or the less harmful 'wood siren', being *taken* by the ear.

When the nightingale is finally introduced directly, it is as an imperial monarch:

> A Nightingale, the Queen of a Sweet Quire,
> Her Empire deems invaded by the Lyre.
> Upon the Frontiers therefore bent to try
> Her now, he'er till now, doubtful Destinie;
> The same Oak chose, her Ambush and her Cage;
> And so of this fam'd War the honor'd Stage.[29]

The duel that is about to ensue between bird and harpist is thus framed as a battle over territory; the nightingale is queen of an 'empire', which the harpist has 'invaded', and whose frontiers he threatens. The 'war' waged is not only one of man and nature, but also a gendered one against the nightingale's queenship and iteration of female power. The term 'empire' also invites analysis, ambiguously evoking both the domain of the natural world as opposed to the urban man-made one, as well as pointing to an extraneous empire in opposition to early modern England—in this historical and cultural context, likely the Ottoman empire.

When the duel between harp and nightingale starts, improvisation is quickly weaponised and the nightingale's 'natural' ability is pitted against the harpist's laboured efforts. The 'lessons' that the harpist has learned 'with much Pains' are instantly sung back to him by the nightingale 'True, Clean, Sweet', and 'Without Book'. In this manner (i.e. playing 'by ear') she is able to sing back his 'Pavin-Grand Pas', 'Almain-Trot', 'Coronto-Amble', 'Saraband' and 'Jigg'. Her ability at playing back whatever she hears from the harpist echoes Sylvester's description of nightingales embellishing upon each others' songs; it is natural to her to match 'without book' anything that she hears. Accordingly, the harpist decides that 'ready-prest close Composition' does not 'advance his war', and decides to try to overpower his rival through 'free loose Voluntaries'. The contrast between descriptors of 'ready-pressed' for pre-printed

---

29  *Strada's Musical Duel*, n.p.

compositions and 'free, loose' for improvised voluntaries highlights the shift that is about to take place, from the realm of composition to that of 'extemporary wits':

> The *Lessons* he, oft seen, with much Pains learn'd,
> She, at first hearing, *True, Clean, Sweet* return'd.
> Vvithout Book *Pavin*-Grand Pas, *Almain-Trot,*
> And the *Coronto-Amble* so soon got.
> Knew the False-Gallop of the *Saraband:*
> And could the Full-Speed of the *Jigg* command.
> Vvhat *Lessons* e're he play'd, *sung* to the *Life.*
> Wisely then stints he this vain Part of Strife.
> When ready-prest close *Composition*
> No whit advanc'd his *War;* he thought upon
> (His sweet *Bird-Rival* so to over-pow'r;
> And sink her in as *smart,* as *sweet* a Show'r)
> His free loose *Voluntaries;* in which kind
> He play'd as soft as A'er, as swift as Wind.
> As 'tis with some Extemporary Wits;
> His sodain better were than studied Hits.[30]

However, the author is quick to note that despite being improvised, the harpist's 'judgment' is 'quick as Phansie' and even 'gives Laws', dispelling anxieties around improvisation as a law-breaking practice, as expressed in debates around extemporary prayer discussed in Chapter 1. While the harpist turns to the genre of voluntary to make his improvisations, the nightingale turns to improvised divisions on a ground, showing that the harpist has mistaken his 'Weapon, and his Foe', who 'hath him now at her wish'd Lock'—the 'looser freedom' of improvisation is her true domain and she is able to show him that both 'invention' and 'memorie' are in her nature: 'She's born the Poet, and Muse of the Wood/Other inspir'd ones Rapture wait from far;/And sometimes long; her Inspirations are/Her Nature'.

This natural ability in improvisation results in the most skilled divisions on a ground, better than the 'boldest hand' could effect:

---

30 *Strada's Musical Duel,* n.p.

> The first was *Nature's Plain-Song,* and her *Grounds;*
> The next her *Descant,* last *Divisions.*
> Yea, all these she so *blends,* as her small Breast
> Had been of all siz'd *Viols* a full *Chest:*
> And all *together* sounding in the Hands
> Of (for all *Parts*) best skill'd *Musicians.*
> For she as well as they, due *Time,* and *Place*
> Knew for sweet *Relish,* and all other *Grace.*
> In *Dropping* Notes her *Voice* would swifter glide,
> Than boldest *Hand* on *Strings* could Posting Ride.[31]

This reference to 'nature's grounds' echoes both Charles Butler's use of the phrase in reference to bees, and John Wilkins's allusion to it as essential knowledge to partake in the kind of musical language he outlines. Its application here to a situation of musical improvisation—the extemporisation of divisions *upon a ground*—draws the use of the word 'ground' as a repeating bass line ever closer to the earth and associations of the natural world with improvisation, as well as to the 'grounds' or essentials of music-making. Nature, in the form of the harmonious cosmos evoked by Christopher Simpson, is the seat of primordial musical knowledge, the domain of the earth out of which the ground bass line originates, the underlying structure to all improvisation.

The origins of improvisation in the natural world give the nightingale an advantage in this mode that the harpist will never match, and he retreats to consider his options and devise a new plan of attack:

> The herein baffl'd *Harper* sounds *Retreat.*
> But such *Retreat* he made, as Men devise
> For longer *Leaps* to take a better *Rise.*
> Such, as for *Flight* in other Wars they feign,
> With more Advantage to *fall on* again.
> So acts our *Harper;* whose *Retirements* be
> But from loose *Phansie,* to fast *Memorie.*[32]

This move from 'loose Phansie' to 'fast Memorie' suggests that he moves from free and 'loose' improvisation to a faster, more controlled form of

---

31 *Strada's Musical Duel*, n.p.
32 *Strada's Musical Duel*, n.p.

extemporisation that relies on his memory, perhaps following the rules for divisions and voluntaries set out by Christopher Simpson and Roger North. It also suggests that the nightingale's realm is that of free and loose improvised divisions, rather than this more artful and stylised mode of music-making. The harpist's new approach is presented in sounds of almost shocking violence:

> Trebles alone then skilfully he moulds
> To the right Accents of mere Women-Scolds:
> Their Tunings, far from Unisons, designs
> For imbred Discords in the Female Minds.
> When touch't, their jarring Accents aptly meant
> The Quarrels of She-Tongues to represent.
> Upon a softer touch submisser Jarrings,
> Before they bark't, the Dogged Womens Snarlings.
> When harder Strokes yet harsher Jars out-hammer;
> This spake the Scolding womens lowder Clamor.
> Many such Strings together when he'd strike;
> Confus'd Brawls of more Scolds at once 'twas like.
> Ill names when try'd, the Strings knowing him mean
> Vvould say, ye filthy Jade! Ye dirty Quean!
> Yea, Pinching of such jarring Strings he'd shew
> Scratchings, as well as Scoldings, of that Crew.
> Streight rudelyer handled put 'em to such Squeeks,
> As would exactly render Female Shrieks.
> Some short Pause made, to work agen he'd go:
> Just as such Scolds, when out of breath, will do.[33]

The 'brawl' created by the harpist presents gendered sounds with jarring and discordant tuning, imitating 'women-scolds' that represent the discord of 'female minds', along with 'quarells of she-tongues', 'dogged womens snarlings' and 'female shrieks'. The strings of the harp themselves speak for the harpist with insults, saying to the nightingale 'ye filthy Jade! Ye dirty Quean!' The mobilisation of such sounds against the nightingale—herself gendered as a female queen, seem puzzling. They recall the poet's earlier comment about the dangers of sirens to men's ears—perhaps the harpist enacts a fantasy in which he brings down the 'queen' using the very tools

---

33   *Strada's Musical Duel*, n.p.

that he is anxious the queen will mobilise against him. Furthermore, this passage highlights an anxiety around improvisation as queenly weapon; the nightingale's superior extemporary facility must be quelled, and quelled with some force. In response, she is unable to compete—

> She fills her *Bag;* and *blows,* and *blows;* but brings
> Forth Nothing, beyond softer *Murmurings.*
> Sweet little *Soul!* She had accustom'd long
> To pleasant *Air,* and well-tun'd peaceful *Song.*
> But could not tune her prettie *Pipe* at all
> To the *Cross-Capers* of such *Jarring Brawl.*[34]

The poem ends with the nightingale singing one final 'funeral note', before succumbing to death whereupon her soul retires into the harp—the instrument absorbs her and her song. This popular story of the nightingale's defeat presents a clear example of improvisation as intrinsic to the natural world, associating her natural skill in making free divisions upon a ground with her rule as 'Queen of a Sweet Quire', the frontiers of whose Empire is invaded by the Lyre (or harp) and its sounds. Matching the power of her queenship over sound and nature, this poem casts improvisation as a site for gendered violence, showing that the queen can only be overwhelmed by a different type of improvisation that moves away from 'phansie' to 'memorie' and its rules. In this domain, the lyre can evoke dangerous 'female' sounds while still maintaining its status as a cultivated musical instrument.

As with the bee, the nightingale's voice and her status as a creature embodying female rule and the power of natural improvisation render her a threat. While Butler figuratively took the sting out of the bee's tail by concealing her improvised piping in the intricacies of a madrigal, in this poem the nightingale's improvisations are 'silence'd in eternal Pause, and Rest', as her dead corpse 'on the Harp drops breathless down'. As her body enters the instrument, the harp 'needs no more Fill of other Vocal Tone:/It self is Voice and Instrument in One./And so at Once both Rings the Fun'eral Peal,/And Sings the Requi'em of sweet Philomel'. The nightingale's voice is taken into the harp, and in a strange parallel to Ovid's metamorphosis, is changed into an instrument that will improvise in accordance with the rules of musical extemporisation rather than according to her nature. From this

---

34  *Strada's Musical Duel,* n.p.

perspective, both Butler and Strada's texts tell the same story of curtailing an improvising queen's songs of nature, presenting a more orderly, rational and humanised version of their extemporisations.

The lyre's consumption of the nightingale is thus a triumph of nurture over nature, and perhaps also of male dominance over the independence and reign of the queen. Yet her positioning as a foreign queen of an empire separate from that of the lyre complicates the story by once again associating the 'otherness' of the natural world with that of a cultural/geographical other. Once again, the nightingale's improvisations are connected to an inherent otherness in her positionality. In this case, this tension between the natural, free improvisations that she sings and the harpist's studied divisions is resolved through her death, not simply to be silenced forever, but to be heard in a muted form through the instrument's body. As an origin story for instrumental music, this narrative reflects the idea that human music-making imitates and improves upon nature, as well as the idea that improvisation found in the natural world was simultaneously more 'naturally' skilful than instrumental improvisation, and yet more in need of silencing.

Reflecting on Richard Crashaw's retelling of Strada's duel, Linda Austern writes that

> the same fatal musical contest is recounted in a young gentlewoman's mid-century manuscript lute-tutor as an illustration of 'the Enthusiasmes and Ravisments of the Lute' and the concomitant superiority of the divinely assisted 'Art of man' over 'the woonders of nature.' Yet her lutenist is assigned no gender, and her nightingale is a cocky male.[35] In this way, the female instrumentalist depicted in the *Mary Burwell Lute Tutor* is subtly invited to share in a form of musical power that overcomes the innate shortcomings of her body and her traditional connection to the natural world.[36]

This 'connection' to the natural world is heard in the young woman's superior improvisations, suggesting that the gendered nature of extemporary accomplishment extended from birdsong to musicking on an instrument.

---

35 For an edition of this tutor book, see Thurston Dart, 'Miss Mary Burwell's Instruction Book for the Lute', *The Galpin Society Journal* 11 (1958), 3–62. See also a discussion of the text's possible colonial overtones in Olivia Bloechl, *Native American Song at the Frontiers of Early Modern Music* (Cambridge: Cambridge University Press, 2008), pp. 15–18.

36 Austern, 'Nature, Culture, Myth', p. 26.

*What are the tyrannies in your practice that you swallow day by day and attempt to make your own, until you will sicken and die of them, still in silence? [List as many as necessary today. Then write a new list tomorrow. And the day after.]*

## A Musical Archive of Nightingales and Bees

In this final section of my chapter, I explore some depictions of nightingales in early modern English music. The bird often featured in masques, songs and sets of variations at the time, either inviting extemporisation by the musician(s), or including improvisatory musical material in the score.

Perhaps one of the most famous pieces of music about the nightingale in early modern England is a piece called the 'English nightingale', or *Engels Nachtegaeltje* as it was known in a collection of variations titled *Der Fluyten Lusthof* (Volume 1, published in Amsterdam in 1644) transcribed from the blind Dutch recorder player and carillonneur Jacob van Eyck's improvisations on popular contemporary songs and melodies.[37]

Audio Recording 4 'Engels Nachtegaeltje'. Track 4 from Fatima Lahham, *bulbul*, FS Records (2022). https://hdl.handle.net/20.500.12434/b736cf1a

My recording illustrates how the melody in this piece is clearly imitative of a bird's song, with the repetitions and improvisatory leaps in van Eyck's variations reflecting the spontaneity and extempory nature of the nightingale's famous songs (see Figures 12a and 12b).

> ...*I find myself preoccupied with the thought of how I could be a bird, trying to imagine the feeling of being in a bird's body, making such sounds...* (creative reflection, December 2021)

---

[37] See Thiemo Wind, *Jacob van Eyck and the Others: Dutch Solo Repertoire for Recorder in the Golden Age*, Muziekhistorische Monografieën 21 (Utrecht: Koninklijke Vereniging voor Nederlandse Muziekgeschiedenis, 2011).

Fig. 12a Jacob van Eyck, 'Engels Nachtegael', in *Der Fluyten Lusthof*, 2nd edn (Amsterdam: Paulus Matthysz, 1644), p. 31, https://s9.imslp.org/files/imglnks/usimg/d/d3/IMSLP354037-PMLP201599-van_eyck_1_edicao_tif.pdf, public domain.

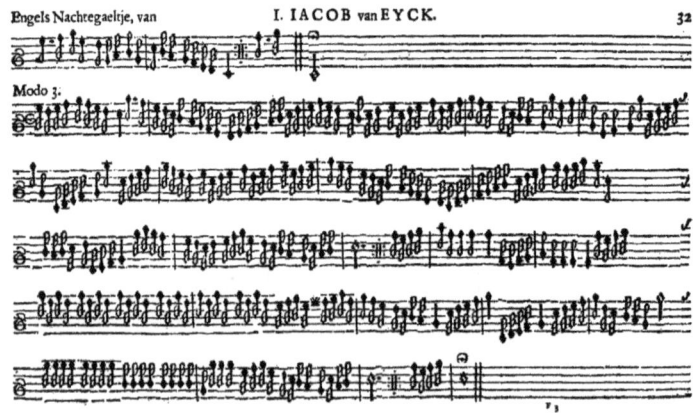

Fig. 12b Jacob van Eyck, 'Engels Nachtegael' (cont.), *Der Fluyten Lusthof*, 2nd edn (Amsterdam: Paulus Matthysz, 1644), p. 32, https://s9.imslp.org/files/imglnks/usimg/d/d3/IMSLP354037-PMLP201599-van_eyck_1_edicao_tif.pdf, public domain.

About thirty years earlier in England, *The Lord's Masque* (1613) by Thomas Campion (1567–1620) had included this melody in a work that was performed alongside *The Tempest* to celebrate the marriage of James I's daughter to Frederick the Elector Palatine. In this masque,

'The Nightingale's Response' imagines the song of Orpheus's silver nightingale responding to his master's harp playing.[38] The classical story of Orpheus as the 'tamer' of wild beasts and creatures through his music was well known in early modern English literature, and the melody's appearance in this masque was perhaps the source for van Eyck's later improvisations on the same melody, which also featured in settings for keyboard, cittern and lute, and appears in Thomas Mace's *Musick's Monument* (1676).[39] Its association with Orpheus suggest that perhaps this melody represents a transcription of the 'tamed' nightingale's improvisations, made 'safe' in a similar fashion to Strada's nightingale.

In fact, to a certain extent, these settings of the nightingale's song for instruments can be heard as depicting the ending of Strada's popular poem: we can now hear the lute 'playing' the nightingale, her voice trapped inside its body. With this in mind, what did the act of playing the nightingale's song on an instrument signify? Was it heard as a way of 'taming' the nightingale's divisions, of controlling and bounding the sounds of nature through more nurtured and foreseen musical means?

The recorder is a particularly interesting case study for this connection between birdsong and musical instrument, since it derives its name from the Latin verb *recordari* (to remember) associating its sound with recollection or remembrance, as well as with the physical operations of memory involved in making music (and particularly, improvising).[40] Numerous sources show, moreover, that the English verb 'to record' was used of birds in the early modern period, for example by the poet and musician Thomas Watson, who writes in his *Entertainment...at Elvetham* (1591): 'Now birds record new harmony,/And trees do whistle melody...'[41]

In Watson's poem the verb is used of the birds themselves, miraculously 'recording' or remembering 'new harmonie'. However, it was also used by Shakespeare in relation to the nightingale to refer to one of the two gentlemen of Verona's 'tuning' and 'recording' of his woes alongside her

---

38   Thomas Campion, *A Score for The Lords' Masque by Thomas Campion: Performed on 14 February, 1613*, ed. by Andrew J. Sabol (London: Brown University Press, 1993), pp. 61, 335.
39   Mace, *Musick's Monument*, p. 201.
40   *The Cambridge Encyclopaedia of Historical Performance in Music,* ed. by Colin Lawson and Robin Stowell (Cambridge: Cambridge University Press, 2018), p. 526.
41   Wilson and Calore, *Music in Shakespeare*, p. 359.

song; in Valentine's words, as he yearns in the forest for his lover, Silvia: 'Here can I sit alone, unseen of any,/And to the nightingale's complaining notes/Tune my distresses and record my woes'.[42] In this passage, Valentine may be remembering his woes alongside the nightingale's song of tragedy, but there is also a musical process to his recollection; he 'tunes' his distresses to the nightingale's 'complaining notes', and perhaps recalls and sounds his own sorrows simultaneously—presumably enacting the same process that the bird is going through.

The recorder's role in 'recording' is ambiguously open, then; through its name, it can recollect melodies, but is also associated with birdsong. In the context of the nightingale's duel, the instrument might also take the role of replacing the bird, swallowing her whole and providing a wooden body through which her voice might echo. This preoccupation with 'taming' birdsong through the recorder, and thus also taming the free and natural improvisations of these birds, is epitomised in a book published a little later, in *The Bird Fancyer's Delight* (c.1715).[43] This collection of tunes was intended to serve as a compendium of musical material with which the flageolet or recorder player could 'train' birds how to sing, and features particular songs for the canary, linnet, bullfinch, woodlark, blackbird, thrush, nightingale and starling. The nightingale's song in the book is stilted and formal, a complete reversal of the spontaneous divisions and mournful songs that we read about in contemporaneous plays and poetry.[44] Whether or not early modern 'bird fancyers' believed they could actually train their caged nightingales in this way, the very fact that this was a plausible aim deserves attention in the history of early modern improvisatory practices and their complicated place between musical rules and the natural world.

---

42  William Shakespeare, *The Two Gentlemen of Verona*, ed. by Barbara A. Mowat and Paul Werstine (The Folger Shakespeare), V.4, 1.4–7, p. 175, https://shakespeare.folger.edu/downloads/pdf/the-two-gentlemen-of-verona_PDF_FolgerShakespeare.pdf

43  *The Bird Fancyer's Delight, or Choice Observations and Directions Concerning the Teaching of All Sorts of Singing Birds after the Flagelet and Flute [recorder] when Rightly Made as to Size and Tone, with Lessons Properly Compos'd within the Compass and Faculty of Each Bird, viz. for the Canary-Bird, Linnet, Bull-Finch, Wood-Lark, Black-Bird, Throustill [thrush], Nightingale and Starling. The Whole Fairly Engraven and Carefully Corrected* (London: Printed for J. Walsh, c.1715), https://imslp.org/wiki/The_Bird_Fancyer's_Delight_(Walsh,_John)

44  *The Bird Fancyer's Delight*, p.11.

## Hearing the Bulbul Who Is Not Being Heard

Audio Recording 5 'Asfour tal men el shebbak'. Track 1 from Fatima Lahham, *bulbul*, FS Records (2022). https://hdl.handle.net/20.500.12434/021a707e

I end this chapter with a musical collaboration of sorts between English clergyman and physician John Covel (1638–1722) and Polish dragoman and musician at the Ottoman court 'Alī Ufukī (c.1610–75). John Covel toured the Levant between 1670–79, and wrote extensively about his travels in his diaries during these years. Covel was also the Master of Christ's College, Cambridge (1688–1723), where I was a PhD student (2018–22) researching the thesis that has now become this book.

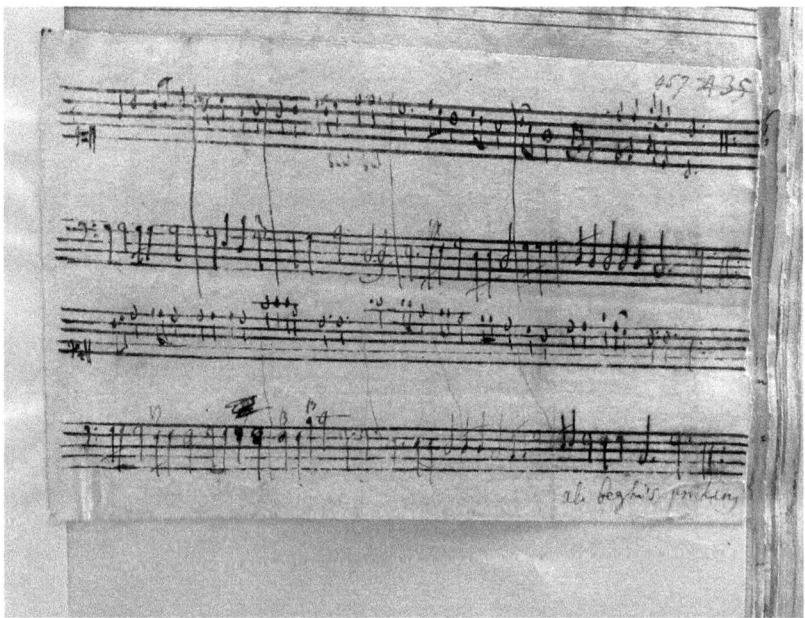

Fig. 13 Fragment from John Covel's collected papers. British Library, London, MS Add MS 22911 (reproduced with permission, all rights reserved).

The fragment shown in Figure 13 is a scrap of paper that I found in his collected papers in the British Library. It shows a melody from 'Alī Ufukī's compendium, the *Mecmuâ-i Sâz u Söz*, to which John Covel added a bass line.⁴⁵ The melody belongs to the song Semā'ī-yı Evc-'Irak *Reng-i ruhı gülizar tebah eyledi bülbül*, and, as we see above, John Covel has added a note—'ali beghi's pricking'—presumably to indicate that the musician had notated ('pricked') the melody for him at some point on his travels in Ottoman Turkey.⁴⁶

The original song's text follows a common theme for Ottoman poetry of this time; it tells of a nightingale and his unrequited love for the rose, which, as mentioned earlier, was often evoked as an analogue for the soul's unrequited yearning for its Creator.

> SEMAI
> [1] Renghi rui ghiulizar tebah [eiledi] Bulbul Dost ieleli ieleli Lella Lelli [eiledi] Bulbul
> [2] Bakti ghiul ruhsarina ebah [eiledi] bulbul Dost etc.
> [3] Bir ahi gigher soz chekiub iadi [ruinle] Dost etc.
> [4] Ghiul gon'gei hurszidi siah eiledi bulbul Dost etc.⁴⁷
>
> (The nightingale spoiled the colour of the face of the rose-cheeked one
> The nightingale looked at the rose's cheeks and sighed 'ah'
> With the memory of your face, it let out a heart-piercing [lit. 'liver-burning'] sigh
> The nightingale made the rosebud mouth of the sun black.)⁴⁸

However, in John Covel's version of the song, the only word of the text that remains is *bülbül* (nightingale) faintly sketched across the third bar. This tiny fragment points not only to the nightingale as cultural ambassador between English and Ottoman cultures but also highlights some of the bird's transposable tongues/identities: in England the nightingale is Philomela, making mournful divisions on her tragic story, in Turkey he is an anguished lover gazing on the unattainable rose.

The presence of this fragment in my archive of nightingales complicates both these versions of the bird, suggesting an improvisatory nightingale who hovers in between. Moreover, when we consider how

---

45 London, British Library, MS Add MS 22911.
46 Judith I. Haug, *Ottoman and European Music in 'Alī Ufukī's Compendium, MS Turc 292: Analysis, Interpretation, Cultural Context*, Volume 2: Critical Report (Munster: ULB, 2020), p. 390.
47 Judith I. Haug, *Ottoman and European Music in 'Alī Ufukī's Compendium, MS Turc 292: Analysis, Interpretation, Cultural Context*, Volume 1: Edition (Munster: ULB, 2020), p. 467.
48 Many thanks to Dr. Jacob Olley for his help with my translation of the Ottoman Turkish text of this poem.

this piece would have been performed according to Covel's copy, again improvisation is surely called for—in adding such an impromptu sounding and incongruous bass to this melody, perhaps Covel himself was simply scribbling down his extemporised bass line, to be changed and improved upon in performance. The dissonant ninth interval on the ninth note of the piece, along with the clunky tracking of the melody's rhythm with the bass line, all suggest a work-in-progress, a sketch or a starting point. An early modern performance of the piece might have also called for divisions on the simple melody, which tips us over into the realm of the imagination—perhaps the only space in which historical materials that touch on improvisation can be assimilated in order to reach a version of 'historically informed improvisation'…

## Conclusion

In this chapter I have searched for the nightingale's voice as a vital clue towards the early modern extemporary. My searches are often fragmentary and inconclusive, frustratingly hovering between the certain and the unknown, printed and improvised, heard and unheard. My historical explorations in this chapter may be enriched by considering them while listening to birdsong today, and reflecting on changes to modes of listening, perceptions of improvisation, and the songs of the birds themselves.

I have mostly taken a human-centric approach to voices and sounds of the natural world, but that is not the only way. After all, nightingales are 'imprinted' by the sensory aspects of their environments to sing differently in different contexts and times.[49] As musicians today studying these contexts for historical improvisation in the early modern natural world, it is important to understand that the environmental factors that caused nightingales to modify their divisions affected what early modern improvisers heard around them, and thus the music they subsequently made in imitation. In turn, these factors affect our own improvisations and understandings of historical improvisation today—how could they not, when the very 'air' around one could affect extemporary processes?

---

49  See Helen Briggs, 'How Lockdown Birds Sang to a Different Tune', *BBC News* (24 September 2020), https://www.bbc.co.uk/news/science-environment-54285627

A question: to what extent might such environmental considerations affect our own engagements with material objects, instruments and texts from the early modern period, and how might we mediate between our own improvising bodies, our imaginations fuelled by historical research, and the desire to practice 'historically informed improvisation'?

# 4. Improvising Text: Historical Performance and a Decolonial Imaginary

> I would like to propose a decolonial imaginary as a rupturing space, the alternative to that which is written in history. I think that the decolonial imaginary is that time lag between the colonial and the postcolonial, that interstitial space where different politics and social dilemmas are negotiated.
> —Emma Pérez, *The Decolonial Imaginary: Writing Chicanas into History* (1999)[1]

Throughout the process of researching and writing this book, I have been deeply inspired by Chicana feminist Emma Pérez's concept of the decolonial imaginary: another way to hear what is not being heard.

In this final chapter, I ask how the 'third space' created by the decolonial imaginary could become a creative tool for more contrapuntal historiography, as well as more multi-layered historical performances. My experiences of this 'third space' have crystallised through creative experiences such as recording J. S. Bach's Partita in A minor (BWV 1013). In the extract below, I reflected on how the sensory and environmental memories that accompanied my learning of the piece showed up in that moment through Mahmoud Darwish's voice, and how I found myself falling between Darwish and Bach to create a third space where both their stories were re-told alongside mine:

> ...*I have recorded the Allemande from J. S. Bach's unaccompanied Flute Partita BWV 1013. First though, I made a loop of a recording of the Palestinian*

---

1   Emma Pérez, *The Decolonial Imaginary: Writing Chicanas into History* (Bloomington: Indiana University Press, 1999), p. 6.

*author Mahmoud Darwish reading a stanza from his poem Fe Dimishq (In Damascus). The stanza translates as 'in Damascus, dialogues revolve, between the violin and oud, about the question of existence, and about the endings...' My intention was to play the Allemande over the top of the reading, to respond to it with my recorder, to dialogue with the poem about the question of existence and improvise the endings with my breath and phrasing.*

*The concept was inspired by my first visit ever to see my family in Damascus over ten years ago, when I was just learning this piece. I played the Allemande on the roof every dusk as I sat by my great-grandmother, and it mixed with all the other sounds of the city. This memory stuck with me so persistently because of the way I felt myself slowly become part of those city sounds with my recorder, despite experiencing many other points of unfamiliarity and incongruence as someone born abroad.*

*When I read Darwish's poem for the first time so many years later, this piece was the first thing that came to mind. Yet when I started recording it in this way, I felt so intimidated: by the idea of capturing so vividly this in-between-ness: not quite Darwish, not quite Bach, not quite a mixture of the two.*

*Slowly, I found a space by following not just the music nor only the poem. On the first few takes I had tried to end all the musical phrases on the last word of the stanza (which is nihayat—endings), but it felt forced. In the end the take I loved most, where I felt most myself, was where I followed neither Bach nor Darwish, but ran in parallel with them, met them when the time was right, brought them together when it was easy and the moment of meeting brought them into dialogue. Nothing forced is good in improvisation.* (creative reflection, December 2021)

## Between 'the Law of Writ and the Liberty'

An imaginative approach to historical texts is not only a modern-day practice, but is frequently implicated in and by early modern texts—even in the works of such an established and canonised author as William Shakespeare.

In Shakespeare's *Hamlet*, for example, Polonius introduces the players in Elsinore with an impressive recommendation. He casts them as 'the best actors in the world', able to perform any genre imaginable as well as capable of 'the law of writ and the liberty'. By this last phrase, Polonius seems to be referring to scripted plays ('the writ') and improvisatory acting traditions ('the liberty'). He makes an important statement on improvisation and/as freedom, and on the relationship between following a script and improvising:

> Introducing the players:
>
> The best actors in the world, either for tragedy, comedy, history, pastoral, pastoral-comical, historical-pastoral, tragical-historical, tragical-comical-historical-pastoral; scene individable, or poem unlimited. Seneca cannot be too heavy, nor Plautus too light. For the law of writ and the liberty, these are the only men.[2]

The Shakespeare scholar Louise George Clubb explains Polonius's distinction between the 'writ' and the 'liberty' as 'the contrast [...] between scripted five-act plays observing the rules (the "writ") and improvised three-act performances from a canevaccio or scenario (the "liberty"), also obeying some of the rules, sometimes'.[3] The 'scenarios' she mentions refer to the tradition of improvised theatre, the *commedia dell'arte*, popular in Renaissance Italy. In this genre, plays would be semi-improvised by players based on pre-written scenes.

As in early modern music-making, the flexible and inextricable relationship between improvisation and text is also evident in theatre practices, with the distinction between 'writ' and 'liberty' proving difficult to pin down. In fact, Clubb goes so far as to liken the difference between scripted and improvised plays as 'not unlike the difference between classical music and jazz, distinct in several ways but most obviously in that one is performed from a full score and the other is improvised on the chord progressions of a tune'—or, to find a more appropriate early modern analogue, a ground bass line. Clubb continues, 'in undertaking to produce pastoral plays in the form Polonius calls the "writ", dramatists were in effect performing a jazz operation, improvising a theatrical structure from a canon of non-theatrical Arcadian literature...'[4]

Looking to extemporary early modern theatre practices can be

---

2 William Shakespeare, *Hamlet*, ed. by Barbara A. Mowat and Paul Werstine (The Folger Shakespeare), II.2, 1.420–6, p. 107, https://shakespeare.folger.edu/downloads/pdf/hamlet_PDF_FolgerShakespeare.pdf

3 Louise George Clubb, 'Pastoral Jazz from the Writ to the Liberty', in *Italian Culture in the Drama of Shakespeare and his Contemporaries: Rewriting, Remaking, Refashioning*, ed. by Michele Marrapodi (Aldershot: Ashgate, 2007), pp. 15–26 (p. 15).

4 Clubb, 'Pastoral Jazz', p. 19.

helpful in terms of thinking through the multiple relationships between 'the writ' and 'the liberty' in contemporaneous musical practice. The study of historical improvisation is rife with paradoxes and contradictions. One such issue is that of demarcating the boundaries between the improvised and the texted; if an improvisation is notated, it loses some of its 'improvised-ness', yet if it is not, we can never know it after the moment of performance. I want to suggest that we can open up a new way of approaching text by thinking about it in the same way as a bass line, suggesting a series of chord progressions and motives for improvisation rather than a fixed order of events. In the world of early modern drama, this approach has been convincingly argued by scholars such as Richard Andrews, who proposed that Shakespeare's *The Tempest* is based on scenarios for improvisation that existed and were in use in Italy well before the play's first performance in 1611.[5] Thus Shakespeare's text is merely a written-out 'version' of the 'theatregrams' or paradigms for a set of pre-existing scenes.

Such a communal or distributed account of creativity echoes the processes of memory I explored in Chapter 1, whereby a musician might memorise modules of music heard elsewhere and assemble them together in the process of improvisation. It also presents a way of thinking about contemporaneous musical texts as 'versions' of that piece made from an underlying structure for improvisation (such as the ground bass line). A binary distinction between the 'purely improvised' and the 'purely texted' is thus ultimately a false one, since neither of the two categories can be found without the other. Instead, I argue that they exist in a series of combinations, depending on the other parameters informing the moment of improvisation.

Here it is interesting to note the similarities with improvisation/composition in Iranian classical music, and the ways in which a clear-cut binary between improvisation and composition has often been used to other non-Western musics, as Laudan Nooshin has explored.[6] Nooshin cites Bruno Nettl's 1974 *Musical Quarterly* article

---

5   Richard Andrews, 'The Tempest and Italian Improvised Theatre', in *Revisiting the Tempest: The Capacity to Signify,* ed. by Silvia Bigliazzi and Lisanna Calvi (Basingstoke: Palgrave Shakespeare Studies, 2014), pp. 45–62.

6   Laudan Nooshin, 'Improvisation as "Other": Creativity, Knowledge and Power—The Case of Iranian Classical Music', *Journal of the Royal Musical Association* 128.2 (2003), 242–96.

in which he challenges 'the idea of improvisation and composition as oppositional categories', and suggests instead 'a continuum of creative practice between music which is primarily "compositional" and that which is primarily "improvisatory", whether musicians are using notation or creating in performance'.[7] Nooshin problematises the distinction between the two and the association of composition with notation even further, pointing out that in the first five sections of her article she discusses compositional practices in a range of performance traditions, without even discussing the role of notation until later.[8] This problematisation of such discrete categories and connections like improvisation/composition, or composition as notation, persists throughout her examination of classical Persian performance practices. For example, Nooshin cites an instance of the musician H. Gholi (d.1915) being asked why he did not compose fixed pieces like his students, to which he replied 'What I compose is what I play'.[9] This attitude is perhaps surprisingly at home in early modern English music-making, rich with ambiguities between the murky spaces of composition, improvisation, print, writing and a score's 'fixity'.[10]

I have explored many instances of these combinations in this book, enjoying the multiplicity of improvisational wealth to be found in early modern texts, musical and otherwise, while trying to understand some of the differences between these instances of improvisation. Within this multiplicity, we can hear distinctions between improvisations that are made by following clear rules to conform to a particular genre (for example, divisions on a ground), and 'free' improvisations, heard for example in the songs of nature, or in descriptions of more 'loose' music-making genres such as the prelude (which I explore later on in this chapter). Additionally, within all the early modern printed texts I have read/listened to in my book, we can see evidence of an improvisatory approach to text—from the copying of passages from travelogues to the

---

7  Nooshin, 'Improvisation as "Other"', p. 254.
8  Nooshin, 'Improvisation as "Other"', p. 256.
9  Nooshin, 'Improvisation as "Other"', p. 261.
10 For an account of encounters between Western 'early music' practice with indigenous music practices, see Dylan Robinson, 'Chapter Three, Contemporary Encounters between Indigenous and Early Music', in Dylan Robinson, *Hungry Listening: Resonant Theory for Indigenous Sound Studies* (Minneapolis: University of Minnesota Press, 2020), pp. 113–47.

translated variations on Strada's nightingale poem by several authors.

The type of improvisation seen in extemporary prayer is clearly different from that of Nicola Matteis's violin playing; the improvisations heard by English travellers in Turkish coffee houses are not the same as those presented in Christopher Simpson's divisions upon a ground; the divisions in poems about the nightingale are not the same as those of the bee in stylised madrigals. Improvisation takes on different guises and characters, different balances of extemporary practice to texted practice, depending on the social, historical, personal, political and geographical contexts.

I argue, then, that the two spheres of 'the writ' and 'the liberty' do not exist separately in any meaningful way, but that the way they interact depends on how different parameters relate in each instance of improvisation. I have sought out historical texts that may be read in an improvisatory fashion, whether that has been travelogues that call for performative readings, or notated examples of improvisations that musicians could either follow strictly, mix in with their own improvisations, or use as an inspiration for entirely improvised performances.

To 'historically-informed' performers, these parameters that create the relationships between text and extemporary practice may seem to form yet another paradox—how can a musician be strictly 'informed by history' while also being responsive to issues of environment and the need to delve into their own imaginations when engaging in 'historically-informed improvisation'? As I have argued earlier and will continue to explore in this chapter, early modern extemporary practices are processes through which musicians build 'memory stores' to be drawn on in moments of improvisation, and thus improvisation is always a contemporary concern. These storehouses are filled not only with musical experiences and passages that can be book-learned, but are also made up of sensory experiences: the sounds of nature that surround us, people we remember, smells of different environments, the memory of certain feelings, travels we may have experienced, and perhaps even our historical researches into these extemporary contexts. Historical improvisation is thus an intensely present matter, while also requiring a rich and nuanced understanding of early modern texts and ways to use them.

# Thomas Mace and Roger North: On *Hab-nab* and the Extemporary Imagination

While there are plenty of early modern writings denouncing certain types of extemporary behaviours there is no clear consensus as to what constituted 'good' improvisation amongst early modern music theorists, who wrote variously about different modes of creative production and their relationships to text and transmission. Rebecca Herissone has written insightfully about the connection between the improvisatory practices of making voluntaries as described by English musician Roger North, and processes of aural transmission and the notation of existing pieces from memory.[11] While it is beyond the scope of this book to engage meaningfully with questions of transmission and arrangement, it is important to note that these practices were inescapably caught up in extemporary culture, so that in some sense it is impossible to conceive of any contemporaneous musical practice that does not somehow pertain to some aspect of improvisation and memory.

Roger North's description of making voluntaries contrasts vividly with the English musician and theorist Thomas Mace's transcriptions and stories of his own improvisations, posing questions around the role of memory, embodiment and imagination in their writing. These texts constantly refer to an integrated understanding of extemporary practice and printed text, and this integration can prompt us to ask questions about the ways in which we read and perform early modern texts, and the role of improvisation in this process.

In his treatise *Musick's Monument* (1676), the English musician Thomas Mace lists some common types of 'lessons' for learning the lute, paying attention to their intersections with written and improvised forms. Of the prelude and voluntary he writes:

> The *Praelude* is commonly a *Piece of Confused-wild-shapeless-kind of Intricate-Play* (as most use It) in which no perfect *Form, Shape*, or *Uniformity* can be

---

11   Rebecca Herissone, *Musical Creativity in Restoration England* (New York: Cambridge University Press, 2013), p. 372.

perceived; but a *Random-Business, Pottering,* and *Grooping,* up and down, from one *Stop,* or *Key,* to another; And generally, so performed, to make *Tryal,* whether the *Instrument* be *well in Tune,* or not; by which doing, after they have *Compleated Their Tuning,* They will (if They be *Masters*) fall into some kind of *Voluntary,* or *Fansical Play,* more *Intelligible;* which (if He be a *Master, Able*) is a way, whereby He may more *Fully,* and *Plainly,* shew *His Excellency,* and *Ability,* than by any other kind of undertaking; and has an *unlimited,* and *unbounded Liberty;* In which, he may make use of the *Forms,* and *Shapes of all the rest.*[12]

The hierarchy of genres is not hard to detect here; the prelude is 'confused' and 'wild', has no 'form' or 'shape', and is employed simply to make sure the instrument is in tune. However, the voluntary, or 'Fansical Play', will progress from the prelude in the hands of an experienced musician, affording them 'unlimited and unbounded liberty' and allowing them to make use of all the forms and shapes of the other genres listed. The final clearly improvised form that Mace lists is the Ground, which, as noted in Chapter 1, he describes as a location for the musician to show the 'bravery' of both invention and hand.[13]

Perhaps surprisingly, then, according to Mace's description of the voluntary, the musician can only find 'liberty' through following the shapes of the other genres and knowing their way around the instrument and musical forms. The freedom he describes is not defined through distance from form, but rather through a facility with genre and knowledge of how to make extemporary music in a way that mediates between the body, the imagination and pre-existing pieces. Figure 14 offers an example of a voluntary in chapter 42 of his book on how to play the theorbo, titled 'A Fancy-Praelude, or Voluntary; Sufficient Alone to make a Good Hand, Fit for All manner of Play, or Use'.[14] As I noted in Chapter 1, extemporary practice could be thought of as a way of *making* the body—here, this happens through the use of a text: the piece is seen as a way to make a 'good hand', or one that is 'good' for improvising.

---

12 Thomas Mace, *Musick's Monument*, Reproduction en fac-similé (Éditions du Centre National de la Recherche Scientifique: Paris, 1958), pp. 128–9 (italics in original).
13 Mace, *Musick's Monument*, p. 129.
14 Mace, *Musick's Monument*, p. 210.

Fig. 14 Thomas Mace, 'A Fancy-Prelude', *Musick's Monument* (London: T. Ratcliffe and N. Thompson, 1676), p. 210, https://archive.org/details/bim_early-english-books-1641-1700_musicks-monument-_mace-thomas_1676/page/n231/mode/2up, public domain.

Mace introduces the piece as an example for how a musician may learn to improvise once their hand is fully made:

> *Here* is *That One Only Lesson for your Hand*; which although It seem long, may be *Divided* (as It were) into *13 Several Strains*; which you may perceive by the *Pauses*, and *Double Barrs*, I have made; and also let *Figures* at the *Beginning* of every *Place*: So that you may (if you please) leave off at any of *Those Places*; But I set it *Thus*, to show you the way and manner of Playing *Voluntary*, which you may well Imitate. This *Lesson* alone will make your *Hand Sufficiently* for the whole *Business* of the *Theorboe*, be It what It will.[15]

---

15  Mace, *Musick's Monument*, p. 209.

He continues, 'Therefore *Practice It well*; for I intend to set no more to That Purpose; for I *Aim at Short Work*: Therefore I'le proceed to the *Directions* of Playing a *Part*; your *Hand* being first made, there will be much *Less Difficulty* in *That*'.[16] In other words, the printed voluntary is there to train the musician and their hand so that they may make their own voluntaries, thereby attaining their own 'unlimited, and unbounded Liberty'.

By contrast, Roger North's conception of the voluntary is one of simply knitting together pre-composed passages that the musician had found in musical scores and committed to memory and 'into' the body. While this process somewhat counter-intuitively centres text in acts of extemporisation, it bears many parallels to the extemporary theatre practices I have discussed above, and can involve a similar destabilisation of printed text. Moreover, it recalls Thomas Mace's notion that through the voluntary the musician may make use of the 'forms and shapes' of all the other genres.

Of the voluntary, North writes that 'there must be so much practise of the art that it shall become habituall. And not onely his mind be filled with the material, but the proper forms also to be at his tongue's end, always ready on occasion—this makes a good orator, or as they now terme it a good extemporary speaker...'[17] The analogy with the art of an orator and the classical art of rhetoric evokes the memory arts I discuss in Chapter 1, and describes a method of 'filling one's mind with the material' and then practising ways to dispose and deliver this material in an improvised manner at a moment's notice.[18] North explains, 'by this he will know the fluency and emphases of musick, and his memory will be filled with numberless passages of approved ayre, and have *ad unguem* all the cursory graces of cadences and semi-cadences, and common descants and breakings, as well as the ordinary ornaments of accord, or touch...'[19]

North's insistence on the importance of using the material that the improviser has assimilated offers another example of how improvisation

---

16  Mace, *Musick's Monument*, p. 209.
17  John Wilson (ed.), *Roger North on Music; Being a Selection from His Essays Written during the Years c. 1695–1728* (London: Novello, 1959), p. 141.
18  See also Thomas Mace on music and oratory in Mace, *Musick's Monument*, p. 152.
19  Wilson (ed.), *Roger North on Music*, p. 141.

did not necessarily preclude text, but rather engaged with it in a variety of ways. Here, North explains that the performer must choose, apply and connect these memorised passages:

> It is not to be expected that a master invents all that he plays in that manner. No, he doth but play over those passages that are in his memory and habituall to him. But the choice, application, and connexion are his, and so is the measure, either grave, buisy, or precipitate; as also the several keys to use as he pleaseth.[20]

In this context, the extemporary parameters are clearly stated, including the measure or mood, and the keys used. To these parameters, we might add too issues of the performer's spirit and invention, the space in which the performance takes place, and the climate or 'ayre' of the country where they find themselves as they play their musical airs.

North continues.

> And among the rest, in the spirit of zeal when he is warme and engaged, he will fulfill of his owne present invention a musick which, joined with the rest, shall be new and wonderfull. I say'd application, which refers to what was sayd before of imitation, as the lying downe after labour is sweet repose is admirably express't in the semicadence of a flat key, adagio; and so of other like conjectures not to be repeated. Then for connection, these passages which a voluntiere serves himself of are (by transitions of his own) so interwoven as to make one style, and will appear as a new work of a good composer, of whom the best (as I will venture to say here) useth the methods of a voluntiere, and more or less borrows ayre from those that went before him, and such as he hath bin most conversant with. (This is exemplified in the game of chess, of which they say he that hath most gambetts hath the advantage, which gambetts are pre-contrived stratagems, which are put forward as occasion is given by the walk of the adversary. So he that hath most musicall passages drawne off from the musick of others and in most variety to be put together with extemporary connection, is the best furnished for voluntary.)[21]

Despite the pre-composed nature of these passages, North ventures that these 'improvisations' will be 'new and wonderfull', and goes on to suggest even that good composers will use the same method of 'borrowing' ayres that went before. He offers an analogy with chess

---

20   Wilson (ed.), *Roger North on Music*, p. 141.
21   Wilson (ed.), *Roger North on Music*, pp. 141–2.

and the preconceived nature of 'gambits' or calculated opening moves that are combined with the chess player's reactions in the moment to succeed.

This comparison to a game, and the quite formulaic notion of simply 'sticking' together musical passages composed by others might seem to render improvisation an achievable goal for an amateur musician such as North. Yet the 'extempory connection' to which he refers proposes a way in which any musician could enter a series of extemporary relationships with text, and textual relationships with improvisation.

North concludes:

> But as I sayd, the connexion, handling, and setting forth is his owne; for no one man is an absolute inventor of art, but comonly takes up and adds to the inventions of predecessors.
>
> ....For in musick nothing is left to accident; all must be done either with designe or by inveterate habit, in a course duely establisht; and the chief industry lyes in procuring variety, and *ne quid nimis*, for the long uniformity of air and manner, tho' at first very good, will grow fastidious.[22]

North's preoccupation with not leaving anything 'to accident' is striking in the context of a practice that was ostensibly defined by a lack of 'premeditation'; it also evokes the 'accidents' and lack of artificial planning in the songs of the natural world, and can perhaps point to some of the reasons for discourses around curbing the divisions of the nightingale as explored in the previous chapter. In contrast to this lack of accidence, Mace's descriptions of his own improvisations (transcribed as lessons in his book), are full of chance.

In the two examples that follow, I explore Mace's depiction of improvisation as a practice of artlessly 'finding' pieces of music, in this case, inspired by two women. The processes described are intensely visceral and built on embodied memory. In the case of the second example, the process is framed in a derogatory fashion as a messy stitching together of different passages— seemingly presenting a very different opinion about such a practice to Roger North. As early modern transcriptions of improvisations, Mace's pieces provide us with important clues about the relationship between instrument, musician, body and text, with the written narrative accompanying each musical piece perhaps as important as the scores themselves.

---

22   Wilson (ed.), *Roger North on Music*, p. 142.

Fig. 15 Thomas Mace, *Musick's Monument* (London: T. Ratcliffe and N. Thompson, 1676), p. 121, https://archive.org/details/bim_early-english-books-1641-1700_musicks-monument-_mace-thomas_1676/page/n231/mode/2up, public domain.

Early in the book, Mace introduces us to a lesson that transcribes one of his own improvisations—one inspired by (and named after) his 'mistress', as shown in Figure 15. He writes that the piece came to him when he was 'past being a suitor' to his now-wife, but not yet married:

> That very *Night*, in which I was *Thus Agitated in my Mind, concerning Her, (My Living Mistress;) She being in* Yorkshire *and My Self in* Cambridge,) *Close Shut up in my Chamber, Still, and Quiet, about 10, or 11 a Clock at Night, Musing, and Writing Letters to Her; Her Mother, and Some other Friends, in Summing up, and Determining the whole Matter, concerning Our Marriage: (You may conceive, I might have very Intent Thoughts, all that Time, and might meet with some Difficulties. (For as yet, I had not gain'd her Mother's consent.) So that I my Writings, I was sometimes put to my Studyings.*

The detail with which he sets the scene is surely not an accident; the particulars of the circumstances are just as important to the resulting improvisation as the musician and instrument are. He continues:

> *At which Times, (My Lute lying upon My Table) I sometimes took It up, and Walk'd about My Chamber; Letting my Fancy Drive, which way It would (for I studied nothing at the time, as to Musick) yet my secret Genius or Fancy, prompted my Fingers, (do what I could) into This very Humour; So that every Time I walk'd, and took up my Lute (in the interim, betwixt Writing, and Studying) This Ayre would needs offer It Self unto Me, Continually; In so much that at the last, (liking it Well), (and lest it should be Lost),) I took Paper, and Set it down, taking no further Notice of It, at that Time; But afterwards, It pass'd abroad, for a very Pleasant, and Delightful Ayre, amongst All; yet I gave It no Name, til a long Time after, no taking any more Notice of It, (in any particular kind) than any other My Composures, of That Nature.*

According to this description, the driving factor behind the improvisation is 'fancy', since Mace claims to have been unschooled in music at this time. He also refers to this faculty of creative imagination as 'secret genius', and credits it entirely with moving his fingers into the piece's 'humour' or mood; once placed in this situation, the ayre 'offers itself' to him 'continually', until Mace finally commits it to paper. The process is mysterious, intuitive, and generated by his experience of separation from his fiancée. Despite his lack of musical training, he is still able to create a piece of music worthy of transcription.

In fact, Mace even claims that the piece was performed 'abroad' where it passed 'for a very Pleasant, and Delightful Ayre', which, whether or not it is true, recalls the idea of improvisation as simulation and Henry Blount's attempts to pass off his untrained improvisations as 'ayers of my country' when travelling in Turkey (see Chapter 2 of this book). In contrast to the care with which North recommends that voluntaries should be made, and the detailed instructions for making divisions passed down by Christopher Simpson, here the process is one of inspiration through a set of direct sensory experiences.

Mace continues with his narrative, revealing to us the after-history of his improvisation:

> *But after I was Married, and had brought my wife home, to Cambridge; It so fell out, that one Rainy Morning I stay'd within; and in my Chamber, My Wife and I, were all alone; She Intent upon Her Needle-Works, and I Playing upon my Lute, at the Table by her; She sat very Still, and Quiet, Listening to All I Play'd, without a Word a Long Time till at last, I hapned to Play This Lesson; which, so soon as I had once Play'd, She Earnestly desired Me to Play It again; For, said She, That shall be Called, My Lesson.*

Once again, Mace's attention to detail is painstaking—we need to know that this occasion took place on a rainy day when he was confined indoors with his now wife, intent on her needle-work while he played his lute by her. These facts are all an integral part of the extemporary process. His wife's recognition of the piece also happens in and through this setting, where they are both somehow connected through a shared environment and sonic experience. When his wife speaks these words of recognition, Mace remembers the occasion of the piece's creation:

> *From which Words, so spoken, with Emphasis, and Accent, It presently came into my Remembrance, the Time when, and the Occasion of Its being produced, and returned to Her This Answer*, viz. *That it may properly be call'd Your Lesson; For when I Compos'd It, You were wholly in my Fancy, and the Chief Object, and Ruler of My Thoughts; telling Her how, and when It was made: And therefore, ever after, I Thus call It, My Mistress; (And most of My Scholars since, call it, Mrs. Mace, to This Day.)*[23]

Mrs Mace's presence is key to the improvisation; she originally inspired it due to 'ruling' her then fiancée's thoughts, and now evokes it again as they sit in Cambridge. Furthermore, her inexplicable connection to the piece causes her husband to recall the original performance.

By relating that his wife recognised herself in the piece, Mace suggests that something about it captured something of her true essence, spirit, humour or intrinsic nature. He explains that the purpose of telling this story is so that the reader may know that 'there are *Times, and particular Seasons, in which the Ablest Master, in his Art*, shall not be able to *Command his Invention*, or produce things, so to his *Content*, or *Liking*, as he shall at other Times; but he shall be (as it were) *Stupid, Dull*, and *Shut up*, as to any *Neat, Spruce*, or *Curious Invention*. But again at other *Times*, he will have *Inventions come flowing in upon him, with so much Ease, and Freedom*, that his greatest Trouble will be, to *Retain, Remember*, or *Set Them down*, in *Good Order*'.

Presumably, then, on the original occasion of finding the piece, Mace's feelings for his wife resulting in an 'overflowing' of inventions, somehow transforming his thoughts of her into musical figures, shapes, and forms.

Accordingly, he continues:

---

23  Mace, *Musick's Monument*, pp. 122–3.

> Yet more particularly, as to the *Occasion of This Lesson*; I would have you take notice, that as it was at such a Time, when I was *Wholly*, and *Intimately possessed, with the True, and Perfect Idea of my Living Mistress*, who was at That time *Lovely, Fair, Comely, Sweet, Debonair, Uniformly-Neat*, and every way *Compleat*. How could (possibly) my *Fancy* Run upon any Thing, at that Time, but upon the very *Simile, Form*, or *Likeness*, of the same Substantial Thing.[24]

This story corroborates my earlier readings of certain texts, in which I claimed that the extemporary process was one deeply affected by the people, places, sights and sounds that one experienced. Here Mace is so preoccupied with thoughts of his wife that she overtakes not only his fancy but also his fingers—his body is literally overwhelmed and the piece comes out as a result.

Moreover, the printed score is transformed through this story from a text whose notations must be replicated through an instrument, to a transcription of an improvisatory moment that encrypts within in it the entire story, Mace's creative process, the environmental factors that went into making the piece, and the interactions between him and his wife. The text is mired in improvisation, so that the performer's interaction with it is troubled. How should a present-day performer proceed? Should we take the score and story as inspiration for our own improvisations? How many of Mace's other pieces are similarly modelled on improvisation, and how many pieces of his contemporaries?

My next example occurs in the fifth lesson of the third set, titled 'Hab-Nab'. While the origin of this piece is also due to Mace's overwhelming thoughts about a woman, this time the process and resulting piece are not cast in a favourable light. As before, Mace includes 'A Story of the Manner, and Occasion of Hab-Nab's Production' along with the notation of the piece. The story starts:

> Now comes a *Lesson*, which has neither *Fugue*, nor very Good *Forme*, yet a *Humour*, although none of the *Best*, which I call *Hab-Nab*. This last lesson (quite *Differing* from all the *whole Number* going before) I have set you here on *Purpose*; because by It, you may the more *Plainly Perceive*, what is meant by *Fugue*: Therefore view every *Barr* in it, and you will find not any one *Barr* like another, nor any *Affinity* in the least kind betwixt *Strain*, and *Strain*; yet the *Ayre pleaseth some sort of People well enough*: But for my

---

24  Mace, *Musick's Monument*, p. 123.

*own Part, I never was pleased with it;* yet because some liked it, I retained It. Nor can I tell, how it came to pass, that I thus made It, only I very well remember, the *Time, Manner, and Occasion of its Production;* (which was on a sudden) without the least *Praemeditation,* or *Study,* and meerly *Accidentally;* and as we use to say, *Ex tempore,* in the *Tuning of a Lute.*[25]

Despite including it in his book, Mace clearly seeks to somewhat distance himself from this piece, pointing out its faults and inconsistencies and scathingly remarking that the ayre will be pleasing enough to 'some sort of people'—but clearly, not to him. He goes on to explain that the way he made this piece was 'without the least Praemeditation, or Study and meerly Accidentally; and as we use to say, Ex tempore, in the tuning of a lute'—thus according with his earlier description of the prelude.

Mace continues to fill us in with the details of the 'occasion' of this improvisation, which he claims came to him as he contemplated one of his students, 'a Person of an Ununiform and Inharmonical Disposition, (as to Musick)':

And the Occasion, I conceive, might possibly contribute something towards It, which was *This. I had, at that very Instant (when I made It) an Agitation in Hand* (viz. *The Stringing up, and Tuning of a Lute, for a Person of an Ununiform and Inharmonical Disposition, (as to Musick;) yet in Her self well Proportion'd, Comely, and Handsome enough; and Ingenious for other Things; but for Musick very Unapt; and Learned It, only to please Her Friends, who had a great Desire she should be brought to It, if possible; but never could, to the least Good purpose; so that at the last we both grew weary;* (For there is no striving against such a Stream.)[26]

In light of my research in Chapter 1 into the body and the potential to affect its appearance through reading/performing certain texts or improvisations, it is notable that Mace describes this woman's physique as almost deceptive—her appearance is 'proportion'd, comely, and handsome', but her disposition when it comes to music is 'ununiform and inharmonical'. Perhaps the improvisation that Mace transcribes is thus a musical depiction of the woman's true nature; through the extemporary, Mace is able to make heard what her appearance belies.

He continues:

---

25 Mace, *Musick's Monument*, p. 150.
26 Mace, *Musick's Monument*, pp. 150–1.

> I say, *This Occasion*, possibly might be the *Cause* of this so *Inartificial a Piece*, in regard that *That Person, at that Time, was the Chief Object of my Mind, and Thoughts*. I call it *Inartificial; because the Chief Observation, (as to a good Performance) is wholly wanting: Yet it is True Musick, and has such a Form, and Humour, as may pass, and give Content to Many; Yet I shall never advise any to make Things Thus by Hab-Nab, without any Design, as was This: And therefore I give It That Name.*[27]

Mace's use of 'inartificial' here is derogatory—to him, music must have artifice in order to be worthy and pleasant. His description of how 'hab-nab' came to be is thus a story of preoccupation with the student spilling into his mind and thoughts and spilling out again in his improvisation. And yet, he concedes that it is 'true musick', and that its form and humour may content many, while making it clear that he does not endorse making anything 'without design', or, 'hab-nab'.[28]

The story concludes with a thought about the difference between composition and improvisation. Mace notes that there are many musicians who pass as composers when in fact they are merely assembling passages here and there from other people's compositions:

> There are *Abundance of such Things* to be met with, and from the *Hands of some*, who fain would pass for Good Composers; yet most of them may be *Trac'd*, and upon *Examination, their Things found, only to be Snaps, and Catches;* which they (having been *long Conversant in Musick*), and can command an *Instrument*, (through *great*, and *long Practice*, some of *Them very well*) have taken here and there (Hab-Nab) from several Ayres, and Things of other Mens Works, and put them Handsomely together, which then pass for their Own Compositions.[29]

Thus 'hab-nab' refers to an assemblage of musical passages put together and resulting in something 'unpremeditated' that falls accidentally from Mace's lute as he is tuning. With this in mind, the piece itself, as shown in Figure 16, is perhaps less offensive than a modern reader may have imagined—with its wandering phrases, basic harmonic structure (I-V-I), and gentle atmosphere, we might be forgiven for hearing it as a ubiquitous prelude of its time.

---

27 Mace, *Musick's Monument*, p. 151.
28 See the OED entry for meanings of 'hab-nab', which include 'however it may turn out', 'anyhow', 'at a venture', 'at random', in *OED Online*, 'Hab, adv. (and n.), https://www.oed.com/view/Entry/82947?redirectedFrom=hab+nab
29 Mace, *Musick's Monument*, p. 151.

Fig. 16 Thomas Mace, *Musick's Monument* (London: T. Ratcliffe and N. Thompson, 1676), p. 150, https://archive.org/details/bim_early-english-books-1641-1700_musicks-monument-_mace-thomas_1676/page/n231/mode/2up, public domain.

Crucially, the piece challenges our ideas of the 'wild', 'confused' and 'shapeless'—what may seem benign and unremarkable to us was heard differently by Mace. Furthermore, if we treat this musical text as a transcription of Mace's improvisation, we can imagine that the piece would sound quite different when brought to life and subjected to improvised timing, ornaments and even 'wrong' notes and chords.

Through reading Mace's transcriptions and narratives alongside North's ideas about the voluntary, I propose that while my central claim—that extemporary practice and printed text exist as a series of possible relationships informed by certain key performance parameters—still holds, the exact way in which this unfolded was by no means uniform or agreed upon. For example, the practice of stitching together passages from other works was a contested one; in this case perhaps Mace's low opinion of the practice and North's account of its efficacy reflect their respective skills and disposition in inventing their own passages. Furthermore, even in cases where one did engage in such a practice, it may not have happened consciously—in Mace's case of hab-nab, he simply made music *ex tempore* as he was tuning his lute, and 'accidentally' happened upon this assemblage, directly contradicting North's statement that there is nothing accidental about improvising. In fact, according to Mace's earlier example of his wife's piece, everything about his extemporary process seems accidental: the improvisation reflects all the accidents of time, place and affect that he experienced.

However, rather than pitting North and Mace against one another, I propose instead that there was no one way of demarcating and thinking of improvisation in this context. In light of my opening exploration of 'the writ' and 'the liberty', I would argue that there are many types of writ and many types of liberty at work here, in constant engagement with one another.

## Text and Act: Dido, Improvising Queen

The 'division books' published in early modern London represent collections of printed improvisations, to be used by the musician as scores to be followed, as inspiration for their own truly 'improvised' divisions, or a mixture of both. John Walsh's *Division Flute* (1706)[30] was published twenty-three years after John Playford's first edition of his *Division Violin* (1684),[31] and features many of the same pieces, transposed up a third for the recorder.

Playford himself is unclear about where he got these divisions from, writing in the preface to his second edition: 'Having for some Years stored my self with a Collection of several Choice Divisions for the Violin upon a Ground, A Consort of Musick which do not require many hands to perform; knowing how acceptable and useful this would be to Practitioners in Musick, I have no with no small Pains and Charge made the same publick'.[32] The pieces are simple in form: the repeated bass

---

30 *The First and Second Part of the Division Flute, Containing the Newest Divisions upon the Choisest Grounds for the Flute as also Several Excellent Preludes Chacon's and Cibells* (London: Walsh, 1706), https://s9.imslp.org/files/imglnks/usimg/5/58/IMSLP79264-PMLP160577-versao_final.pdf

31 *The Division-Violin: Containing a Collection of Divisions upon Several Grounds for the Treble-Violin, Being the first Musick of this Kind Made Publick. The Second Edition, Much Enlarged* (London: Playford, 1685), https://s9.imslp.org/files/imglnks/usimg/4/42/IMSLP96722-PMLP198850-Playford_John-_division_violin.pdf

32 *The Division-Violin*, p. 1.

line that runs through is overlaid with a melody part (for violin, or, in the case of the *Division Flute*, for recorder) which is varied each time it repeats, usually (but not always) increasing in complexity.

'Readings Ground', reproduced in Figure 17 from Walsh's print, illustrates the genre well: the 'Ground Bass' at the bottom of the page is played repeatedly while the recorder 'improvises' the printed divisions over the top. We can see that the set of divisions ends with four rounds of a new topic (the last sixteen bars of the melody part), marked in Playford's version as a 'Jigg', and that before that there are sixteen four-bar sections.

Fig. 17 'Readings Ground', in John Walsh, *The Division Flute* (London: Walsh, 1706), p. 1, public domain.

Following the descriptions of Mace and North, we might imagine that each four-bar module could be used interchangeably. The nature and intended uses of the piece challenges the narrative fixity of its presentation in a printed score. Going a little further, we may also imagine that the modules could be interchanged and/or exchanged with the performer's own improvised divisions, either for one or more rounds of the bass. With this approach, we can start to use printed divisions as a bank of musical ideas on which the improviser could draw, considering the score merely as an example of one route that could be taken by a performer in a single performance.

Such an analytic method takes an approach similar to creating a 'choose your adventure' book out of a linearly-written novel, and recalls Laurence Dreyfus's model of 'paradigmatic' analysis developed with regard to the music of J. S. Bach. Dreyfus proposes that we imagine pieces of music not as 'static objects' but 'as a residue of human thoughts and actions', taking the historical notion of 'invention' as a tool with which to unpack the actions of the composer (in his case, Bach) and to build a picture of some of the possible actions they could have taken—and thus consider what they did *not* do as well as what they did. Taking an approach grounded in rhetoric, Dreyfus explores not only the musical transformations that are available to the composer, but also considers how they arranged these transformations to form the final narrative of the piece, hearing it in rhetorical terms as an act of *dispositio*.[33]

Rather than tracing compositional actions and the notion of compositional disposition in this way, I propose to try and go back to the moment just before improvisation, when a performer had some textual tools available to them and was about to make their own 'version' of the piece. Such a process would consider how notation may represent rhetorical devices at the point of performance, rather than seeking to unravel the minutiae of 'composed' melodic figuration, which I suggest is incidental to the underlying paradigms that guide the improviser. This approach is grounded in a historical understanding of how early modern English writers such as Thomas Mace and Roger North theorised improvised practices such as 'hab-nab', or a knitting together of pre-contrived materials that the musician may choose to perform in a

---

33   Laurence Dreyfus, *Bach and the Patterns of Invention* (Cambridge: Harvard University Press, 1996).

different order, with a different measure, and in a different key.

This model of reading and performing a text recalls my earlier explorations of extemporary theatre practices. As I noted above, scholars such as Richard Andrews have analysed Shakespeare's *Tempest* as a 'version' of some pre-existent scenes for improvisation, or 'theatregrams', as Andrews calls them. We can perhaps imagine that the relationship between Shakespeare's text and the corresponding scenes or paradigms that appear in the 1611 collection of actor-manager Flaminio Scala, are similar to that of printed divisions and the original bass line and opening theme that they elaborate. Excitingly, considering such a practice in the context of such a canonic work as Shakespeare's *Tempest* can have broader implications for our approach to musical scores more generally; it draws attention to moments in early modern musical texts that are now generally considered to be 'fixed', and instead of simply asserting that they may represent an improvisatory process, calls for moments of contemporary improvisation.

As a case study, I take Henry Purcell's opera *Dido and Aeneas* Z.626, and focus on Dido's famous lament as a place to experiment with an extemporary approach to text, as well as a place to listen to some connections between gender, coloniality and improvisation[34] Purcell's opera tells the ancient tale of Queen Dido of Carthage who falls in love with the Roman traveller Aeneas, and takes her own life after he abandons both her and their affair in favour of continuing his empire-building mission. In the famous scene of Dido's lament (Act 3), the queen sings over eleven repetitions of the well-known ostinato bass that consists of a chromatic falling fourth 'lament' bass followed by a cadence.

There is no shortage of modern-day analyses of Dido's lament. But to what extent is it significant that her aria is written as a ground, and to what extent *is* she the ground, as an analogue for the natural world? In light of some of my earlier explorations, it is perhaps not of little consequence that the Queen of a 'foreign' empire represented onstage in seventeenth-century London would express the height of her passion

---

34  The opera was written no later than July 1688, according to Bryan White's reading of a letter by Rowland Sherman from Aleppo, Syria, that mentions Purcell's work. See Bryan White, 'Letter from Aleppo: Dating the Chelsea School Performance of Dido and Aeneas', *Early Music* 37.3 (2009), 417–28.

through the ground bass, so close to the earth in which she would she soon be laid. Notwithstanding Purcell's role in composing a work in a traditionally improvised genre, the work's popular associations as 'Dido's lament' almost position her as composer/improviser rather than performer of his music—even though the notes are dictated in the score, we might reimagine a completely different set of divisions over the same repeating bass line.

Early modern depictions of Dido (or Elissa, as she was known interchangeably) in England do not start or end with Henry Purcell—Christopher Marlowe had reimagined her in his play *Dido, Queen of Carthage* (c.1593), Shakespeare evokes her in *The Tempest*,[35] and twentieth-century singers such as London-born 'Dido' (Florian Cloud de Bounevialle O'Malley Armstrong) and the Lebanese singer Elissa would all take inspiration from her in different ways.

How could Dido's ground be rethought within the extemporary contexts of early modern England that I have explored in my book? As the expression of her despair at this moment, the environment, her feelings and sensory experiences are all evoked through her performance, rendering her body the 'text' that she reads to her death. In Chapter 2, I explored the effects of travel on improvisation, and descriptions of people improvising abroad; here Dido's improvisations are inextricable from her status as a Carthaginian queen, and the song she sings is surely reflective of the 'air' and environmental factors her body has imbibed through living there.

This brings us to the question of nature and its othering, often through colonial means. I have mentioned already the coincidences between a musical 'ground' and the ground on which we walk, the earth in which Dido's body would be laid. And there are so many symbolic references to other contemporaneous depictions of improvising creatures in the natural world; to take Strada's nightingale in Chapter 3 as an example, we see a striking parallel between the nightingale's body being absorbed by the lute, and Dido's body being absorbed by the ground. Only it is perhaps unclear which ground it is that has subsumed her; is it the earth, or is it the musical form? In some senses, it may be that Purcell's ground bass marshals her into a correct and orderly form of musical

---

35   William Shakespeare, *The Tempest*, ed. by Stephen Orgel (Oxford: Oxford University Press, 1987), 2, II.1, l.75–99, pp. 131–2.

improvisation, much as the lutenist hoped to curtail the nightingale's wild and free divisions. Ultimately, we are once again asked to reckon with the contradictory freedoms and bounds of musical improvisation in early modern England; between the writ, and the liberty.

To the 'historically-informed' performer encountering Dido's lament, I therefore suggest that the various intersecting histories of the extemporary I have explored have a bearing on the way in which improvisation might be mobilised here. The options for a performer might, in fact, be endless; my recording of the piece is just one example.

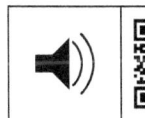

Audio Recording 6 'Dido's Lament'. Track 13 from Fatima Lahham, *hulhul*, FS Records (2022). https://hdl.handle.net/20.500.12434/4915edfd

We might follow Purcell's text to the letter; we might adopt the method of 'hab-nab' and cobble together some alternative divisions heard from other sources; we may become overtaken by thoughts of Dido and let our fancy take over, as Thomas Mace describes; we may improvise freely and wildly as we heard the nightingale did; we may even somehow attain Mace's 'unlimited and unbounded Liberty' in the process. As I suggested earlier, the relationship between early modern text and extemporary practice can be said to have existed in constant shifting relations to one another, the result of combining the various parameters that make up an improvised performance, changing on each occasion.

The examples and case studies of improvised performances that have arisen throughout my book have all existed in separate and various relationships to different parameters of environment/humour/sensory experience/fancy, as have my own performances on the accompanying recordings. When I suggest ways to reimagine Dido, it is thus impossible to prescribe any one way to do so in writing or notation, since the reimagination will be largely dependent on the particular factors at play in the moment of performance. My recording thus exists as one version of the possible interactions between parameters, brought together through my performance and the tools available to me in that moment: my body, instrument, texts, space and imagination. Nevertheless, it is important to recognise that recordings still 'fix' a version, or even sonically print a particular narrative of events (and imprint those on a listener). In this regard, perhaps we could think of 'printing' as a much broader category, encompassing not only ways of affixing ink to paper but including all attempts to notate the same thing in the same way multiple times. It is in fact not merely a mechanical process but a way to reconceive relationships between the body and the world, externalising and determining processes of embodied memory.

Thus, as I explore further in the conclusion at the end of my book, when I offer my own 'versions' of the bee's improvisation, of Jacob van Eyck's English nightingale, or Dido's lament, it is important to recognise that they are precisely that: versions. The nature of a book is that it is written, recorded and fixed, and for this reason I ask the reader to mobilise their own improvisatory powers, when reading—or listening—to my work.

My example above of Dido's improvisation requires a certain use of creative imagination, or perhaps what Thomas Mace would call 'fancy'. Any reimagination of Dido's lament might lead to telling a different story about her; an alternative narrative about her death and its causes. This mobilisation of the historical imagination has been present in various forms throughout my book, and in fact I suggest that it is necessary for the study of improvisation practices, as we reimagine extemporary practices and the alterative narratives and stories they may uncover. In identifying these processes of reimagination throughout my book, I have proposed an 'extemporary imagination', that might offer new ways of imagining historically, reconceptualising histories and improvising musically in the present moment.

By way of a brief example, let us go back to my previous interlude's bee, caught in the moment of nectar pursuit. Let us imagine that the bee is about to alight on the flower, and that both insect and plant exist in the potential that their union may bring about. At this moment, the bee's buzz and the flower's 'ears' guide the improvised encounter; the bee finding the right buzz frequency for the particular flower, and the flower tuning in to the buzz. The bee's sonic performance is a unique expression of its present moment of relation to the flower, and the flower's disposition is altered by the sonic presence of the bee—they exist in a state of reciprocity. Broadly speaking, their encounter is one of improvisation: a series of interactions between bee, flower and all aspects of their environment that could only exist in that particular order and at that particular time.

If we historicise the bee, and imagine it through early modern perceptions, we might add a further layer to the scene and propose that the bee's buzz is formed through the marks of its past histories; its previous flowers; its earlier flights. These processes by which I have imagined the hypothetical bee and flower do not only reconceptualise ways of listening to nature or trying to re-imagine historical ears, but, I suggest, also require a certain type of improvisation themselves. It is this nature of re-imagined improvisation narratives that I describe as the 'extemporary imagination'; a way of entering into the 'live-ness' of improvisation and recalling moments of presence while maintaining historical understandings. This type of time-travel becomes particularly useful for applying historical research to historical performance practice, as my recordings throughout the book have attempted to illustrate.

Our imaginations are our own. When you choose to embrace imagination in your historical music-making or writing about musical histories, you may attempt what Emma Pérez described as the historian's political project—'to decolonise otherness'—or you may choose something else, as do many of the early modern English authors I read in this book.[36]

*If we have been 'socialized to respect fear more than our own needs for language and definition', ask yourself: what am I afraid to improvise? [So, answer this today. And every day.]*

---

36   Pérez, *The Decolonial Imaginary*, p. 6.

# Epilogue

> Not *otherwise*, as in, the political horizon awaits; *otherwise* as in, a firm embrace of the unknowable; the unknowable as in, a well of infinity I want us to fall down together.
> —Lola Olufemi, *Experiments in Imagining Otherwise* (2021)[1]

The practice and field of 'historical performance'[2] might seem to trade in the 'unknowable'. In fact, the problems of a movement that seemingly places emphasis on historical 'reconstruction' or 'authenticity' are well-rehearsed within HP, and it is perhaps at those cracks that improvisation appears.[3]

In my own work I have made no attempts to know the unknowable. Instead, in Lola Olufemi's words, I choose to 'embrace' it. To ask how the speculative pursuit of reimagining historical improvisation could foster an imaginative will to fall down a well of infinity together; how it could 'result in more liberatory performances of early music'.[4] Through researching processes of early modern improvisation, I believe we can experiment with practices of imagination that challenge the linear historicity of past-present-future, rendering 'historical improvisation' more broadly a mode of making music that is alive to the multiple past and present contexts of its performers and performances.

Additionally, researching historical improvisation practices has

---

1. Lola Olufemi, *Experiments in Imagining Otherwise* (Maidstone: Hajar Press, 2021), p. 7.
2. NB: I use the terms historical performance and historically informed performance (and their acronyms HP/HIP) interchangeably.
3. For example, see Nicholas Kenyon, *Authenticity and Early Music: A Symposium* (Oxford: Oxford University Press, 1988).
4. Kailan R. Rubinoff, '(Re)creating the Past: Baroque Improvisation in the Early Music Revival', *New Sound* 32, Special issue on improvisation, ed. by Marcel Cobussen and Mira Veselinovic-Hofman (2009), https://libres.uncg.edu/ir/uncg/f/K_Rubinoff_Recreating_2009.pdf

enabled me to uncover alternative stories of early modern English music history, situating my musical research within histories of the body, sounds of nature, Anglo-Ottoman relations and the coloniality of the travelogue. I argue that these contexts are not disconnected from our current socio-political realities as musicians improvising in the twenty-first century.

It is my hope that my work may pave the way for historically informed musicians to become politically engaged in our music-making, understanding the histories that inform the music we make, and turning to improvisation as a way to create music that is alive with the possibilities of new futures. It is important also to acknowledge work that has been done on engaging the early music movement in more critical and racially, colonially and politically literate ways.

Geoffrey Baker's article of 2008 focussed on Latin American baroque music to call on Philip Bohlman's description of musicology as a political act, urging practitioners of early music 'to transform performance into a post-colonial act'.[5] While I would argue for a practice that is *anti-* or *de-*colonial rather than simply 'post', this article was an important moment of reckoning for performers engaging with the colonial legacies of baroque music. Olivia Bloechl's 2015 essay on the critical study of race in early modern European music has also made waves of change in the landscape of early modern music histories and racial literacy,[6] while Kailan Rubinoff's chapter on 1968 situates the early music movement within counter-cultures and political protest, shedding light on a much-neglected part of the history of the early music movement that deserves much more study.[7] More recently, Melodie Michel[8] and Eric Lubarsky[9]

---

[5] Geoffrey Baker, 'Latin American Baroque: Performance as a Post-Colonial Act?', *Early Music* 36.3 (2008), 441–8 (p. 447).

[6] Olivia Bloechl, 'Race, Empire, and Early Music', in *Rethinking Difference in Music Scholarship*, ed. by Olivia Bloechl, Melanie Lowe and Jeffrey Kallberg (Cambridge: Cambridge University Press, 2015), pp. 77–107.

[7] Kailan R. Rubinoff, 'A Revolution in Sheep's Wool Stockings: Early Music and "1968"', in *Music and Protest in 1968*, ed. by Beate Kutschke and Barley Norton (Cambridge: Cambridge University Press, 2013), pp. 237–54.

[8] Melodie Michel, 'Early Music and Latin America: Transhistorical Views on the Coloniality of Sound', PhD thesis, UC Santa Cruz, 2021, https://escholarship.org/content/qt63b2j65k/qt63b2j65k_noSplash_a5c96dec830086c3f4071a143f6fd146.pdf?t=qsxuoo

[9] Eric Lubarsky, 'Reviving Early Music: Metaphors and Modalities of Life and Living in Historically Informed Performance', PhD dissertation, Eastman School

have contributed PhD dissertations on early music and Latin America, and modalities of living and HP, respectively.

These calls for more critical and politically-engaged models of HP have been reflected by musical projects that embrace a more cross-cultural perspective. Jordi Savall and Hespèrion XXI must of course be mentioned here, along with cross-collaborative albums such as *Istanbul* (2009), *Armenian Spirit* (2012), *The Routes of Slavery* (2017) and *Ibn Battuta, The Traveller of Islam* (2019). Additionally, groups such as the Pera Ensemble have specialised in historical music of the Ottoman empire, while Saraband and soprano Fadia el-Hage present performances of J. S. Bach that highlight some of the connections between Arabic classical music and Western baroque music.

Inspired by some of the alternative histories sought out through these cross-cultural collaborative recordings, throughout this book, I have grappled with the types of histories we consider relevant to historical musicology, and that we consider as informing 'historically-informed performance.'

As I researched this book, I started teaching a new course on historical improvisation at the Royal College of Music in London. I designed the course at the end of 2019, with the intention of exploring 'historical improvisation both as a practical skill and as a way to explore some of the histories by which we are usually *not* informed as historically-informed performers'. The rest of the course description echoed some of the central concerns of my book topic:

> You will learn to improvise over some popular repeating bass lines of the sixteenth–eighteenth centuries, studying historical texts alongside contemporary theory to re-imagine how the notion of 'history' is constructed, and how that intersects with the present-ness of performance and improvisation. The course aims to inspire you to form inclusive understandings of creativity, history, and identity, encouraging you to create your own historical archive that informs your music-making, and to think critically about your role as a 'historically-informed' musician in today's society.

However, by the time I started teaching, the decision was taken to move teaching online due to the pandemic. As we worked our way through

---

of Music, 2017, https://www.proquest.com/dissertations-theses/reviving-early-music-metaphors-modalities-life/docview/2001524940/se-2

the course texts I had carefully selected and paired with historical musical materials for improvisation, the strain and disconnect caused by constant news of illness and death, the weight of transnational grief, internet issues, the difficulties of improvising online and the impossibility of improvising collectively made me question further the way I was using 'history' in my practice. Why were we all making such a concerted effort not to include our present circumstances in the intensely personal practice of improvisation? How could our imaginations not be implicated in such a practice? And what kinds of histories inevitably kept making their ways into our archives, or being left out?

A year later, I taught the same course again. This time we met in person, sat in a circle, got our instruments out and made music together. In this practical setting, improvisation clearly presented itself as a way to imagine otherwise—to think musically against the grain of a classical conservatoire training that prizes perfection, to unpick the authority of a written score. It also challenges the histories we choose to study and by which we are informed, asking whose voices are left unwritten in any given text.

My book has asked how we can use different kinds of histories to inform our improvisation, rather than propose that any kind of reconstruction of how 'historical' improvisation sounded might be possible. On the contrary, I believe that this former approach imbues improvisation with the potential to transform the field of historical performance more broadly. By approaching historical improvisation in this way, I believe that the field of historical performance might become an exciting area for creatively developing critical-historical perspectives that can bring multiple current contexts into dialogue with the texts we encounter, resulting in historical re-conceptualisation and reimagination.

And suddenly, it is the end. And how should I write about the endings? About the question of what has existed? What I have written, deleted and re-written. I come back to the description of improvisation that starts my introduction: *the way creativity seeks freedom; an alternative way to imagine the world.* Imagination is usually a silent activity. What does it mean to make it audible? And in the end, is that what improvisation is? How we re-imagine the world differently, how we hear each other do that, how we imagine and re-imagine together?

*Improvisation: a way to seek the otherwise. The way we make home in places that bear our names. The way I sing to the same skies as the bee and the nightingale. How our memories collide in a sonic corridor where each door could open onto a new future. How we label our contradictions; a name we give to the acts we can't explain.*

# Bibliography

## Primary Sources

### Unpublished

London, British Library, London, MS Add MS 22911

National Archives, Kew, SP 10/73, part 2, folio 73v

### Published

Attar, Farid, *The Conference of the Birds*, translated by Afkham Darbandi and Dick Davis (London: Penguin Books, 1984)

Bacon, Francis, 'Of Studies', *Essays or Counsels, Civil and Moral*, 1627, http://fountainheadpress.com/expandingthearc/assets/francisbaconstudies.pdf

Blount, Henry, *A Voyage into the Levant: A Breife Relation of a Journey, Lately Performed by Master H.B. Gentleman, from England by the Way of Venice, into Dalmatia, Sclavonia, Bosnah, Hungary, Macedonia, Thessaly, Thrace, Rhodes and Egypt, unto Gran Cairo: with Particular Observations Concerning the Moderne Condition of the Turkes, and Other People under that Empire* (London: Printed by I. L. for Andrew Crooke, 1636), https://archive.org/details/avoyageintoleva00blougoog

Butler, Charles, *The Feminine Monarchie or a Treatise Concerning Bees, and the Due Ordering of Them Wherein the Truth, Found out by Experience and Diligent Observation, Discovereth the Idle and Fondd Conceipts, Which Many Haue Written anent this Subiect. By Char: Butler magd* (Oxford: Printed by Ioseph Barnes, 1609), https://archive.org/details/bim_early-english-books-1475-1640_the-feminine-monarchie-_butler-charles_1609

Butler, Charles, *The Feminine Monarchie: Or the Historie of Bees Shewing their Admirable Nature, and Properties, their Generation, and Colonies, their Gouernment, Loyaltie, Art, Industrie, Enemies, Warres, Magnanimitie, &c. together with the*

*Right Ordering of Them from Time to Time: And the Sweet Profit Arising Thereof. Written out of Experience by Charles Butler. magd.* (London: Printed by Iohn Hauiland for Roger Iackson, 1623), https://archive.org/details/RAM2023-1081

Campion, Thomas, *A Score for The Lords' Masque by Thomas Campion: Performed on 14 February, 1613*, ed. by Andrew J. Sabol (London: Brown University Press, 1993)

Cotgrave, Randle, *A Dictionarie of the French and English Tongues* (London: Printed by Adam Islip, 1611), http://www.pbm.com/~lindahl/cotgrave/534small.html

Drake, Richard, *A Manual of the Private Devotions and Meditations of The Right Reverend Father in God Lancelot Andrews, Late Lord Bishop of Winchester Translated out of a Fair Greek MS. of His Amanuensis by R.D., B.D.* (London: Printed for W.D. by Humphrey Moseley, 1648), https://quod.lib.umich.edu/e/eebo2/A25391.0001.001?view=toc

Dumont, Jean, *A New Voyage to the Levant Containing an Account of the Most Remarkable Curiosities in Germany, France, Italy, Malta, and Turkey: With Historical Observations Relating to the Present and Ancient State of Those Countries / by the Sieur du Mont; Done into English, and Adorn'd with Figures* (London: T. H., 1696), https://quod.lib.umich.edu/e/eebo/A36827.0001.001?view=toc

Dumont, Jean, *Nouveau voyage du Levant/par le sieur D.M. contenant ce qu'il a vû de plus remarquable en Allemagne, France, Italie, Malthe, & Turquie: où l'on voit aussiles Brigues secretes de Mr. de Chateau-neuf, Ambassadeur de France à la Cour ottoman, & plusieurs histoires galantes* (La Haye: Chez Etienne Foulque, 1694)

Evelyn, John, *Diary of John Evelyn, Volume IV: Kalendarium, 1673–1689*, ed. by E. S. de Beer (Oxford: Oxford University Press, 1955)

Florio, John, *A Worlde of Wordes, or Dictionarie of the Italian and English Tongues* (London: Arnold Hatfield, 1598), https://archive.org/details/worldeofwordesor00flor

Freeman, Ireneus, *Logikē latreia the Reasonablenesse of Divine Service: Or Non-Conformity to Common-Prayer, Proved not Conformable to Common Reason: In Answer to the Contrary Pretensions of H. D. in a Late Discourse Concerning the Interest of Words in Prayer and Liturgies/by Ireneus Freeman* (London: Printed and sold by Tho. Basset, 1661), https://ota.bodleian.ox.ac.uk/repository/xmlui/handle/20.500.12024/A48963

Gillespie, George, *Reasons for Which the Service Booke, Urged upon Scotland Ought to Bee Refused* (Edinburgh: Printed by G. Anderson, 1638), https://quod.lib.umich.edu/cgi/t/text/text-idx?c=eebo2;idno=A11744.0001.001

Godwin, Francis, *The Man in the Moone: Or, a Discovrse of a Voyage thither by Domingo Gonsales the Speedy Messenger* (London: Printed by John Norton, to be sold by Ioshua Kurton and Thomas Warren, 1638), https://name.umdl.

umich.edu/A42948.0001.001

Godwin, William, *Enquiry Concerning Political Justice* (Batoche Books, 2000), https://oll.libertyfund.org/titles/godwin-an-enquiry-concerning-political-justice-vol-ii

Hole, Matthew, *The Expediency of a Publick Liturgy, to Preserve the Reverence of Publick Worship a Sermon Preach'd at Bridgewater, for the Satisfaction of an Eminent Dissenter / by Matthew Hole* (London: Printed for Matt. Wotton, 1697), https://quod.lib.umich.edu/e/eebo2/A44142.0001.001?view=toc

Hotteterre le Romain, Jacques, *Principes de la flute traversiere, de la Flute a bec, et du Haut-bois*, Op. 1 (Amsterdam: Estienne Roger, n.d.), https://imslp.org/wiki/Principes_de_la_flute_traversiere,_de_la_Flute_a_Bec,_et_du_Haut-bois,_Op.1_(Hotteterre,_Jacques)

Johnson, Richard, *A Most Royall Song of the Life and Death of Our Late Renowned Princesse Queene Elizabeth* (London: Printed by G. Eld for Iohn Wright, 1612), n.p., https://name.umdl.umich.edu/A04551.0001.001

Lewthwat, Richard, *A Justification of Set Forms of Prayer and in Special of the Liturgy of the Church of England; in Answer to, and Confutation of Vavasor Powel's Fourteen Considerations, against All Composed and Imposed Forms of Prayer. By Richard Lewthwat, M.A. and Rector of Wethersdale in Suffolk* (London: Printed by A. Godbid and J. Playford, for Robert Clavel, 1679), http://hdl.handle.net/20.500.14106/A48298

Locke, John, *Second Treatise of Government and A Letter Concerning Toleration*, ed. by Mark Goldie (Oxford: Oxford World's Classics, 2016)

Mace, Thomas, 'A Fancy-Prelude', *Musick's Monument* (London: T. Ratcliffe and N. Thompson, 1676), https://archive.org/details/bim_early-english-books-1641-1700_musicks-monument-_mace-thomas_1676/page/n231/mode/2up

Mace, Thomas, *Musick's Monument*, Reproduction en fac-similé, 1676 (Paris: Éditions du Centre National de la Recherche Scientifique, 1958)

Matteis, Nicola, *Other Ayrs Preludes Allmands Sarabands with Full Stops for the Violin by Nicola Matteis, The Second Part* (n.p.: n.d.), https://s9.imslp.org/files/imglnks/usimg/5/5e/IMSLP99060-PMLP203526-Matteis_Nicola_2._Other_ayrs_preludes_allmands_sarabands.pdf

Matteis, Nicola, *Ayres For the Violin to Wit...The Third and Fourth Parts Composed by Nicola Matteis* (n.p.: n.d.), https://s9.imslp.org/files/imglnks/usimg/7/75/IMSLP99061-PMLP203526-Matteis_Nicola_3._Ayres_for_the_violin.pdf

Maundrell, Henry, *A Journey from Aleppo to Jerusalem at Easter, A.D. 1697* (Oxford: Printed at the Theatre, 1703), https://archive.org/details/gri_journeyfroma00maun

al-Nābulusī, 'Abd al-Ghanī, *Al-Ḥaqīqa wa-l-majāz fī al-riḥla ila Bilād al-Shām wa Miṣr wa-l-Ḥijāz*, ed. by Ahmad ʿAbd al-Majīd Harīdī (Cairo: Al-Hay'a al-

Misriyya), https://archive.org/details/hakika-majaz

North, Roger, *Roger North on Music; Being a Selection from His Essays Written during the Years c. 1695–1728*, ed. by John Wilson (London: Novello, 1959)

Parker, Martin, *The Nightingale Vvarbling forth her Owne Disaster; or the Rape of Philomela. Newly Written in English Verse, by Martin Parker* (London: Printed by George Purslowe for William Cooke, 1632), https://quod.lib.umich.edu/e/eebo2/A08974.0001.001?view=toc

Playford, John, *Division-Violin: Containing a Collection of Divisions upon Several Grounds for the Treble-Violin, Being the first Musick of this Kind Made Publick. The Second Edition, Much Enlarged* (London: Playford, 1685), https://s9.imslp.org/files/imglnks/usimg/4/42/IMSLP96722-PMLP198850-Playford_John-_division_violin.pdf

Prete, Frederick R., 'Can Females Rule the Hive? The Controversy over Honey Bee Gender Roles in British Beekeeping Texts of the Sixteenth-Eighteenth Centuries', *Journal of the History of Biology* 24.1 (1991), 113–44

Ray, John, *Travels through the Low Countries: Germany, Italy and France, with Curious Observations* (London: J. Walthoe et al., 1673), https://archive.org/details/travelsthroughlo02rayj/page/n5/mode/2up

Ross, Alexander, *The Alcoran of Mahomet, Translated out of Arabick into French, by the Sieur du Ryer, Lord of Malezair, and Resident for the French King, at Alexandria. And Newly Englished, for the Satisfaction of All that Desire to Look into the Turkish Vanities. To Which is Prefixed, the Life of Mahomet, the Prophet of the Turks, and Author of the Alcoran. With a Needful Caveat, or Admonition, for Them Who Desire to Know What Use May Be Made of, or if There Be Danger in Reading the Alcoran* (London: Printed and to be sold by Randal Taylor, 1688), https://archive.org/details/alcoranofmahomet00dury

Shakespeare, William, *Romeo and Juliet*, ed. by Barbara A. Mowat and Paul Werstine (The Folger Shakespeare), https://shakespeare.folger.edu/downloads/pdf/romeo-and-juliet_PDF_FolgerShakespeare.pdf

Shakespeare, William, *The Two Gentlemen of Verona*, ed. by Barbara A. Mowat and Paul Werstine (The Folger Shakespeare), https://shakespeare.folger.edu/downloads/pdf/the-two-gentlemen-of-verona_PDF_FolgerShakespeare.pdf

Shakespeare, William, *Hamlet*, ed. by Barbara A. Mowat and Paul Werstine (The Folger Shakespeare), https://shakespeare.folger.edu/downloads/pdf/hamlet_PDF_FolgerShakespeare.pdf

Shakespeare, William, *The Tempest*, ed. by Stephen Orgel (Oxford: Oxford University Press, 1987)

Simpson, Christopher, *The Division-Viol, or The Art of Playing Ex Tempore upon a Ground by Christopher Simpson*, A Lithographic Facsimile of the Second Edition, 1677 (Faber Music: Curwen Edition, 1965)

Spinola, George, *Rules to Get Children by with Handsome-faces: Or, Precepts for the*

*Paptists, that Get Children by Book and for the Extemporary Sectaries, that Get Children without Book, to Consider What They Have to Doe, and Look Well before They Leape* [...] *Composed by George Spinola. Published According to Order* (London: Printed for T.S., 1646), http://hdl.handle.net/20.500.14106/A93684

*Strada's Musical Duel in Latine / Much Enlarg'd in English by the Addition of Several Traverses between the Harper and the Nightengale ; Together with a More Particular Account of the Issue of the Contest* (London: Printed by J.W. for William Gilbert, 1671), https://quod.lib.umich.edu/cgi/t/text/text-idx?c=eebo2;idno=A61709.0001.001

Taylor, Zachary, *A Disswasive from Contention Being a Sermon Preached and Designed for the Last Itineration of the King's Preachers in the County Palatine of Lancaster / by Zachary Taylor* (London: Printed by John Gain for William Cadman, 1683), http://hdl.handle.net/20.500.14106/A64270

Terence, *Phormio*, ed. by Robert Maltby (Oxford: Oxbow Books, 2012)

Thévenot, Jean de, *Relation d'un voyage fait au Levant: dans laquelle il est curieusement traité des estats sujets au Grand Seigneur... et des singularitez particulières de l'Archipel, Constantinople, Terre-Sainte, Égypte, pyramides, mumies* ["sic"], *déserts d'Arabie, la Meque, et de plusieurs autres lieux de l'Asie et de l'Affrique... outre les choses mémorables arrivées au dernier siège de Bagdat, les cérémonies faites aux réceptions des ambassadeurs du Mogol et l'entretien de l'autheur avec celuy du Pretejan, où il est parlé des sources du Nil / par Monsieur Thevenot* (Paris: n.p., 1664), https://gallica.bnf.fr/ark:/12148/bpt6k106525z/f83.item

Thévenot, Jean de, *The Travels of Monsieur de Thevenot into the Levant in Three Parts, viz. into I. Turkey, II. Persia, III. the East-Indies / Newly Done out of French* (London: Printed by H. Clark, for H. Faithorne, J. Adamson, C. Skegnes, and T. Newborough, 1687), https://archive.org/details/travelsofmonsieu00thev/page/n7/mode/2up

Ufukī, 'Alī, *Ottoman and European Music in 'Alī Ufukī's Compendium, MS Turc 292: Analysis, Interpretation, Cultural Context*, ed. by Judith I. Haug, Volume 1: Edition (Munster: ULB, 2020)

Ufukī, 'Alī, *Ottoman and European Music in 'Alī Ufukī's Compendium, MS Turc 292: Analysis, Interpretation, Cultural Context*, ed. by Judith I. Haug, Volume 2: Critical Report (Munster: ULB, 2020)

van Eyck, Jacob, *Der Fluyten Lusthof*, 2nd edn (Amsterdam: Paulus Matthysz, 1649), https://s9.imslp.org/files/imglnks/usimg/9/9t/IMSLP98063-PMLP201599-fluyten_lust_hof_1649.pdf

Walsh, John, *The Bird Fancyer's Delight, or Choice Observations and Directions Concerning the Teaching of All Sorts of Singing Birds after the Flagelet and Flute* [recorder] *when Rightly Made as to Size and Tone, with Lessons Properly Compos'd within the Compass and Faculty of Each Bird, viz. for the Canary-Bird, Linnet, Bull-Finch, Wood-Lark, Black-Bird, Throustill* [thrush], *Nightingale and Starling. The Whole Fairly Engraven and Carefully Corrected* (London: Printed for J. Walsh, c.1715), https://imslp.org/wiki/The_Bird_Fancyer's_Delight_(Walsh,_John)

Walsh, John, *The First and Second Part of the Division Flute, Containing the Newest Divisions upon the Choisest Grounds for the Flute as also Several Excellent Preludes Chacon's and Cibells* (London: Walsh, 1706), https://s9.imslp.org/files/imglnks/usimg/5/58/IMSLP79264-PMLP160577-versao_final.pdf

Willis, John, *Mnemonica, or, the Art of Memory Drained Out of the Pure Fountains of Art & Nature, Digested into Three Books : Also A Physical Treatise of Cherishing Natural Memory, Diligently Collected out of Divers Learned Mens Writings / by John Willis* (London: Printed and to be sold by Leonard Sowersby, 1661), p. 137, http://hdl.handle.net/20.500.14106/A66483

Wilkins, John, *Mercvry, or, the Secret and Svvift Messenger Shewing, How a Man May with Privacy and Speed Communicate his Thoughts to a Friend at Any Distance* (London: Printed by I. Norton, for Iohn Maynard and Timothy Wilkins, 1641), http://hdl.handle.net/20.500.14106/A66051

## Secondary Sources

Abivardi, Cyrus, 'Honeybee Sexuality: An Historical Perspective', in *Encyclopedia of Historical Entomology*, ed. by John L. Capinera (Dordrecht: Springer, 2005), pp. 1103–04

Agnew, Vanessa, *Enlightenment Orpheus: The Power of Music in Other Worlds* (Oxford: Oxford University Press, 2008), https://doi.org/10.1093/acprof:oso/9780195336665.001.0001

Agnew, Vanessa, 'Gooseflesh: Music, Somatosensation, and the Making of Historical Experience', in *The Varieties of Historical Experience*, ed. by Stephan Palmié and Charles Stewart (London: Routledge, 2019), pp. 77–94, https://doi.org/10.4324/9780429456527

Ahmed, Sara, *Living a Feminist Life* (Durham: Duke University Press, 2017)

Akhimie, Patricia, and Andrea, Bernadette (eds), *Travel and Travail: Early Modern Women, English Drama and the Wider World* (Lincoln: University of Nebraska Press, 2018), https://doi.org/10.2307/j.ctv8xnh57

Almas, Lamiya Mohamad, 'The Women of the Early Modern Turk and Moor Plays' (PhD thesis, University of Minnesota, 2009), https://conservancy.umn.edu/server/api/core/bitstreams/1bb98efa-e909-419f-9e78-23ee54893e6a/content

Andrews, Richard, '*The Tempest* and Italian Improvised Theatre', in *Revisiting the Tempest: The Capacity to Signify*, ed. by Silvia Bigliazzi and Lisanna Calvi (Basingstoke: Palgrave Shakespeare Studies, 2014), pp. 45–62, https://doi.org/10.1057/9781137333148

Andrews, Walter G., and Kalpaklı, Mehmet, *The Age of Beloveds: Love and the Beloved in Early-modern Ottoman and European Culture and Society* (Durham: Duke University Press, 2005), https://doi.org/10.1515/9780822385905

Austern, Linda P., 'Nature, Culture, Myth, and the Musician in Early Modern England', *Journal of the American Musicological Society* 51.1 (1998), 1–47, https://doi.org/10.2307/831896

Baker, Geoffrey, 'Latin American Baroque: Performance as a Post-Colonial Act?', *Early Music* 36.3 (2008), 441–8, https://doi.org/10.1093/em/can082

Baeten, Somayeh, *Birds, Birds, Birds: A Comparative Study of Medieval Persian and English Poetry, especially Attar's 'Conference of Birds', 'The Owl and the Nightingale', Chaucer's 'The Parliament of Fowls', and the Canterbury Tales* (Munich: Utzverlag, 2020)

Bass, John, 'Improvisation in Sixteenth-Century Italy: Lessons from Rhetoric and Jazz', *Performance Practice Review* 14.1(2009), https://doi.org/10.5642/perfpr.200914.01.01

Boal, Augusto, *Theatre of the Oppressed*, translated by Charles A. and Maria-Odilia McBride and Emily Fryer (London: Pluto Press, 2008)

Blasdale, Walter C., 'The Early History of the Persian Cyclamen', *The National Horticultural Magazine* (October 1949), 156–61

Bloechl, Olivia, *Native American Song at the Frontiers of Early Modern Music* (Cambridge: Cambridge University Press, 2008)

Bloechl, Olivia, 'Race, Empire, and Early Music', in *Rethinking Difference in Music Scholarship*, ed. by Olivia Bloechl, Melanie Lowe and Jeffrey Kallberg (Cambridge: Cambridge University Press, 2015), pp. 77–107, https://doi.org/10.1017/CBO9781139208451.003

Bloechl, Olivia, 'Music in the Early Colonial World', in *The Cambridge History of Sixteenth-Century Music*, ed. by Iain Fenlon and Richard Wistreich (Cambridge: Cambridge University Press, 2019), pp. 128–75, https://doi.org/10.1017/9780511675874.006

Briggs, Helen, 'How Lockdown Birds Sang to a Different Tune', *BBC News* (24 September 2020), https://www.bbc.co.uk/news/science-environment-54285627

Brown, Katherine, 'Reading Indian Music: The Interpretation of Seventeenth-Century European Travel-Writing in the (Re)construction of Indian Music History', *Ethnomusicology Forum* 9.2 (2000), 1–34, https://doi.org/10.1080/09681220008567299

Bush, Douglas E., and Richard Kassel, *The Organ: An Encyclopedia* (London: Routledge, 2006)

Butler, Gregory G., 'The Fantasia as Musical Image', *The Musical Quarterly* 60.4 (1974), 602–15

Caspari, Maya, and Ruth Daly, 'Reading Otherwise: Decolonial Feminisms', *Parallax* 29.2 (2023), 139–53

Chew, Samuel, *The Crescent and the Rose: Islam and England during the Renaissance* (New York: Oxford University Press, 1937)

Clubb, Louise George, 'Pastoral Jazz from the Writ to the Liberty', in *Italian Culture in the Drama of Shakespeare and his Contemporaries: Rewriting, Remaking, Refashioning*, ed. by Michele Marrapodi (Aldershot: Ashgate, 2007), pp. 15–26

Cumming, Julie E., 'Renaissance Improvisation and Musicology', *Journal of the Society for Music Theory* 19.2 (2013), https://doi.org/10.30535/mto.19.2.4

Dart, Thurston, 'Miss Mary Burwell's Instruction Book for the Lute', *The Galpin Society Journal* 11 (1958), 3–62

Darwish, Mahmoud, *A River Dies of Thirst: Journals*, translated by Catherine Cobham (New York: Archipelago Books, 2009)

Dove, Michael R., 'Chapter 1, Historic Decentering of the Modern Discourse of Climate Change: The Long View from the Vedic Sages to Montesquieu', in *Climate Cultures: Anthropological Perspectives on Climate Change*, ed. by Jessica Barnes and Michael R. Dove (New Haven and London: Yale University Press, 2015), pp. 25–47

Dreyfus, Laurence, *Bach and the Patterns of Invention* (Cambridge: Harvard University Press, 1996)

Engel, William, Rory Loughnane and Grany Williams (eds), *The Memory Arts in Renaissance England: A Critical Anthology* (Cambridge: Cambridge University Press, 2016), https://doi.org/10.1017/cbo9781316091722

Feghali, Layla K., *The Land in Our Bones: Plantcestral Herbalism and Healing Cultures from Syria to the Sinai* (Berkeley: North Atlantic Books, 2024)

Feldman, Walter, *Music of the Ottoman Court: Makam, Composition and the Early Ottoman Instrumental Repertoire* (Berlin: Verlag fur Wissenschaft und Bildung, 1996)

Fischlin, Daniel, and Porter, Eric (eds), *Playing for Keeps: Improvisation in the Aftermath* (Durham: Duke University Press, 2020), https://doi.org/10.1215/9781478009122

Frank, Marcie, Jonathan Goldberg and Newman, Karen (eds), *The Distracted Globe: Worldmaking in Early Modern Literature* (New York: Fordham University Press, 2016), https://doi.org/10.1515/9780823270316

Fudge, Erica, *Brutal Reasoning: Animals, Rationality, and Humanity in Early Modern England* (Ithaca: Cornell University Press, 2019), https://doi.org/10.7591/9781501727191

Gooley, Dana, *Fantasies of Improvisation: Free Playing in Nineteenth-Century Music* (New York: Oxford University Press, 2018), https://doi.org/10.1093/oso/9780190633585.001.0001

Greenblatt, Stephen, *Renaissance Self-Fashioning: From More to Shakespeare* (Chicago: The University of Chicago Press, 1980)

Greve, Martin (ed.), *Writing the History of Ottoman Music* (Würzburg: Ergon Verlag in Kommission, 2015), https://doi.org/10.5771/9783956507038

Guido, Massimiliano, 'Climbing the Stairs of the Memory Palace: Gestures at the Keyboard for a Flexible Mind', in *Studies in Historical Improvisation: From Cantare super Librum to Partimenti*, ed. by Massimiliano Guido (Abingdon: Routledge, 2017), pp. 41–52

Guido, Massimilano, 'Introduction, Studies in Historical Improvisation: A New Path for Performance, Theory and Pedagogy of Music', in *Studies in Historical Improvisation: From Cantare super Librum to Partimenti*, ed. by Massimiliano Guido (Abingdon: Routledge, 2017), pp. 1–6

Gumbs, Alexis Pauline, *Undrowned: Black Feminist Lessons from Marine Mammals* (Edinburgh: AK Press, 2020)

Habib, Imtiaz, *Black Lives in the English Archives, 1500–1677: Imprints of the Invisible* (Farnham: Ashgate, 2008), https://doi.org/10.4324/9781315569468

Haines, John, 'The Arabic Style of Performing Medieval Music', *Early Music* 29.3 (2001), 369–80, https://doi.org/10.1093/earlyj/XXIX.3.369

Hall, Kim F., *Things of Darkness: Economics of Gender and Race in Early Modern England* (Ithaca: Cornell University Press, 1995)

Harris, Rachel A., *Soundscapes of Uyghur Islam* (Bloomington: Indiana University Press, 2020), https://doi.org/10.2307/j.ctv1574p9g

Hayes, Gerald, 'Charles Butler and the Music of Bees', *The Musical Times* 66.988 (1925), 512–15

Haynes, Bruce, *The End of Early Music: A Period Performer's History of Music* (Oxford; Oxford University Press, 2007), https://doi.org/10.1093/acprof:oso/9780195189872.001.0001

Herissone, Rebecca, *Musical Creativity in Restoration England* (New York: Cambridge University Press, 2013), https://doi.org/10.1017/cbo9781139013741

Herissone, Rebecca, and Alan Howard (eds), *Concepts of Creativity in Seventeenth-Century England* (Woodbridge: The Boydell Press, 2013), https://doi.org/10.1515/9781782042310

Hodgson, Marshall, *The Venture of Islam*, Vols 1–3 (Chicago: University of Chicago Press, 1975)

Irving, D. R. M., *Colonial Counterpoint: Music in Early Modern Manila* (Oxford: Oxford University Press, 2010), https://doi.org/10.1093/acprof:oso/9780195378269.001.0001

Irving, D. R. M., 'Rethinking Early Modern "Western Art Music": A Global History Manifesto', *IMS Musicological Brainfood* 3.1 (2019), 6–10, https://brainfood.musicology.org/vol-3-no-1-2019/rethinking-early-modern-western-art-music/

Jacobs, Nicole A., 'John Milton's Beehive, from Polemic to Epic', *Studies in Philology* 112.4 (2015), 798–816, https://doi.org/10.1353/sip.2015.0028

Kenyon, Nicholas, *Authenticity and Early Music: A Symposium* (Oxford: Oxford

University Press, 1988)

Kitto, John, *The Pictorial History of Palestine and the Holy Land* (London: Charles Knight and Co., 1844)

Lawson, Colin, and Robin Stowell (eds), *Cambridge Encyclopaedia of Historical Performance in Music* (Cambridge: Cambridge University Press, 2018), https://doi.org/10.1017/9781316257678

Lee, Sam, *The Nightingale* (London: Penguin Books, 2020)

Lewis, George and Piekut, Benjamin (eds), *Oxford Handbook to Critical Improvisation Studies,* Vols 1–2 (New York: Oxford University Press 2016), https://doi.org/10.1093/oxfordhb/9780195370935.001.0001 (Vol. 1), https://doi.org/10.1093/oxfordhb/9780199892921.001.0001 (Vol. 2)

Locke, Ralph, *Music and the Exotic from the Renaissance to Mozart* (Cambridge: Cambridge University Press 2015), https://doi.org/10.1017/cbo9780511998157

Lorde, Audre, *Your Silence Will Not Protect You* (London: Silver Press, 2017)

Lubarsky, Eric, 'Reviving Early Music: Metaphors and Modalities of Life and Living in Historically Informed Performance', PhD dissertation, Eastman School of Music, 2017, https://www.proquest.com/dissertations-theses/reviving-early-music-metaphors-modalities-life/docview/2001524940/se-2

Lugones, María, 'Playfullness, "World"-Travelling, and Loving Perception', *Hypatia* 2.2 (1987), 3–20

MacBeth, George (ed.), *The Penguin Book of Animal Verse* (Harmondsworth: Penguin Books, 1965)

Maclean, Gerald, *Looking East: English Writing and the Ottoman Empire Before 1800* (Basingstoke: Palgrave Macmillan, 2007), https://doi.org/10.1057/9780230591844

Maltby, Judith, '"Extravagencies and Impertinencies": Set Forms, Conceived and Extempore Prayer in Revolutionary England', in *Worship and the Parish Church in Early Modern Britain,* ed. by Alec Ryrie and Natalie Mears (Farnham: Ashgate, 2013), pp. 221–43

Marrapodi, Michele (ed.), *Italian Culture in the Drama of Shakespeare and his Contemporaries: Rewriting, Remaking, Refashioning* (Aldershot: Ashgate, 2007)

Matar, Nabil I., 'Renaissance Cartography and the Question of Palestine', in *The Landscape of Palestine: Equivocal Poetry,* ed. by Ibrahim Abu-Lughod, Roger Heacock and Khaled Nashef (Birzeit: Birzeit University Publications, 1999), pp. 139–51

Matar, Nabil I., 'The Sufi and the Chaplain: Abd al-Ghani al-Nabulusi and Henry Maundrell', in *Through the Eyes of the Beholder: The Holy Land, 1517–1713,* ed. by Judy A. Hayden and Nabil Matar (Leiden: Brill, 2012), pp. 165–84

Matar, Nabil, *Turks, Moors, and Englishmen in the Age of Discovery* (New York:

Columbia University Press, 1999)

Matar, Nabil, *Europe Through Arab Eyes, 1578–1527* (New York: Columbia University Press, 2008), https://doi.org/10.7312/mata14194

Matar, Nabil, *Islam in Britain, 1558–1685* (Cambridge: Cambridge University Press, 1998)

Matar, Nabil, and MacLean, Gerald, *Britain and the Islamic World, 1558–1713* (Oxford: Oxford University Press, 2011), https://doi.org/10.1093/acprof:oso/9780199203185.001.0001

Mears, Natalie, and Alec Ryrie (eds), *Worship and the Parish Church in Early Modern Britain* (Farnham: Ashgate, 2013), https://doi.org/10.4324/9781315546254

Michel, Melodie, 'Early Music and Latin America: Transhistorical Views on the Coloniality of Sound', PhD thesis, UC Santa Cruz, 2021, https://escholarship.org/content/qt63b2j65k/qt63b2j65k_noSplash_a5c96dec830086c3f4071a143f6fd146.pdf?t=qsxuoo

Mignolo, Walter D., and Catherine E. Walsh, *On Decoloniality: Concepts, Analytics, Praxis* (Durham: Duke University Press, 2018), https://doi.org/10.1215/9780822371779

Morgan, Tan, et al., 'Floral Sonication is an Innate Behaviour in Bumblebees that Can Be Fine-Tuned with Experience in Manipulating Flowers', *J Insect Behaviour* 29 (2016), 233–41

Morrison, Toni, *Mouth Full of Blood* (London: Chatto and Windus, 2019)

Nassar, Issam, 'Review: Maundrell in Jerusalem: Reflections on the Writing of an Early European Tourist', *Jerusalem Quarterly* 9 (2000), https://www.palestine-studies.org/en/node/78133

Natif, Mika, *Mughal Occidentalism: Artistic Encounters between Europe and Asia at the Courts of India, 1580–1630* (Leiden: Brill, 2018)

Nettl, Bruno, and Melinda Russell (eds), *In the Course of Performance: Studies in the World of Musical Improvisation* (Chicago: The University of Chicago Press, 1998)

Nooshin, Laudan, 'Improvisation as "Other": Creativity, Knowledge and Power—The Case of Iranian Classical Music', *Journal of the Royal Musical Association* 128.2 (2003), 242–96, https://doi.org/10.1093/jrma/128.2.242

Norgaard, Martin, 'Descriptions of Improvisational Thinking by Artist-Level Jazz Musicians', *Journal of Research in Music Education* 59.2 (2011), 109–27

Olley, Jacob, 'Towards a Global History of Music? Postcolonial Studies and Historical Musicology', *Ethnomusicology Review* (28 February 2016), https://ethnomusicologyreview.ucla.edu/content/towards-global-history-music-postcolonial-studies-and-historical-musicology

Olufemi, Lola, *Experiments in Imagining Otherwise* (Maidstone: Hajar Press, 2021)

Owens, Jessie Ann, *Composers at Work: The Craft of Musical Composition, 1450–1600* (New York, Oxford University Press, 1997)

Pappa, Joseph, *Carnal Reading: Early Modern Language and Bodies* (Newark: University of Delaware Press, 2011)

Parker, Kenneth (ed.), *Early Modern Tales of Orient: A Critical Anthology* (London: Routledge, 1999)

Pérez, Emma, *The Decolonial Imaginary: Writing Chicanas into History* (Bloomington: Indiana University Press, 1999)

Pfeifer, Helen, *Empire of Salons: Conquest and Community in Early Modern Ottoman Lands* (Princeton: Princeton University Press, 2022), https://doi.org/10.23943/princeton/9780691195230.001.0001

Quijano, Aníbal, 'Coloniality and Modernity/Rationality', *Cultural Studies* 21.2–3 (2007), 168–78, https://doi.org/10.1080/09502380601164353

Racy, Ali Jihad, 'The Many Faces of Improvisation: The Arab Taqasim as a Musical Symbol', *Ethnomusicology* 44.2 (2000), 302–20, https://doi.org/10.2307/852534

Raymond, Joad (ed.), *Cheap Print in Britain and Ireland to 1660* (Oxford: Oxford University Press, 2011), https://doi.org/10.1093/acprof:osobl/9780199287048.001.0001

Reardon-Smith, Hannah, Louise Denson and Vanessa Tomlinson, 'Feministing Free Improvisation', *TEMPO* 74.292 (2020), 10–20

Robinson, Dylan, *Hungry Listening: Resonant Theory for Indigenous Sound Studies* (Minneapolis: University of Minnesota Press, 2020), https://doi.org/10.5749/j.ctvzpv6bb

Rosenberg, Ruth, *Music, Travel and Imperial Encounter in 19th-Century France* (London: Routledge, 2015), https://doi.org/10.4324/9781315772295

Rubinoff, Kailan R., '(Re)creating the Past: Baroque Improvisation in the Early Music Revival', *New Sound* 32, Special issue on improvisation, ed. by Marcel Cobussen and Mira Veselinovic-Hofman (2009), https://libres.uncg.edu/ir/uncg/f/K_Rubinoff_Recreating_2009.pdf

Rubinoff, Kailan R., 'A Revolution in Sheep's Wool Stockings: Early Music and "1968"', in *Music and Protest in 1968*, ed. by Beate Kutschke and Barley Norton (Cambridge: Cambridge University Press, 2013), pp. 237–54, https://doi.org/10.1017/cbo9781139051682.015

Saïd, Edward W., *Orientalism* (London: Routledge and Kegan Paul, 1975)

Saïd, Edward W., *Culture and Imperialism* (London: Random House 1994)

Schimmel, Annemarie, *A Two-Colored Brocade: The Imagery of Persian Poetry* (Chapel Hill: University of North Carolina Press, 1992)

Schmidt-Relenberg, Markus, 'Horen, Tanz und Extase nach Badraddin ibn Salim al-Maliki: Text, Ubersetzung und Kommentar / Al-Maliki' (PhD thesis, Kiel

University, 1986)

Schubert, Peter, 'Counterpoint Pedagogy in the Renaissance', in *The Cambridge History of Western Music Theory*, ed. by Thomas Christensen (Cambridge: Cambridge University Press, 2002), pp. 503–33, https://doi.org/10.1017/chol9780521623711.018

Schülting, Sabine, Sabine Lucia Müller and Ralf Hertel (eds), *Early Modern Encounters with the Islamic East: Performing Cultures* (Farnham: Ashgate: 2012), pp. 67–84

Scott, Derek B., 'Orientalism and Musical Style', *The Musical Quarterly* 82.2 (1998), 309–35

Senay, Banu, *Musical Ethics and Islam: The Art of Playing the Ney* (Illinois: University of Illinois Press, 2020), https://doi.org/10.5622/illinois/9780252043024.001.0001

Shull, Jonathan, 'Locating the Past in the Present: Living Traditions and the Performance of Early Music', *Ethnomusicology Forum* 14.1 (2006), 87–111, https://doi.org/10.1080/17411910600634361

Simone, AbdouMaliq, *Improvised Lives: Rhythms of Endurance in an Urban South* (Cambridge: Polity Press, 2019)

Sirriyeh, Elizabeth, *Sufi Visionary of Ottoman Damascus: 'Abd al-Ghani al-Nabulusi, 1641–1731* (Abingdon: Routledge, 2011)

Smith, Bruce R., *The Acoustic World of Early Modern England: Attending to the O-Factor* (Chicago: University of Chicago Press, 1999)

Stinson, John Alexander, 'Roger North's Essay of Musicall Ayre: An Edition from the Autograph with Introduction and Commentary' (master's thesis, Australian National University, 1977), https://openresearch-repository.anu.edu.au/handle/1885/133223

Swann, Elizabeth L., *Taste and Knowledge in Early Modern England* (Cambridge: Cambridge University Press, 2020), https://doi.org/10.1017/9781108767576

Taff, Dyani Johns, 'Precarious Travail, Gender and Narration in Shakespeare's *Pericles, Prince of Tyre* and Margaret Cavendish's *The Blazing World*', in *Travel and Travail: Early Modern Women, English Drama and the Wider World* ed. by Patricia Akhimie and Bernadette Andrea (Lincoln: University of Nebraska Press, 2018), pp. 273–91

Taylor, Foluke, 'OtherWise: Writing Unbearable Encounters through the Register of Black Life', *LIRIC Journal* 2.1 (2022), 120–41

Taylor, Foluke, *Unruly Therapeutic: Black Feminist Writings and Practices in Living Room* (New York: Norton, 2023)

Tramontana, Felicita, 'The Spread of Catholicism in Seventeenth-Century Palestinian Villages', in *Space and Conversion in Global Perspective*, ed. by Giuseppe Marcocci, Aliocha Maldavsky, Wietse de Boer and Ilaria Pavan (Leiden: Brill, 2014), pp. 81–102

Treitler, Leo, 'Speaking of the I-Word', in *The Oxford Handbook of Critical Improvisation Studies, Vol. 2*, ed. by Benjamin Piekut and George E. Lewis (n.p.: Oxford Handbooks Online, 2014), https://doi.org/10.1093/oxfordhb/9780199892921.013.19

Trouillot, Michel-Rolph, *Silencing the Past: Power & the Production of History* (Boston: Beacon Press, 1995)

Tuck, Eve, and K. Wayne Yang, 'Decolonization Is Not a Metaphor', *Decolonization: Indigeneity, Education & Society* 1.1 (2012), 1–40

Vergès, Françoise, *A Decolonial Feminism*, trans. by Ashley J. Bohrer with the author (London: Pluto Press, 2021), https://doi.org/10.2307/j.ctv1k531j6

Walter, John, 'Affronts and Insolencies: The Voices of Radwinter and Popular Opposition to Laudianism', *English Historical Review* 122.495 (2007), 35–60

Watt, Tessa, *Cheap Print and Popular Piety, 1550–1640* (Cambridge: Cambridge University Press, 1991)

Wegman, Rob C., 'From Maker to Composer: Improvisation and Musical Authorship in the Low Countries, 1450–1500', *Journal of the American Musicological Society* 49 (1996), 409–79

White, Bryan, '"Brothers of the String": Henry Purcell and the Letter Books of Rowland Sherman', *Music & Letters* 92.4 (2011), 519–81, https://doi.org/10.1093/ml/gcr116

White, Bryan, 'Letter from Aleppo: Dating the Chelsea School Performance of Dido and Aeneas', *Early Music* 37.3 (2009), 417–28, https://doi.org/10.1093/em/cap041

Widdess, Richard, 'Schemas and Improvisation in Indian Music', in *Language, Music and Interaction*, ed. by Ruth Kempson, Christine Howes and Martin Orwin (London: College Publications, 2013), pp. 197–209

Willis, Tara Aisha, 'A Litany on An/notations', *Performance Research*, 23.4–5 (2018), 85–7, https://doi.org/10.1080/13528165.2018.1524675

Wilson, Christopher R., and Michaela Calore, *Music in Shakespeare: A Dictionary* (London: Bloomsbury Publishing, 2014)

Wilson, Nick, *The Art of Re-enchantment: Making Early Music in the Modern Age* (Oxford: Oxford University Press, 2013), https://doi.org/10.1093/acprof:oso/9780199939930.001.0001

Wilson, Richard, *Secret Shakespeare: Studies in Theatre, Religion and Resistance* (Manchester: Manchester University Press, 2004), https://doi.org/10.7765/9781526184153

Wind, Thiemo, *Jacob van Eyck and the Others: Dutch Solo Repertoire for Recorder in the Golden Age*, Muziekhistorische Monografieën 21 (Utrecht: Koninklijke Vereniging voor Nederlandse Muziekgeschiedenis, 2011)

Wood, Jennifer Linhart, *Sounding Otherness in Early Modern Drama and Travel: Uncanny Vibrations in the English Archive* (Cham: Palgrave Macmillan, 2019)

Woodfield, Ian, 'The Keyboard Recital in Oriental Diplomacy, 1520–1620', *Journal of the Royal Musical Association* 115.1 (1990), 33–62

Woodfield, Ian, *English Musicians in the Age of Exploration* (New York: Pendragon Press, 1995)

Wright, Owen, *Demetrius Cantemir: The Collection of Notations, Vol. 1: Text* (London: SOAS, 1992)

Wright, Owen, *Demetrius Cantemir: The Collection of Notations, Vol. 2: Commentary* (Farnham: Ashgate, 2011), https://doi.org/10.4324/9781315095035

Wright, Owen, *Music Theory in the Safavid Age: The Taqsim Al-Nagamat* (Abingdon and New York: Routledge, 2019), https://doi.org/10.4324/9781315161624

Wright, Owen, 'Turning a Deaf Ear', in *The Renaissance and the Ottoman World*, ed. by Anna Contadini and Claire Norton (Farnham: Ashgate, 2013), 143–65, https://doi.org/10.4324/9781315237428-17

Yri, Kirsten, 'Thomas Binkley and the Studio der Frühen Musik: Challenging "The Myth of Westernness"', *Early Music* 38.2 (2010), 273–80, https://doi.org/10.1093/em/caq025

# Index

Ahmed, Sara 3
al-Maliki, Badraddin ibn Salim 83
al-Nabulusi, Abd al-Ghani 73, 81, 106
Aleppo 81–82, 84, 145
'Alī Ufukī 119
   *Mecmuâ-i Sâz u Söz* 119
Andrews, Richard 126, 145
archive 36, 84, 115, 120, 153–154
Attar, Farid ud-Din 103–104
   *The Conference of the Birds* 103–104
Austern, Linda 92, 98, 114

Bach, J. S. 123–124, 144, 153
Bacon, Francis 59
Baeten, Somayeh 104
Baker, Geoffrey 152
bees 1, 6, 14–15, 20, 41, 83, 87–96, 98, 111, 113, 128, 148–149, 155
Bloechl, Olivia 152
Blount, Henry 14, 56–66, 69–72, 80, 136
   *Voyage into the Levant* 14, 56–64, 69–70
body/bodies 6, 9, 22, 26, 28–31, 33–34, 36, 42–46, 50–51, 55, 57, 59–60, 65, 67, 72, 74, 77, 80, 98, 106, 113–115, 117–118, 122, 130, 132, 134, 138–139, 146–148, 152
Burnet, Gilbert 32
Butler, Charles 14, 87–91, 93–94, 96, 111, 113–114
   *The Feminine Monarchie* 14, 88–91
   *The Principles of Musik* 87
Butler, Gregory 27

Cairo 13, 69–70
Calore, Michela 98
Campion, Thomas 116–117
Catholicism 13, 15, 36, 93–94
Caxton, William 33
   *The Recuyell of the Historyes of Troye* 33
Charlemagne 104
Charles I, King 57, 93–94
Charles II, King 15, 21
Charles VI, King 66
Chaucer, Geoffrey 33
   *Canterbury Tales* 33
citation 3, 6
Civil War 15, 36, 49
Clubb, Louise George 125
coloniality 1, 3–5, 10–12, 54, 73, 75, 79–80, 87, 94, 98, 102, 145, 152
*commedia dell'arte* 125
composition 7–8, 19–20, 26–27, 70, 87, 110, 126–127, 140, 144
   in opposition to improvisation 126–127, 140
contrapuntal analysis 4–5, 123
Covel, John 119–121
Crashaw, Richard 114
creativity 1, 5–8, 17, 58, 85, 126, 138, 153–154
Cromwell, Oliver 21
Crooke, Helkiah 27, 90
   *Mikrokosmographia* 27
Cumming, Julie E. 7

Dallam, Thomas 14, 104–106
Darwish, Mahmoud 77, 123–124

Daubney, Henry 40, 44
decoloniality
  decolonial feminism 1–3
  decolonial imaginary 123
  decolonial theory 1, 11–12
  in contrast to decolonisation 11
de Worde, Wynkyn 33
Dido (singer) 146
division (music) 20–25, 29–31, 35, 37, 59, 70, 84, 89, 94, 98–100, 103, 106–107, 110–114, 117–118, 120–121, 127–128, 134, 136, 142–147
Drake, Richard 38, 42, 59
Dumont, Jean 66–69, 78
  *A New Voyage to the Levant* 67–69

ears 3, 28, 30–31, 33, 35, 50–51, 58–60, 63, 65, 81, 98, 101, 108–109, 112, 148–149
East India Company 54
Egypt 54, 64, 69
el-Hage, Fadia 153
Elizabeth I, Queen 13–14, 36, 53–55, 92, 102–104
England 4–5, 7–8, 11, 14–15, 17–18, 20, 22, 27–28, 33–34, 36, 44, 50, 53–57, 66, 73, 78, 80, 82, 84, 87, 90, 92, 97–98, 100–101, 106–107, 109, 115–116, 120, 146–147
ethnography 56
Evelyn, John 32
Eyck, Jacob van 14, 115–117, 148
  *Der Fluyten Lusthof* 14, 115–116

Feghali, Layla K. 82
feminism 1–3, 17, 54, 81, 123
Fischlin, Daniel 9
Florio, John 18
  *World of Words* 18
Frederick V, Elector Palatine 116
Freeman, Ireneus 14, 40–44, 46–47

gender 14–15, 70, 87, 93, 98, 102, 107, 109, 112–114, 145
Gholi, H. 127
Gillespie, George 41, 43

Glorious Revolution, the 15, 36, 49
Godbid, William 21
Godwin, Francis 14, 94–95
  *The Man in the Moone* 14, 94–95
Great Fire of London 14, 21
Great Plague of London 14, 21
Greenblatt, Stephen 56, 61
Guido, Massimiliano 6–7, 27

Hartman, Saidiya 3
Harun al-Rashid, Caliph 104
Haynes, Bruce 8
Henry VIII, King 13
Herissone, Rebecca 7–8, 129
Hespèrion XXI 153
Higden, Ranulf 33
  *Policronicon* 33
historical performance (HP) 1, 6, 8–10, 89–90, 149, 151, 153–154
historiography 2, 5, 12, 15, 66, 123
Hole, Matthew 19
Hotteterre, Jacques 69
Howard, Alan 7

identity 1, 8–9, 11, 28, 53, 56, 100, 106–107, 120, 153
imagination 2–3, 7–8, 26–27, 42, 44–45, 53, 56, 58, 75, 80, 85, 90, 96, 121–122, 128–130, 136, 147–149, 151, 154
imperialism 4–5, 11, 46, 54–57, 72–73, 78, 90, 92, 109
improvisation/extemporisation
  etymology 17–20
  historical improvisation 6–9, 17, 121, 126, 151, 153–154
  improvisation studies 6, 8–10, 20
  improvised/extemporary music 21, 30, 32–33, 37, 39, 50, 66, 70, 130, 148
  improvised/extemporary prayer 9, 20, 32, 36–42, 44–46, 50, 59, 69, 110, 128
  improvised/extemporary sound 94
  improvised/extemporary theatre 125, 132, 145
  negative interpretation of 43–44, 50,

71
instrument  25–26, 32, 64–68, 92, 95, 105–106, 108, 113–114, 117–118, 122, 130, 134–135, 138, 147, 154
Irving, David  5
Islam  5, 14–15, 40, 53

Jacobs, Nicole  93
James I, King  92, 116
Johnson, Richard  55–56

Kitto, John  72–73

language/speech  19–20, 26–27, 29, 43, 55, 59–60, 70, 72–73, 87, 90–92, 94–99, 108, 111
Laud, William, Archbishop  36
Lebanon  10, 54, 70, 74, 78, 82
L'Estrange, Roger  21
Levant Company  14, 54, 84, 105
Lewis, George  9
Lewthwat, Richard  18
listening  1, 3, 20, 30, 54, 63, 70, 81, 84, 89, 96, 121, 148–149
literacy  22, 33–34, 80, 152
Locke, John  48–49
Lorde, Audre  2, 12
Lubarsky, Eric  152
Lugones, María  53–54, 63, 75, 80, 84

Mace, Thomas  14, 29, 97–98, 117, 129–132, 134–142, 144, 147–148
  *Musick's Monument*  14, 29, 97–98, 117, 129–132, 135, 137–141
Maclean, Gerald  55
madrigal  87, 89–92, 113, 128
Maltby, Judith  36–37
Marlowe, Christopher  146
  *Dido, Queen of Carthage*  146
Matar, Nabil  10, 12, 14, 73
Matteis, Nicola  30–33, 50–51, 128
  *Ayrs*  30–32
Maundrell, Henry  13–14, 70–84
  *A Journey from Aleppo to Jerusalem*  13–14, 71–72, 74–79, 81
Mehmed III, Sultan  14, 104

memory  7, 15, 20, 26–28, 36, 42, 44, 57–58, 60–61, 75, 85, 112, 117, 120, 123–124, 126, 128–129, 132–134, 148, 155
metaphor  7, 11, 50, 56, 59, 93, 100, 102–103
Michel, Melodie  152
Mignolo, Walter  11–12, 45
Milton, John  92
monarchy  87–88, 90, 92–94
moon  14–15, 94–96, 102
Morrison, Tony  3
Murad III, Sultan  102
musicology  6–7, 12, 24, 152–153

Nettl, Bruno  126
Nichol, Robert  98
nightingale  1, 6, 94, 98–104, 106–115, 117–118, 120–121, 128, 134, 146–148, 155
Nooshin, Laudan  126–127
Norgaard, Martin  29
North, Roger  26, 30, 50, 112, 129, 132–134, 142, 144
notation  87, 89–91, 94, 96, 127, 129, 138, 144, 147

Olufemi, Lola  151
orality  8, 10, 17, 22, 33–34, 37, 98
organ  13–14, 26, 59, 104–106
orientalism  55–56, 70–71, 78–79
Ottoman empire  4–5, 10–11, 53–58, 60, 62–63, 66, 73, 90, 100–102, 104–105, 109, 119–120, 153
Ovid  99, 113
Owens, Jessie Ann  7

Palestine  10, 13, 54, 73, 81, 93, 106
Pappa, Joseph  42
paradigmatic analysis  144
Parker, Martin  97, 99, 101
Pera Ensemble  153
Pérez, Emma  123, 149
Petrucci, Ottaviano  33
Piekut, Benjamin  9
Pius V, Pope  53

Playford, John  21, 142–143
  *The Division Violin*  22, 142
politics  5, 10–11, 41, 48, 55–57, 90, 93, 123, 128, 149, 151–152, 159
Porter, Eric  9
prayer  9, 15, 19, 20, 32, 33, 36, 37, 38, 39, 40, 41, 42, 43, 44, 45, 46, 47, 48, 49, 50, 59, 69, 93, 110, 128. *See also* improvisation/extemporisation: improvised/extemporary prayer
  Common Prayer  14, 36–37, 39, 46–47
Prete, Frederick  93
print culture  10, 22, 28, 33–34, 37, 41, 43–46, 53, 72, 80, 98, 121, 127, 129, 132, 138, 141–142, 144, 148
Protestantism  15, 37, 41, 53
Purcell, Henry  145–147
  *Dido and Aeneas*  145

Quijano, Aníbal  11

Ray, John  18
recorder (instrument)  1, 21, 66, 115, 117–118, 124, 142–143
Rubinoff, Kailan  152

Safiye, Empress  14, 102–104
Saïd, Edward  4, 78
Sandys, Miles  28
Saraband  153
Savall, Jordi  153
Schubert, Peter  7
Schülting, Sabine  57, 60, 65
Sedgwick, John  40
Shakespeare, William  5, 98, 101, 117–118, 124–126, 145–146
  *Hamlet*  124–125
  *Romeo and Juliet*  101
  *The Tempest*  116, 126, 145–146
  *Two Gentlemen of Verona*  117–118
Sherman, Rowland  84, 145
silence  17, 72–74, 77, 80, 113, 115
Simpson, Christopher  14, 21–26, 29–31, 33–37, 46, 50, 111–112, 128, 136
  *The Division-Viol or The Art of Playing Extempore upon a Ground*  14, 21, 24–25, 29–30, 34–35
Smith, Bruce R.  90
speech. *See* language/speech
Spinola, George  44–45
Strada, Famiano  107–114, 117, 128, 146
  *Musical Duel*  107–113
Sylvester, Joshua  107
symbolism  92, 101–102, 104, 107
Syria  10, 13, 28, 54, 82, 84, 145

Taylor, Foluke  1, 3
Taylor, Zachary  18
Terentius  51
theatre  20, 125, 132, 145. *See also* improvisation/extemporisation: improvised/extemporary theatre
theatregrams  126, 145
Thévenot, Jean de  62–63, 100
transcription  64, 87–92, 94, 96, 107, 115, 117, 129, 134, 136, 138, 141
travelogue/travel text  9, 15, 53–54, 56–57, 59, 62, 66, 71–75, 79–81, 85, 92, 100, 106, 127–128, 152
Treitler, Leo  17, 27
Trouillot, Michel-Rolph  74
Tuck, Eve  11

Udall, Nicholas  18
Ufki, Ali  66

Villoteau, Guillaume-André  64
violence  20, 54, 61, 112–113

Walsh, John  23, 142–143
  *The Division Flute*  22–23, 142–143
Ward, Samuel  37
Watson, Thomas  117
Wegman, Rob  7
White, Bryan  84, 145
Wilkins, John  94, 95, 96, 111
Willis, John  58
Willis, Tara Aisha  6
Wilson, Christopher  98
Wilson, Nick  8

Wood, Jennifer Linhart  105
'world-travelling'  54

Yang, K. Wayne  11

# About the Team

Alessandra Tosi was the managing editor for this book.

Adèle Kreager and Lila Fierek proofread this manuscript. Adèle compiled the index.

Jeevanjot Kaur Nagpal designed the cover. The cover was produced in InDesign using the Fontin font.

Jeremy Bowman typeset the book in InDesign and produced the paperback and hardback editions and created the EPUB. The main text font is Tex Gyre Pagella and the heading font is Californian FB.

Cameron Craig produced the PDF edition.

The conversion to the HTML edition was performed with epublius, an open-source software which is freely available on our GitHub page at https://github.com/OpenBookPublishers

This book was peer-reviewed by Prof. Amanda Eubanks Winkler, Director of the Department of Music at Mason Gross School of the Arts, Rutgers University, and an anonymous referee. Experts in their field, these readers give their time freely to help ensure the academic rigour of our books. We are grateful for their generous and invaluable contributions.

# This book need not end here...

## Share

All our books — including the one you have just read — are free to access online so that students, researchers and members of the public who can't afford a printed edition will have access to the same ideas. This title will be accessed online by hundreds of readers each month across the globe: why not share the link so that someone you know is one of them?

This book and additional content is available at
https://doi.org/10.11647/OBP.0451

## Donate

Open Book Publishers is an award-winning, scholar-led, not-for-profit press making knowledge freely available one book at a time. We don't charge authors to publish with us: instead, our work is supported by our library members and by donations from people who believe that research shouldn't be locked behind paywalls.

Join the effort to free knowledge by supporting us at
https://www.openbookpublishers.com/support-us

### We invite you to connect with us on our socials!

BLUESKY
@openbookpublish
.bsky.social

MASTODON
@OpenBookPublish
@hcommons.social

LINKEDIN
open-book-publishers

### Read more at the Open Book Publishers Blog
https://blogs.openbookpublishers.com

# You may also be interested in:

### Acoustemologies in Contact
Sounding Subjects and Modes of Listening in Early Modernity

*Emily Wilbourne and Suzanne G. Cusick (editors)*

https://doi.org/10.11647/OBP.0226

### Tellings and Texts
Music, Literature and Performance in North India

*Francesca Orsini and Katherine Butler Schofield (editors)*

https://doi.org/10.11647/OBP.0062

### Nouvelles études sur les lieux de spectacle de la première modernité

*Pauline Beaucé and Jeffrey M. Leichman (editors)*

https://doi.org/10.11647/OBP.0400

### Auld Lang Syne
A Song and its Culture

*Morag Josephine Grant*

https://doi.org/10.11647/OBP.0231

www.ingramcontent.com/pod-product-compliance
Lightning Source LLC
Chambersburg PA
CBHW051127160426
43195CB00014B/2372